THE PROLIFERATION
OF RIGHTS

The Proliferation of Rights

Moral Progress or Empty Rhetoric?

Carl Wellman

WASHINGTON UNIVERSITY, ST. LOUIS

Westview Press
A Member of the Perseus Books Group

Copyright © 1999 by Westview Press, A Member of the Perseus Books Group

Published in 1999 in the United States of America by Westview Press, 5500 Central Avenue, Boulder, Colorado 80301-2877, and in the United Kingdom by Westview Press, 12 Hid's Copse Road, Cumnor Hill, Oxford OX2 9JJ

Library of Congress Cataloging-in-Publication Data
Wellman, Carl.
  The proliferation of rights : moral progress or empty rhetoric? /
by Carl Wellman.
    p.   cm.
Includes bibliographical references and index.
ISBN 0-8133-2820-9 (hardcover). — ISBN 0-8133-2821-7 (pbk.)
  1. Law and ethics.   2. Human rights.   3. Political rights.
4. Law—Philosophy.   I. Title.
K258.W448   1999
340'.112—dc21   98-28117
                                                                                CIP

The paper used in this publication meets the requirements of the American National Standard for Permanence of Paper for Printed Library Materials Z39.48-1984.

10   9   8   7   6   5   4   3   2   1

Contents

Acknowledgments

Several years ago, Spencer Carr, who was then a senior editor for Westview Press, asked me whether it was advisable to publish a little book on the proliferation of rights. I responded enthusiastically that it was a great idea, for the subject was both very important and of interest to a wide audience. At the same time, I said that I was too busy with other projects to undertake this one and recommended several others for the job. Only gradually, as I reflected on the potential of such a book, did I reconsider and agree to write what follows. First and foremost I owe a debt of gratitude to Spencer Carr for the germinal idea for this book.

I am also grateful to several colleagues, both here at Washington University and in Oxford, who have rendered valuable assistance as I struggled to draft some of the chapters. Most notable are Joel Anderson, Marilyn Friedman, James Griffin, and Joseph Raz.

Special thanks go to Larry May, Christopher Wellman, and an anonymous reviewer for Westview Press who read the entire manuscript and accurately pointed to some serious deficiencies at the same time that they gave many very helpful suggestions of ways to improve the text.

Finally, I am glad to acknowledge Catherine Murphy, senior editor for Westview Press, for her cooperative attitude, knowledgeable assistance, and wise advice as I have struggled to transform a manuscript into a publishable book.

Carl Wellman

1

Some Critical Questions

Early in the twentieth century, most jurists and moral philosophers assumed that rights and duties were logically correlative. Just as the creditor's right to be repaid the borrowed sum implies the debtor's duty to repay the amount borrowed, so a father's duty to provide for the needs of his child implies the child's right to financial support from her father. But in 1930, W. D. Ross, a moral philosopher who distinguished radically between the moral rightness of an act and the moral goodness of an action, argued against this assumption by pointing out that we have both moral and legal duties to treat animals humanely. These are duties we owe to the animals, not to our fellow human beings, because they are grounded primarily on our consideration for the feelings of the animals themselves. These duties cannot, however, logically imply any correlative rights of the animals, because we mean by a right something that can be justly claimed, and nonhuman animals are incapable of making any claim to humane treatment from us. As one would expect, this argument was widely accepted in the 1930s as a convincing refutation of the correlation of rights and duties. Almost all philosophers and jurists thought it obvious that animals could be said to have moral rights only in some metaphorical sense.

Today many vegetarians argue that our practice of raising animals merely to gratify our appetite for meat is grossly immoral because slaughtering cattle, sheep, and pigs violates their fundamental moral right to life. Some moral reformers argue seriously that zoos ought not to exist, because confining wild animals in cages or fenced areas violates their moral right to liberty. Environmentalists have even gone so far as to argue that trees and woodlands, such as giant redwoods and virgin forests, can and ought to have legal rights not to be destroyed. These are signs of the times, for during the second half of the twentieth century there has been a vast proliferation of rights.

This recent proliferation of rights is a complex social phenomenon consisting of three interwoven strands. Moral reformers have asserted the existence of a large number of unfamiliar, sometimes strange, moral rights. They normally do not imagine that these are new rights; rather, they take themselves to be describing moral rights that have always existed but have gone unrecognized. Thus the first strand consists in the proliferation of alleged moral rights, rights that may or may not be real. On the other hand, the second strand consists in the proliferation of new legal rights, the creation of real, not merely alleged, rights. The number and variety of legal rights in the United States and in many other countries really have increased rapidly as more and more rights have been introduced by legislation or judicial decision. These two strands have been interwoven in political discourse, for moral reformers often argue for the introduction of some new legal right on the ground that it is required to protect some fundamental moral right. In a similar manner, political conservatives frequently object that the introduction of a new legal right would be a violation of some traditional moral right. Hence, the third strand is the proliferation of the language of rights in political discourse. This book will describe and assess all three strands in the proliferation of rights.

Trouble in Paradise

As this proliferation of rights has spread into more and more areas of modern life, it has produced increasing resistance, both theoretical and political. A few examples may illustrate why so many moral philosophers, jurists, and private citizens find these developments troubling.

Alleged Moral Rights

Article 24 of the United Nations *Universal Declaration of Human Rights* asserts, "Everyone has the right to rest and leisure, including . . . periodic holidays with pay." Although this is an official affirmation by a highly respected international organization, almost everyone has regarded it as suspect. A genuine human right justifies the strongest kind of moral claim, and however much one might desire a paid holiday, holidays with pay are not believed to be something to which every human being has a moral right. By asserting this alleged right, the United Nations has probably encouraged unrealistic expectations and diverted attention from far more urgent and practicable moral claims.

Maurice Cranston, a British political philosopher, has expressed this criticism most emphatically:

> A human right is something of which no one may be deprived without a grave affront to justice. . . . Thus the effect of a Universal Declaration which is overloaded with affirmations of so-called human rights which are not human rights at all is to push *all* talk of human rights out of the clear realm of the morally compelling into the twilight world of utopian aspirations.[1]

The most general complaint about the proliferation of moral rights is that this inflation of rights devalues the currency, so that assertions of these merely alleged rights discredit those who claim their genuine moral rights.

Although labor unions have succeeded in obtaining the legal right to strike throughout the United States, in most states it is illegal for workers who are deemed essential, such as teachers in the public schools and firefighters, to strike. Nevertheless, every fall the schools in many cities and towns remain closed for days or even weeks because the teachers are on strike, and occasionally the firefighters in a community will also strike. Teachers and firefighters typically justify their civil disobedience by appealing to their moral right to strike against the unjust terms offered by the school board or the municipal council with which they are negotiating a new contract. Many public officials and private citizens deny that the alleged right of essential workers to strike is real. Such people regard this claim as a purely selfish demand on the part of the teachers and firefighters who refuse to recognize and fulfill their moral responsibilities. Similarly, many moral philosophers argue that because rights are essentially individualistic, the proliferation of moral rights encourages an egoistic pursuit of self-interest and the neglect of social responsibilities.

Legal Rights

The recent proliferation of legal rights strikes many as equally troublesome. Until 1973, it was illegal for a woman to procure an abortion. Then in the landmark case of *Roe v. Wade,* the United States Supreme Court recognized the legal right of a pregnant woman to have an abortion, at least during the first two trimesters of her pregnancy. Although this new legal right was at first welcomed as a solution to a variety of social problems connected with the birth of unwanted babies—such as the physical and psychological harms, including infertility and death, resulting from large numbers of illegal abortions—many persons have had second thoughts.

The demand for and exercise of this new legal right has caused a backlash that has heightened social conflict and threatens to disrupt law and order in our society. The rhetoric of right-to-life groups has incited some extremists to bomb a number of clinics that provide prenatal medical services and occasionally to murder physicians known to have performed abortions. The absoluteness of legal rights, with their clearly defined contents and ability to override other considerations, has intensified and frozen the conflict between those who insist upon the right of the pregnant woman to have an abortion whenever she so chooses and those who regard abortion as a clear violation of the moral and legal right to life of the unborn child. Thus the introduction of a new legal right has provoked a vehement, often violent, reaction that has prevented any reasonable compromise that might otherwise have constituted an acceptable solution to the social and moral problems posed by undesired pregnancies.

Of course, it may be that the underlying moral dispute is so intractable that no compromise was possible. Still, it is worthy of note that during the years that the *Roe* case was progressing from trial court upward to the Supreme Court, several state legislatures were introducing the right to therapeutic abortion: abortion to preserve the health of the pregnant woman, to prevent the birth of a seriously defective child, or to terminate a pregnancy resulting from rape or incest. Because this new legal right is more limited than the right to abortion on demand introduced by *Roe v. Wade* (the right to have an abortion whenever the pregnant woman so chooses for whatever reason, or for no reason at all), some argue that the establishment of this right could have been an acceptable solution to the social problem posed by the most serious unwanted pregnancies.

Another new legal right is equally controversial. A series of decisions in the federal courts from 1977 to 1986 introduced and firmly established in U.S. law the right not to be sexually harassed in the workplace. Few deny that workers are sometimes sexually harassed (typically female employees by male employers or subordinates by supervisors), and most conscientious persons recognize that this is morally wrong. Nevertheless, there is lively debate as to whether the creation of a new legal right is an appropriate remedy for this kind of wrongdoing. When sexual harassment takes a serious form—such as unwelcome physical contact, the threat of force, or the threat of being fired—this new right is usually unnecessary because the female employee can appeal to her existing legal rights against assault and battery under tort law or against sexual discrimination under civil rights law. When sexual harassment takes a less serious form, the best solution is personal negotiation and informal resolution, rather than the intrusion of state regulation and legal enforcement into the interactions of persons within the office or the factory.

To be sure, sexual harassment will often persist in spite of every effort to prevent it by nonlegal means. Still, conferring a legal right not to be sexually harassed upon a female employee is frequently no solution at all. Such an employee often will not be in a position to claim her right, either because she is dependent upon the income she earns from her job (and hence cannot afford to antagonize her employer) or because her employer or supervisor has the power to retaliate should she demand that he cease and desist from sexual harassment. If she has the temerity to claim her legal right, she and her employer or supervisor become adversaries in court; and even if she does not make such a claim, the existence of this legal right transforms them into potential adversaries. In this way, the legal right against sexual harassment perverts what often could and always should be a cooperative and congenial personal relationship in the workplace.

Political Discourse

These two strands in the proliferation of rights, the moral and the legal, go hand in hand, for moral reformers often demand the introduction of some new legal right as necessary in order to protect some alleged moral right. This produces the third strand in the recent proliferation of rights, the expansion of the language of rights in political discourse. More and more social and political debates appeal to alleged moral rights and support the creation of new legal rights. The children's rights movement, for example, has advocated the introduction of new legal rights against child abuse and has attempted to secure children's liberties in order to protect the analogous moral rights proclaimed in the UN *Declaration of the Rights of the Child* (adopted in 1959) and the *Convention on the Rights of the Child* (adopted in 1989).

Historically the children's rights movement was born from the development of human rights and the civil rights movement. But many people argue that the rhetoric of rights is inappropriate to the dependent status of children. Colonial peoples, racial minorities, and women in male-dominated societies can sometimes achieve autonomy and equality by claiming their fundamental moral rights against those in power. This achievement is possible because their dependence is imposed upon them arbitrarily by their oppressors, and they already possess the capacities required to exercise their human rights. But the dependence of children upon their parents or guardians is natural, not artificial, and at least young children lack the psychological capacities necessary to exercise or even claim any rights that might be conferred upon them. They must, and typically will, grow out of their dependence as they mature and develop their abilities.

In addition, some moral philosophers argue that the language of rights fails to address the real needs of children. It wrongly assumes that they are already autonomous individuals who can stand on their own feet and claim their rights against their parents. But what children really need is not to be liberated and empowered to live independently as much as to receive loving care and nurture by their parents or guardians. When children or their advocates claim their rights against their parents, this makes them adversaries, undermines what is normally an intimate relationship between them, and destroys the spontaneity that enables their parents to give them the unconditional love and affection they need to develop and maintain the self-esteem essential to becoming competent autonomous adults. As the rhetoric of rights has expanded in political discourse, it has crowded out the different and more relevant voice of the ethic of care. Child neglect and abuse are all too common and grave moral wrongs, but they can be effectively addressed only by defining and insisting upon the moral responsibilities of children's caregivers. This requires a different language, one that focuses upon personal relationships and upon the unselfish conduct of those responsible for the well-being of children.

The call for changes in the ways we treat animals has also contributed to the proliferation of the language of rights in political discourse. Traditionally many of those most concerned about the mistreatment of nonhuman animals have taken political action through the animal welfare movement. In more recent years, advocates of animal rights have infiltrated this movement, and the language of rights has come to predominate in its political discourse. Many believe this shift in vocabulary is both unnecessary and counterproductive. It is unnecessary because appeals to the welfare of animals have been widely successful in achieving both legal prohibitions against the cruel treatment of domestic animals and the humane regulation of scientific experimentation on all animals. It is counterproductive because it invites comparison with the rights of human beings. The psychological differences between human and nonhuman animals cause many citizens either to doubt that animals have any real moral rights or to discount those rights when they seem to conflict with human rights. In debates about the permissibility of animal experimentation, for example, the comparison of animal with human rights has been effectively exploited in the slogan, "your child or your dog."

Even worse, the rhetoric of animal rights has proven to be politically dangerous. Its association with radicalism has attracted extremists into what has become the animal rights movement. These extremists have often engaged in violent actions that most animal lovers regard as highly immoral: They have thrown acid upon persons wearing fur coats or jackets, have broken display windows, and have even committed arson in shops selling cosmetics tested upon animals. In England some extremists have gone so far as to attach bombs to the vehicles of scientists who use animals in their medical research. Thus the domination of political discourse by the language of rights is of dubious social value and is perhaps very harmful.

As these three strands in the proliferation of rights continue and even accelerate, jurists, moral philosophers, and citizens debate their theoretical credentials and practical consequences. Are these alleged moral rights genuine or illusory, and in any case, is our increased tendency to claim rights a selfish individualism that damages our most intimate personal relationships and neglects or even denies our social responsibilities? Are these new legal rights solving our urgent social problems and making our legal system more just? Or are they exacerbating the problems we face and, in the process, undermining social cooperation and transforming us into a more and more litigious society? Does the increased use of the language of rights in political rhetoric distort social issues and exclude more useful vocabularies? On the whole, is the recent proliferation of rights moral progress or empty and sometimes dangerous rhetoric? It is to these questions that I will turn in the chapters to follow.

Hohfeld's Fundamental Legal Conceptions

Before I turn to these questions, however, let me prepare the reader by offering a brief explanation of some expressions used by jurists and moral philosophers. Wesley Newcomb Hohfeld, a jurist who taught in the Yale Law School early in this century, argued that the language of legal rights is confusing and ambiguous because it fails to distinguish between four fundamentally different legal relations.

1. *A claim.* One party x has a legal claim against some second party y that y perform some action A if and only if y has a legal duty to x to do A. For example, a creditor's claim to be repaid the amount borrowed by a debtor is logically equivalent to the debtor's duty to the creditor to repay the debt. Similarly, the student's legal claim to confidentiality against her adviser is identical with his legal duty to her not to reveal any confidential information about her without her permission.

2. *A liberty.* One party x has a legal liberty in face of some second party y to perform some action A if and only if x has no legal duty to y not to do A. Thus a student has a legal liberty to turn on his television set in his room even when his roommate is trying to study if and only if he has no legal duty to his roommate to refrain from doing so. Again, a professor's academic liberty to express unpopular ideas in the classroom in spite of the objections of his college president concerned not to alienate potential donors is equivalent to the absence of any duty of the professor to the president not to express unpopular ideas in his classes.

3. *A power.* One party x has a legal power over some second party y to bring about some legal consequence C for y if and only if some voluntary action of x would be legally recognized as having this consequence for y. For example, the owner of a book has the legal power to give it to a friend because if he hands his book to the friend and says, "this is yours," any court of law would recognize that the friend has by that action acquired the legal rights to use, possess, and dispose of that book. Likewise, the student

has a legal power to waive her right to confidentiality because if, for example, she gives her adviser permission to inform some potential employer of her grades, then her action of giving consent extinguishes his legal duty not to do so.

4. *An immunity.* One party x has a legal immunity against some second party y from some specific legal consequence C if and only if y lacks the legal power to do any action that would be recognized by the law as having the consequence C for x. For example, a student is immune from having her parent waive her right to confidentiality: If her proud parent says or writes to her adviser "I give you permission to release my daughter's grades to our local newspaper," the adviser's legal duty not to release this information remains unaffected. Similarly, a student who owns a television has a legal immunity against his roommate that his roommate not sell his TV, perhaps to ensure quiet whenever he wishes to study, because no action of his roommate would be legally recognized as transferring ownership of the television set to another person.

Although Hohfeld argued that only a legal claim really constitutes a legal right in the strict sense, most jurists have recognized the importance of distinguishing between the four legal advantages in the way that Hohfeld does and have used his fundamental legal conceptions to classify four species of legal rights: claim-rights, liberty-rights, power-rights, and immunity-rights. Many, although by no means all, moral philosophers have subsequently applied these distinctions to moral rights. Thus the promisee has a moral claim-right against the promisor that he keep his promise; a male student has a moral liberty-right to wear his hair long even when the school authorities object; a patient has a moral power-right to render experimental medical treatment upon her morally permissible by giving her consent; and at the same time a patient has an immunity-right against her physician's making it morally permissible to subject her to medical experimentation because his act of consenting does not have this moral consequence.

Core and Associated Elements

Philosophers and jurists have proposed various theories of the nature of moral and legal rights. I believe that a right is a complex structure of Hohfeldian positions, especially of claims, liberties, powers, and immunities. The "core" of a right defines its essential content, that to which the right-holder has a right. For example, the core of the creditor's legal right to be repaid is the creditor's legal claim against the debtor that the debtor repay the amount borrowed by the due date. This constitutes a real right, however, only together with a number of "associated elements," other Hohfeldian positions that, if respected, confer upon the possessor of the right both freedom and control over this core. These elements include the creditor's legal power to waive her claim to repayment and thereby cancel the debtor's duty to repay the amount borrowed, the legal liberty to waive or not waive her claim as she chooses, and a legal immunity against the debtor's extinguishing her core claim simply by saying, "I hereby cancel my debt to you."

Similarly, the defining core of the human right to free speech is the moral liberty of each individual human being to speak out or remain silent on any subject no matter how controversial or politically objectionable. Associated elements in this fundamental human right include the moral claim against the government that it not attempt to silence the right-holder by coercive measures and the moral immunity against the government's extinguishing her moral liberty of free speech by declaring a state of emergency.

Not everyone, of course, accepts my theory of the nature of a right. But those who agree with me that Hohfeld's distinctions between claims, liberties, powers, and immunities are useful need not reject my terminology of "core" and "associated elements." They can simply insist that associated elements are externally connected with any legal or moral right rather than intrinsic to its very nature.

The Road Ahead

We are now prepared to begin our philosophical journey. However one conceives of a right and whatever language one uses to describe specific rights, one cannot remain oblivious to, and should not remain uninterested in, the many debates regarding the proliferation of alleged moral rights, the introduction of new legal rights, and the increased use of the language of rights in political discourse. Although these three strands in the proliferation of rights permeate our society, and to a lesser extent other societies in the Western world, the issues debated differ markedly in different arenas. One of the earliest and most fundamental issues in these debates concerns the development of human rights. Hence, this will be the subject of the next chapter.

Although Chapter 2 will begin with a summary of the historical origins of the idea of human rights and will discuss several new human rights in the order in which they have appeared in recent years, it is not intended to be an essay on modern history. It uses the development of human rights merely to illustrate the temporal dimension of the proliferation of rights. Its purpose is to explain the nature of the three generations of human rights that have recently been affirmed and to report the continuing legal and moral debates they have generated. It will be important for the reader to note both that these very different kinds of rights raise quite different issues and that the considerations relevant to legal rights differ from those bearing on alleged moral rights.

Similarly, Chapter 3 is neither a historical nor a sociological account of the civil rights movement. It describes several new civil rights of African-Americans and reports both the legal reasoning underlying them and the moral arguments over them. Of special interest is the way in which these are tied together. A close reading of the opinions of the judges deciding civil rights cases shows clearly how often they formulate their reasoning in moral terms and rest their arguments on moral premises. At the same time, moral assessments of new legal rights frequently appeal to facts about legal institutions, such as whether a new civil right can be effectively enforced and what unintended social consequences its introduction might have.

Women's rights, the subject of Chapter 4, are especially interesting because feminists have been divided on whether the appeal to rights should be central to the struggle for the equality and well-being of women. Although the original goal of the women's rights movement was to secure rights for females equal to those enjoyed by males, some feminists have come to believe that this effort is futile, and others have even argued that claiming rights is both politically harmful and morally suspect. The focus of this chapter is upon these issues, issues that lead far beyond questions about the rights of women to questions about the justification for creating any new legal right and about whether one ought to debate any political issue in the language of rights.

The animal rights movement introduces a very different and philosophically difficult question: Are nonhuman animals possible right-holders? No one doubts that African-Americans and women are capable of possessing rights; the only questions concern what moral rights they do have and what legal rights they ought to have. Although many moral reformers assert that animals have moral rights to life and not to be tortured, many philosophers deny that it makes any more sense to ascribe rights to animals than to say that sticks and stones have rights. This controversy and the related debate about ascribing environmental rights to forests and lakes are central to Chapter 5.

Chapter 6 reports the reasons for and arguments against several new medical rights. These reflect the recent revolution in biomedical ethics. Moral issues that have traditionally been debated in terms of the professional duties of physicians and medical researchers are today discussed primarily in terms of the rights of the patient and the subject of medical experimentation. This change in moral theory has contributed to the introduction of several new legal rights held by patients and the subjects of medical research. An underlying issue posed by this chapter is whether the authority to make medical decisions ought to rest primarily with the physician or with the patient.

Throughout the first six chapters, I attempt to remain neutral for the most part and to give an unbiased report of the recent proliferation of rights and a balanced account of the arguments presented for and against the creation of new legal rights and for and against the assertion of new alleged moral rights. In the concluding chapter, I go beyond providing a general overview of the central issues to give my own evaluation. My purpose is not to inform the reader of the truth, although I do believe that my assessments are correct, but to stimulate the reader to think through the issues for herself and to arrive at her own considered evaluation of the proliferation of rights.

Notes

1. Maurice Cranston, "Human Rights, Real and Supposed," in *Political Theory and the Rights of Man*, ed. D. D. Raphael (Bloomington: Indiana University Press, 1967), p. 52.

Suggestions for Further Reading

Brabeck, Mary. 1993. "Moral Judgment: Theory and Research on Differences between Males and Females." In *An Ethic of Care*, ed. Mary Jeanne Larrabee. New York: Routledge. Brabeck provides a brief description of the ethic of care and its differences from the ethic of justice and rights.

Cranston, Maurice. 1967. "Human Rights, Real and Supposed." In *Political Theory and the Rights of Man*, ed. D. D. Raphael. Bloomington: Indiana University Press. This is the classic critique of the conception of economic and social human rights.

Gilligan, Carol. 1982. *In a Different Voice*. Cambridge Mass.: Harvard University Press. Gilligan's psychological research is the germinal source for the vast literature on the ethic of care.

Hohfeld, Wesley Newcomb. 1919. *Fundamental Legal Conceptions*. New Haven: Yale University Press. Hohfeld distinguishes between and gives illustrations of each of his fundamental conceptions on pages 23–64.

Lindgren, J. Ralph, and Nadine Taub, eds. 1993. *The Law of Sex Discrimination*. Minneapolis/Saint Paul: West Publishing Company. Pages 201–223 are a clear, accurate account of the law of sexual harassment.

O'Neill, Onora. 1988. "Children's Rights and Children's Lives." *Ethics* 98, pp. 445–463. O'Neill argues that the natural dependence of children upon their parents usually renders the appeal to their rights unhelpful.

Roe v. Wade. 1973. 410 US 113. This is the decision of the Supreme Court that first recognized the constitutional right of pregnant women to seek and obtain an abortion.

Ross, W. D. 1930. *The Right and the Good*. Oxford: Clarendon Press. Ross rejects the possibility of animal rights on pages 49–50.

Schrag, Francis. 1980. "Children: Their Rights and Needs." In *Whose Child?* ed. William Aiken and Hugh LaFollette. Totowa, N.J.: Littlefield, Adams and

Company. Schrag argues that the appeal to children's rights undermines the selfless loving care they urgently need from their parents.

Silverstein, Helena. 1996. *Unleashing Rights*. Ann Arbor: University of Michigan Press. There is an excellent discussion of the benefits and drawbacks of using the language of animal rights in political discourse on pages 81–122.

Wellman, Carl. 1978. "A New Conception of Human Rights." In *Human Rights*, ed. Eugene Kamenka and Alice E-S Tay. London: Edward Arnold. This is a brief overview of the author's conception of rights.

_____. 1995. "Rights: I. Systematic Analysis." In *Encyclopedia of Bioethics*, ed. Warren T. Reich. rev. ed. New York: Macmillan. A brief informative description of the most important aspects of legal and moral rights.

Wolgast, Elizabeth H. 1987. *The Grammar of Justice*. Ithaca: Cornell University Press. On pages 36–38 Wolgast argues that children need the loving care of responsible parents, not any appeal to their rights.

2

The Development
of Human Rights

Let us turn now to an examination of three generations of human rights. The rights to seek and enjoy asylum are similar to the civil and political rights traditionally recognized in political theory and democratic constitutions. The right to work has been widely asserted to be a moral right and has become a legal right only in the twentieth century. The right to existence of any people has been alleged to be a moral right most recently and has yet to become established in international or national law. One goal of this chapter will be to understand the nature of these quite different kinds of human rights, both as alleged moral rights and as rights in international law.

Each of these human rights has occasioned vigorous debates. Considered in their legal guise, these rights raise questions concerning whether they can be effectively protected by international courts and political action and, if so, whether this protection would be desirable. Debates concerning declarations of these rights as fundamental moral rights focus on both whether one should take them to be mere ideals or aspirations rather than rights in any strict sense and, however they are interpreted, whether there are reasons to justify their assertion. Hence, a second goal of this chapter will be to understand the arguments advanced in these debates. I will, for the most part, delay my own evaluation of these recent developments until the concluding chapter.

Although the term "human rights" did not gain currency until after the Second World War, the idea it expresses is an ancient one, for what we call human rights today are the descendants of the traditional natural rights of man. These are the fundamental moral rights each and every individual possesses simply as a human being. They are natural both because they are grounded on human nature and because their existence is independent of any artificial social institutions, such as the positive law created by human legislation and enforced in the courts. At the same time, these fundamental moral rights were originally thought to be analogous to legal rights in the sense that they are conferred upon the right-holder by law—not the law posited in any society but the natural law conceived of either as the commands of God or the moral rules self-evident to the natural light of reason. These natural rights, especially the inalienable rights to life, liberty, and property, are central to the political theory used to justify the American and French Revolutions. Because the primary purpose of the state is to protect the natural rights of the individual, any government that violates these rights may legitimately be resisted and replaced by one that will respect these fundamental moral rights of its citizens.

Thus natural rights were traditionally thought to be independent of human legislation and a moral standard to which one could appeal in the criticism or reform of any legal system. Nevertheless, the history of natural rights in theory and practice reveals a continuous interaction between moral philosophy and the law. The concept of a natural right was first defined by William of Ockham, the fourteenth-century philosopher who united the Stoics' conception of a natural law of the divine reason immanent in nature with the conception of a legal right found in Roman jurisprudence. Hugo Grotius, the seventeenth-century founder of the modern philosophical theory of natural rights, also contributed mightily to the development of the modern international law governing the relations between nation states. John Locke, the seventeenth-century moral and political philosopher who was highly influential in the framing of the constitutions adopted in America and France after their respective revolutions, was himself deeply influenced by the development of English constitutional law from the Magna Carta to the Bill of Rights of 1689. William Blackstone, the great eighteenth-century commentator upon the common law, even believed that the traditional rights of Englishmen coincided almost perfectly with the natural rights of all mankind. It is no wonder, then, that the recent development of human rights reflects both philosophical theory and legal practice.

During the nineteenth century, natural rights theories were increasingly ignored or even rejected. Probably this was due in large part to the influence of Jeremy Bentham, an exponent of classical utilitarianism, which maintained that the moral standard of individual actions and social institutions is whether they promote or prevent human happiness. Alarmed by the violence of the French Revolution, he argued that declarations of natural rights are groundless, dogmatic assertions leading to anarchy and that the only real rights are legal rights. Later moral philosophers were by and large skeptical of the existence of any personal God to legislate the law of nature and of any self-evident truths to enunciate it. Political philosophers looked to utilitarianism rather than natural rights theory as the basis for social criticism and legal reform. Most jurists adopted legal positivism, the view that whatever rules are posited or willed by legislative or judicial action are valid law. According to legal positivism law and morals, including legal and moral rights, are logically distinct and radically separate. Lawyers became almost completely absorbed in the empirical facts of legislation and adjudication and uninterested in the moral standards they thought irrelevant to their legal practice.

In the twentieth century, however, there was a marked revival of interest in the natural rights of man. This revival reflected two world wars that not only caused the death of vast numbers of individuals and the destruction of immense amounts of property but also exposed the world to the dreadful experience of totalitarian regimes, especially in Nazi Germany, that grossly violated the basic rights of so many human beings. These fundamental moral "rights of man" were renamed "human rights" to avoid any insinuation that only males are qualified to possess them and to eliminate the dubious presuppositions of traditional theories of natural rights.

Hence, the development of human rights as such began in 1945 when the *United Nations Charter* reaffirmed faith in fundamental human rights and announced that one of its primary purposes was "to achieve international co-operation . . . promoting and encouraging respect for human rights and for fundamental freedoms for all without distinction as to race, sex, language, or religion."[1] It will be useful to adopt the usual genealogy in which the first generation of human rights are civil and political rights; the second generation are the economic, social, and cultural rights; and the third generation are the human rights of solidarity. As one would expect from the biological metaphor, these successive generations overlap somewhat in their temporal development.

First Generation Rights

The first generation of human rights consists of civil and political rights. Civil rights are rights possessed by every citizen, or in a wider and more relevant sense, by every inhabitant of some state or society. These are basic rights, such as the right to own property or to a fair trial, belonging to every individual person. Political rights, such as the right to vote or to stand for public office, are those that enable the individual to participate either directly or indirectly in the establishment or administration of the government. These categories are not mutually exclusive; for example, the right to free speech is a civil right that also enables the citizen to take part in political campaigns and to criticize public officials or policies.

Historical Origins

These civil and political rights are known as the first generation of human rights because they are, for the most part, of ancient lineage. Their philosophical foundations were laid in the seventeenth and eighteenth centuries. John Locke argued that the law of nature confers on each human being the inalienable moral rights to life, liberty, and property. Although all persons would possess these rights in a state of nature, a condition in which they live without any legally organized society, their natural rights would be frequently violated. Hence, individuals enter into a social contract by which they agree to limit their natural liberty by forming a commonwealth and subsequently a government in order to secure these fundamental moral rights. However, if the state neglects the common good or violates individual rights, then the citizens have a right to revolt and to form a new state.

This and similar political theories underlie the classic natural rights documents. The American *Declaration of Independence* of 1776 asserts "that all men are created equal; that they are endowed, by their Creator, with certain unalienable rights; that among these are life, liberty, and the pursuit of happiness." The French *Declaration of the Rights of Man and of the Citizen* of 1789 proclaims "The purpose of all civil association is the preservation of the natural and imprescriptible rights of man. These rights are liberty, property and resistance to oppression."

The process of establishing these fundamental moral rights of man in the constitutional law of the modern nation states began at least with the Magna Carta of 1215 and the English Bill of Rights of 1689. It continued with the inclusion of bills of rights in the constitutions ratified in France and the United States after their revolutions, an example that was later imitated by many other nations. The inclusion of human rights in international law began even earlier under the influence of Hugo Grotius and other natural law philosophers. More recently, natural rights have been protected by international treaties and recognized by the international *Cour Permanente de Justice*. Thus the United Nations could very reasonably have taken itself to be *reaffirming* traditional moral and legal principles when it announced in the preamble to its charter that "We the peoples of the United Nations determine . . . to reaffirm faith in fundamental human rights in the dignity and worth of the human person, in the equal rights of men and women and of nations large and small . . . do hereby establish an inter-national organization to be known as the United Nations." Three years later in its *Universal Declaration of Human Rights* it first defined these rights in general terms.

When one compares the more than twenty-six civil and political rights listed in Articles 3–21 of the *Universal Declaration of Human Rights* with the rights to life, liberty, and the pursuit of happiness named in our *Declaration of Independence*, it might appear that the first generation of human rights vastly outnumbers the previously accepted natural rights. This would be to misunderstand the logical structure of traditional theories of fundamental civil and political rights. These theories distinguish between primary rights that are not grounded on some logically prior right and the other rights derived from them. Derived rights may be either more specific forms of some generic right, as the right to freedom of the press is a special case of the right to free speech, or auxiliary rights that serve to protect some primary right, as the right to *habeas corpus* (by which a person can demand to be brought before a judge to obtain release from unlawful confinement) serves to prevent the violation of the individual's right to liberty. The same sort of logical structure is presupposed by the *Universal Declaration*. Article 3 affirms the human rights to life, liberty, and security of person; most of the following rights are assumed to be derived from these primary rights. Also, one must not overlook the manner in which national and international law had previously defined a wide variety of civil and political rights in order to recognize and protect the fundamental natural rights of all persons.

The Rights to Asylum

Nevertheless, the United Nations has introduced a few new civil and political rights. One new right declared by the United Nations is the human right to asylum. As early as 1625 Grotius had asserted the natural right of a state to grant asylum on the ground that this humane act is not contrary to friendship between states. This right to grant asylum gradually became established in international law. But this right of a state was not a human right, not a right of the individual human being. What was new about the UN declaration was that every human being has the right to asylum. No such right then existed in international law; nor was this right generally accepted in moral theory. Although some moral philosophers held that the state has a humanitarian duty to grant asylum to a refugee fleeing from persecution, they did not assert that this is because the refugee has any correlative right to asylum.

Article 14 of the *Universal Declaration of Human Rights* reads in part, "Everyone has the right to seek and to enjoy in other countries asylum from persecution." Although this is frequently called "the right of asylum," it is really a pair of rights. One is the liberty-right to seek asylum from persecution, for example, by asking to be granted asylum or simply by fleeing to another country; the other is the liberty-right to enjoy asylum from persecution, that is, of remaining within the territory of another country and refusing to return to the pursuing state. Asylum is a sanctuary, a place of refuge and safety. The individual is at liberty to seek and enjoy asylum, but only when he or she is a refugee in the restricted sense of someone subjected to or threatened with persecution. The United Nations seems to have adopted a broad conception of persecution, which includes ill treatment for reasons of race, color, national or ethnic origin, religion, nationality, kinship, membership of a particular social group, or the holding of a particular political opinion—including the struggle against colonialism and apartheid, foreign occupation, alien domination, and all forms of racism. What unifies this list of diverse reasons for asylum is that ill treatment on any of these grounds violates one or more human rights. Although some nations argued that the liberty-rights to seek and enjoy asylum would be of very little value unless the individual also possessed a claim-right to be granted asylum, a right implying a duty of other countries to grant asylum to any genuine refugee, the United Nations has refused to recognize this additional right because it would conflict with the unquestioned right of the sovereign state to refuse to grant asylum at its discretion.

Since 1948, the human rights to seek and to enjoy asylum from persecution have become firmly established in international law. In addition to defining the core liberties of the individual to seek and to enjoy asylum in another country, these rights include several associated elements—legal positions of other parties that tend to confer freedom or control over the exercise of these liberties upon the right-holder. For example, although no state has a legal duty to admit a refugee at its frontier, it does have a legal duty not to forcibly return any refugee, even one who has entered the country illegally, to the pursuing state. This duty not to return an alien is limited by any extradition treaty binding upon the state; however, most such treaties require the extradition of common criminals but not of refugees from persecution. Any state has the traditional liberty-right to grant asylum at its discretion, and the pursuing state has a duty under international law to respect any asylum granted by another state.

The alleged moral rights to seek and enjoy asylum as defined by the United Nations and other international bodies have the same complexity. There are associated moral duties and liberties corresponding to the duties and liberties under international law. In 1967, Article 3 of the *Declaration on Territorial Asylum* added the moral duty, not yet recognized as a legal duty, of any state not to reject a refugee at the frontier. Although this does require the state to admit the refugee to its territory, this may be only for temporary asylum. Thus each state is declared to have a moral duty to admit refugees only as long as this does not require any excessive sacrifice by that state.

Critique

Considered as legal rights, there can be no doubt that the human rights to seek and to enjoy asylum are real. They have been increasingly recognized in the authoritative sources of international law. But international lawyers and political scientists insist that what can and should be doubted is their effectiveness. Because there is no human right to be granted asylum in any other country, the individual who seeks asylum has no assurance of finding and enjoying it. Moreover, the legal rights to asylum have clearly failed to provide adequate refuge for the vast numbers of human beings fleeing from persecution. This is illustrated dramatically by the case of Rwanda, where about 500,000 Tutsi fled to avoid annihilation by the Hutu and then, after the Tutsi regained power, over 2 million Hutu fled to escape retaliation. The refugee problem became most obvious and urgent in the United States recently with the flood of Cuban refugees seeking to escape persecution. Nevertheless, inadequacy is not the same as complete ineffectiveness. Most states have fulfilled their duty not to forcibly return refugees to the state where they face persecution and have refused to extradite individuals who may be political offenders but not common criminals. What is needed is probably not so much a stronger human right to asylum in international law as a more effective international action to reduce persecution.

Human rights organizations report that the rights to seek and to enjoy asylum, when considered as moral rights, also have a genuine but very limited effectiveness. Although states have no legal duty to admit refugees, most of them try to fulfill their moral duty not to reject at the frontier anyone fleeing from persecution, even if only to offer temporary asylum. Also the duty of other states merely "to consider . . . appropriate measures to lighten the burden" on any state flooded with refugees has been more effective than one might have predicted. On a variety of occasions, several states have combined under the auspices of the United Nations to provide relief to large numbers of refugees and to enable them either to return to their original countries safely or to be admitted to some other country for protection.

Are the human rights to seek and enjoy asylum as declared and defined in various documents of the United Nations real moral rights? That is, are those pronouncements that affirm them rationally justified or merely dogmatic assertions? This depends not upon whether they are asserted or even widely accepted as such but on whether they have adequate moral grounds. Unfortunately, no UN document contains moral reasoning to justify its assertions that there are rights to seek and to enjoy asylum, and moral philosophers have neglected to inquire into the grounds of these rights. My guess is that they should be regarded as auxiliary rights, rights grounded upon their necessity for the protection of other prior human rights. This is suggested by the facts that they are rights to asylum from persecution and that persecution consists in the violation of certain human rights. To be sure, the rights to seek and enjoy asylum do not protect the individual from having his or her human rights violated, but to the degree that they are effective they do lessen the danger of exercising or insisting upon these other human rights by providing for some escape from retaliation, should it occur.

Second Generation Rights

In addition to civil and political rights, the UN *Declaration* of 1948 includes a number of economic, social, and cultural rights. These have come to be known as second generation rights because no rights of this kind were affirmed in either the American *Declaration of Independence* of 1776 or the French *Declaration of the Rights of Man and the Citizen* of 1789. To be sure, Thomas Paine, an eighteenth-century radical advocate of natural rights, did include social provisions regarding education, welfare, and work in *The Rights of Man*, published in 1792; and then the French *Declaration* of 1793 did affirm the right to education. But these rights did not fit easily into the traditional natural rights theories and were not very widely recognized as fundamental moral or constitutional rights until this century. Although the right to education was introduced into many legal systems long ago, this was done by simple legislation rather than constitutional amendment, and the same is true of the various welfare rights more recently enacted. Only in 1936 did the USSR Constitution give fundamental status to the rights to work, to rest and leisure, to maintenance in old age and in case of sickness or disability, and to education.

How should one define these second generation human rights? The usual label "economic, social, and cultural rights" is not very illuminating, for it tells us neither what distinguishes these rights from the more traditional civil and political rights nor what these kinds of economic, social, and cultural rights have in common. We can learn something of what distinguishes these rights from more traditional rights by consulting the early history of human rights.

When it adopted its *Universal Declaration of Human Rights*, the United Nations understood that these declared rights could not be secured in practice until they were spelled out in terms that could be embodied in international law and in national constitutions. But as it drafted a more detailed covenant, it came to recognize that economic, social, and cultural rights must be institutionalized very differently from more traditional civil and political rights. For one thing, although rights such as the rights to life or liberty or due process could be enforced in the courts, this enforcement would require the construction of schools and hospitals, the improvement of irrigation and agriculture, the industrialization of production, and the creation of an elaborate system of welfare agencies to ensure the rights to education, to an adequate standard of living, and to social security. For another thing, and as a consequence, although the civil and political rights could be introduced almost immediately into every legal system, the economic, social, and cultural rights could be achieved only gradually and over a considerable period of time in the less affluent nations. Because of these differences, first and second generation human rights were articulated in two separate UN covenants.

What, then, do the various rights included in the *International Covenant on Economic, Social, and Cultural Rights* have in common? They all presuppose the recognition that the welfare of the individual human being depends upon certain social conditions, such as an opportunity to earn one's living by productive labor, the availability of physicians with access to hospitals, and public or private agencies to provide subsistence in the event of unemployment or disability. These rights also presuppose the conviction that because these conditions cannot be effectively achieved by individual effort, one's society has a moral obligation, and ought to have a legal duty, to provide them. Hence, second generation human rights might best be thought of as social welfare rights.

The Right to Work

A good example of a social welfare right is the human right to work. It is not at all clear whether Article 23 of the *Universal Declaration of Human Rights* affirms a single but complex right to work or a number of distinct rights concerning work. Later human rights documents, beginning in 1961 with the *European Social Charter*, distinguish between the right to work itself and the right to just or fair working conditions. Probably the most authoritative definition is contained in Article 6 of the UN *International Covenant on Economic, Social, and Cultural Rights* of 1966: "The States Parties to the present Covenant recognize the right to work, which includes the right of everyone to the opportunity to gain his living by work which he freely chooses or accepts, and will take appropriate steps to safeguard this right." Thus the core of this human right is the claim of every individual human being against his or her state to be provided with the opportunity to gain a living by work and to freely choose between working positions. This right implies the correlative duty of one's government to take the appropriate steps to provide this opportunity. The underlying assumption is clearly that the welfare of the individual human being requires this opportunity and that only the state has the ability to fulfill this fundamental human need.

Because each of the key concepts in this definition of the right to work is vague, some explanation is required. Work is a purposive, presumably useful, activity involving effort or exertion. This distinguishes the right to work from other rights such as the right to rest and leisure or the right to take part in the cultural life of one's society. Finally, the conditions should allow the individual a reasonable choice between working positions in society. This does not mean that the individual should be able to work when and where and how he or she most desires, but at the very least it does exclude forced labor, except perhaps as punishment of a convicted criminal.

Legal Doubts

Human rights frequently exist both as fundamental moral rights and as rights in force under international law. However, jurists have questioned the reality of social welfare rights considered as legal rights. Are economic, social, or cultural rights genuine legal rights today? If not, could they become so as the international law of human rights continues to develop?

One challenge to the reality of social welfare rights under international law arises from what David Trubek, a jurist who has published extensively on international law, has called the principle of progressive realization. Article 2 of the *International Covenant on Economic, Social, and Cultural Rights* reads in part: "Each State Party to the present Covenant undertakes to take steps . . . with a view to achieving progressively the full realization of the rights recognized in the present Covenant by all appropriate means." For example, the steps to be taken to achieve the full realization of the right to work include the creation of vocational guidance and training programs as well as of policies to achieve full and productive employment. But steps like these would not ensure the enjoyment of the right to work for each and every individual human being in a society. A genuine right, such as the creditor's right to be paid, imposes a present duty upon some second party, in this case the debtor. The debtor's duty is not merely to take steps to earn the money to repay the loan or to do his best to repay the loan in the future; it is to pay in full on the due date. And if payment is not forthcoming, the right-holder can take legal action to claim performance of the duty correlative to her right. Hence, some jurists argue that the principle of progressive realization defines a social ideal but does not recognize any legal right.

Other jurists reply that the *Covenant* does more than define an ideal to be achieved in the indefinite future; it imposes definite obligations upon the states parties today. Those states that have ratified this international treaty have bound themselves to legislate specific economic, social, and cultural programs to satisfy certain fundamental human needs. Thus each human being does have a right that demands of his or her government that it actually adopt the appropriate policies and effectively administer the agencies necessary to ensure the enjoyment of each social welfare right.

Even granted that the *Covenant* does impose programmatic obligations—such as the obligations to provide institutions for vocational training and to take steps to achieve full employment—these would fall short of ensuring for every individual her right to work. Some job-seekers will still lack the opportunity to gain their living by work they have chosen or accepted freely. There is and always must remain a gap between any obligation to undertake programs to achieve social goals and any corresponding duty to each and every individual that would enable him or her to enjoy a human right. Thus what international law calls economic, social, and cultural rights are really social ideas rather than individual rights.

Another challenge to the reality of social welfare rights as legal rights is that they permit such extensive derogations and limitations that they do not impose any binding obligation upon the states parties that have ratified treaties such as the *International Covenant*. Any real right implies one or more correlative obligations, and to be bound by an obligation is to have one's freedom of action constrained in some manner. But any state can always evade any burdensome obligation by taking advantage of one of the provisions in the human rights treaties. Under the *Covenant* each state undertakes only to take steps "to the maximum of its available resources" (Article 2.1), and developing countries "may determine to what extent they would guarantee the economic rights recognized in the present Covenant to non-nationals" (Article 2.3). Moreover, Article 4 permits each state to abridge the recognized rights by "such limitations as are determined by law . . . and solely for the purpose of promoting the general welfare in a democratic society." Because each state can interpret the meaning and force of these derogations for itself, it can always decide that it lacks the resources to realize these social welfare rights or that the attempt to guarantee them to needy individuals would conflict with policies required to maximize the general welfare.

However Louis Henkin, a specialist on international law and a recognized authority on human rights, believes that these derogations and limitations do not render the undertakings of the states parties illusory, provided that international bodies and other states scrutinize the interpretation and application of the relevant provisions in international human rights treaties. The question remains, of course, as to how effectively international supervision would enforce social welfare rights.

Accordingly, a third challenge to the reality of social welfare rights is that they are not enforceable. Any real legal right must be enforceable in the courts. If a debtor fails or refuses to repay a loan, for example, the creditor has the power to take legal action to force the debtor to pay the amount owed or to pay compensation for any damages suffered as a consequence of the violation of his or her right. Without some such power to sue, the alleged right would be a merely paper right rather than a real right because the document in which it is said to exist makes no difference in the way the legal system really functions.

The *International Covenant on Economic, Social, and Cultural Rights* provides for what Trubek has aptly called a system of generic implementation. Articles 16 and 21–23 require the states parties to submit reports on both the measures they have adopted and the progress they have made in achieving the recognized rights. These reports shall be transmitted by the secretary-general of the United Nations to the Economic and Social

Council. This council may submit recommendations of a general nature (not mentioning any particular state) to the General Assembly and to the specialized agencies of the United Nations and may assist such bodies in deciding on the advisability of international measures likely to contribute to the progressive implementation of the social welfare rights. This method is clearly designed to assist the states parties and not to embarrass or censure any that fail to ensure the recognized rights. It is not, and is not intended to be, a system of legal enforcement. Many jurists conclude that there are no real social welfare rights under existing international law. Others point to the fact that many such rights are already enforced in the domestic law of several welfare states to show that social welfare rights could, given the necessary modifications in the system for their implementation, become real rights under international law also.

What should a jurist or philosopher of law conclude from these debates? Probably that there are no economic, social, or cultural human rights under existing international law. It may well be that no international social welfare rights are real legal rights because none of them imposes any definite obligation upon any state party and none can be enforced through the courts of human rights. Even if a few such rights are currently enforceable, they are not human rights in the strict sense because individual human beings lack access to these courts. However, it seems that at least some social welfare rights could become real rights if the human rights documents were amended in a way that would impose more definite duties upon the states and would give the individual right-holders the power to go to court to enforce their rights.

Moral Arguments

Rights Are Negative. Jurists and international lawyers tend to be concerned with institutional issues: whether social welfare rights could be enforced in the courts and what role individual right-holders might have in any judicial processes. Moral philosophers, on the other hand, focus more on conceptual and moral issues: what the expression "a human right" does or should mean and what moral implications would follow from the recognition of any alleged right.

Thus some moral philosophers argue that so-called social welfare rights cannot be human rights in the strict sense because human rights are essentially negative. They distinguish between negative rights—such as one's right not to be killed, which imposes a duty upon others not to kill one—and positive rights—such as the creditor's right to be repaid, which imposes upon the debtor the correlative duty to pay the amount borrowed by the due date. Moral philosophers maintain that human rights are essentially negative rights, rights correlative to the duties of others, primarily governments, *not* to mistreat individuals in fundamentally immoral ways. Hence, genuine human rights could not impose any positive social obligations to promote individual welfare. Robert Nozick, a libertarian philosopher who holds that government welfare programs violate the basic rights of those taxed to support them, expresses this conception of a right succinctly when he addresses the question of whether every right necessarily confers upon its holder a right to enforce that right: "Yet rights of enforcement are themselves merely *rights*; that is, permissions to do something and obligations on others not to interfere."[2]

Why should one accept this purely negative conception of rights? Nozick himself grounds his theory of rights upon a Kantian moral theory. Along with many others, he believes that the import of moral rights cannot be explained by a utilitarian theory. If rights were justified by their utility, their contribution to human welfare, then it would be permissible or even required to violate someone's rights whenever it would be useful to do so. This implies that one might, for example, have an obligation to punish an innocent person in order to prevent a riot in which large numbers of persons might be seriously harmed. Such an act would clearly be morally wrong because it would be using an innocent person merely as a means to benefit others. To avoid this immoral conclusion, Nozick contrasts rights with goals. Rights are not goods or benefits to be pursued by human action; they are side constraints that limit what one may do to right-holders in promoting one's own welfare or even the general welfare. Rights must be purely negative because their moral function is to constrain or limit permissible kinds of action; they tell one only what one must *not* do in the pursuit of one's goals. The import of moral rights can be explained best with recourse to Kantian theory, in which the most basic moral principle is the respect for persons. What commands our respect in each individual person is his or her practical rationality, the ability to choose and act on moral reasons. Therefore, one ought always to treat others as ends-in-themselves, as individuals capable of choosing for themselves how to live their own lives. This is why moral rights are essentially both freedoms to act as one chooses and obligations on the part of others not to interfere with one's liberty of action.

There are at least two ways in which moral philosophers have tried to avoid this Nozickian challenge to social welfare rights. One is to rebut his rejection of all utilitarian theories of moral rights. David Lyons, a contemporary moral philosopher and interpreter of utilitarianism, has advanced an interpretation of John Stuart Mill that would enable us to integrate human rights into his utilitarian moral philosophy. Another way to avoid the Nozickian challenge is to explain how a moral right could impose some positive obligation even according to Kantian theory. Immanuel Kant, an eighteenth-century German philosopher, argued that one has a moral duty to rescue someone in dire need of help, and this might well imply that the individual in distress has a right to be rescued. Kant could argue that although a right is a purely negative side constraint, a drowning person's right to life implies an obligation that one who could save her life *not* refrain from doing so.

Nozick is not the only one to deny the existence of positive human rights. There is another sort of reasoning advanced to defend a purely negative conception of human rights. It is not based upon any Kantian theory of the grounds of moral rights or any general conception of the nature of rights; it is based upon our paradigms of human rights, those traditional natural rights that were the first generation of civil and political rights. An examination of the great natural rights documents, such as the American *Declaration of Independence* and the French *Declaration of the Rights of Man and of the Citizen*, shows clearly that their essential purpose is to protect individuals from state action. Hence, the function of human rights is purely negative; it is to limit state interference with individual liberty.

This reasoning is not, however, conclusive. Some moral philosophers accept this characterization of the traditional natural rights documents but suggest that they reflect the political issues of their times rather than the nature of human rights. When the main threat to individual welfare was governmental oppression, it was only natural that moral and political philosophers would assert negative rights. But when new social and economic institutions result in vast unemployment, the poverty of many dependent children, and great financial insecurity of elderly individuals, then it is time to recognize a second generation of social welfare rights. Others reject the view that our paradigms of natural rights are purely negative. The rights to life and liberty impose upon the state not merely the negative duties to refrain from the arbitrary killing or imprisonment of individuals but also the positive duties to provide police protection so that other individuals will not kill or kidnap one. Similarly, the right to due process requires the state to create and maintain an expensive system of courts before which its citizens can obtain fair trials in criminal and civil cases.

Scarce Resources.   Even granted that moral rights often imply positive duties, there remains the problem of scarce resources. Most moral philosophers accept the Kantian principle that there can be no moral obligation to do the impossible. Maurice Cranston asserts the corollary: No right can imply a duty to do the impossible. Hence, the primary test for the reality of any moral right is practicability. He argues that the alleged social welfare rights fail this test.

If social welfare rights were a second generation of human rights, they would be universal rights—rights of *all* human beings to certain benefits, such as work or social security, essential for their welfare. But many societies lack the resources to fulfill the duties that would be implied by such rights. Periodic famines make it impossible for some African countries to protect all their citizens at all times from malnutrition, even from starvation. Many countries lack the physicians, hospitals, and medicines that would be required to provide everyone with necessary medical care in the event of sickness. Even affluent societies are finding themselves unable to contain the costs of medical care sufficiently to ensure high quality care to all their citizens. And we in the United States are discovering how frightfully expensive it is to provide the disabled and the handicapped with an opportunity to work. Cranston and others conclude that social welfare rights cannot be real human rights because many societies lack the resources to make them practicable.

There are at least three ways to rebut this argument against second generation human rights. One is to limit the content of social welfare rights in a way that reduces the implied duties sufficiently to render them practicable. The *International Covenant on Economic, Social, and Cultural Rights* does this when it requires only that "Each State Party to the present Covenant undertakes to take steps . . . to the maximum of its available resources." Similarly, D. D. Raphael, a British moral and political philosopher, argues that it is always possible for a society to do something to control unemployment or to provide security against hunger. After all, we do not conclude that there is no human right to life simply because no amount of police protection will prevent all homicides. Thus any social welfare right implies the correlative duty of one's state to do as much as it can to fulfill the demands of the right.

Paradoxically, a second way to respond to the problem of scarce resources is to multiply the number of correlative duties implied by any human right. Henry Shue, a moral philosopher who has argued that American foreign policy ought to take human rights more seriously, suggests that the basic right to subsistence implies three types of correlative duties—duties to avoid depriving anyone of subsistence, duties to protect everyone from such deprivation, and duties to aid the deprived. He points out that the first sort of duty is purely negative and that the second type is no more demanding than the duties implied by such first generation human rights as the rights to life or liberty. He then argues that by fulfilling these two types of duties, any society can greatly reduce the amount of resources needed to aid those who find themselves deprived of the means of subsistence. Presumably an analogous argument could be advanced to defend other social welfare rights.

Finally, H. J. McCloskey, an Australian philosopher who has articulated one of the more important theories of rights, rejects the correlativity of rights and duties. He holds that a right is an entitlement to do, have, enjoy, or have done. Although any right will imply one or more claims against others, it is a mistake to identify a right to something with a claim against some duty-bearer. According to McCloskey's theory, a social welfare right is an entitlement to the efforts of others to aid and promote one's seeking after or enjoying some good. But the duties implied by such a right will depend upon the circumstances and never demand more than is practicable.

The Violation of Fundamental Rights.   A third argument against the existence of social welfare rights is that they would require the state to violate fundamental moral rights of its citizens. As all the international documents defining these rights show, each economic, social, or cultural right imposes upon the state the appropriate programmatic obligations. Any governmental program, such as one to provide unemployment benefits or medical care to those in poverty, would have to be funded through taxation of the incomes or real estate of the more fortunate members of society. Robert Nozick argues that such taxation would violate their human right to property. The central core of a property right is the right to determine what shall be done with one's property. But the state violates this right when it takes a portion of one's property and thereby deprives one of the choice of whether to give this amount to charity or to spend it oneself. The taxation of one's income also violates the individual's human right to liberty. To take away part of one's income is, in effect, to force one to work part of the time for the state. This constitutes forced labor and amounts to a partial ownership in one's person. In this respect it violates the human right to liberty much as the institution of slavery does.

One criticism of this argument, a criticism advanced by Tony Honoré, a contemporary British jurist, is that human rights are more limited than Nozick recognizes. Nozick does admit that one's right to property is limited by the Lockean rights of others. Regarding the core right to decide what shall be done with one's property, he says, "My property rights in my knife allow me to leave it where I will, but not in your chest."[3] Thus the scope of the human right to property is limited by the human right to life. But why assume that the only limits to one's property rights are the three natural rights asserted by Locke—the rights to life, liberty, and property? If there is a second generation of human rights, these will also limit the individual's human rights to property and liberty. And if these Lockean rights are thus limited, then taxation need not infringe them. To assume that the fundamental rights of the individual are not limited by social welfare rights is to beg the question.

Another criticism of Nozick's reasoning is that he mistakenly presupposes that the rights to property and liberty are absolute, that they are never overridden by other rights. In a footnote, Nozick writes, "The question of whether these side constraints are absolute . . . is one I hope largely to avoid."[4] However, he cannot evade this issue. Samuel Scheffler, a contemporary moral philosopher, proposes a wider range of human rights, including social welfare rights. He admits that these may conflict under some circumstances, but explains that this does not show that any of them are unreal. This is because our fundamental moral rights are prima facie rather than absolute. A prima facie right is a right that imposes a duty upon some second party *unless* it is outweighed by some more important moral factor; an absolute right is one that always imposes a correlative duty whatever the circumstances. Thus taxation to fund social welfare programs will be morally justified when, but perhaps only when, the social welfare rights of the deprived override the property rights of the more fortunate members of society.

The debate about whether second generation human rights are real moral rights continues. Although it would be premature to predict its outcome, perhaps one can draw some tentative conclusions. The repeated attempts to introduce such rights into international law have been only partially successful because it has proven difficult to define with precision the obligations they are supposed to impose, and no effective procedures for enforcing them have been firmly established. There are very plausible arguments against the moral credentials of social welfare rights, but by far the most serious of these is posed by the problem of scarce resources. Still, there are equally plausible replies to each of these moral arguments. Thus both the legal and moral status of second generation human rights remain to be decided.

Third Generation Rights

Today a third generation of human rights is emerging in international law and moral theory. Although there is almost no doubt about the birth of several new rights, there is very considerable uncertainty about what, if anything, they have in common and how, if at all, they differ from human rights of the first and second generations.

These new human rights are most often labeled rights of solidarity. Solidarity is the mutual support or cohesiveness within a group, especially among individuals with strong common interests, sympathies, or aspirations. Solidarity enters into the definition of this third generation of human rights in two ways. First, they are rights of social groups rather than of individual human beings. They include the rights of all humanity to peace and to a healthy environment and the rights of any people to self-determination and to its own culture. Second, they hold against all humanity. Because they demand worldwide action, the duties they impose fall primarily upon international institutions—including the United Nations, regional organizations such as the Council of Europe and the Organization of American States, and a variety of more specialized associations of nation states, such as the Organization for Economic Cooperation and Development and the North Atlantic Treaty Organization.

The difference between third generation human rights and those of the first two generations is one of degree. Civil and political rights, especially the economic, social, and cultural rights, impose duties upon states and international organizations as well as upon individual persons; conversely, third generation rights impose duties upon individuals as well as upon social groups. What is new, or at least relatively new, is the assertion of human rights of groups with correlative obligations falling collectively upon all humanity. What is distinctive about each generation of human rights is probably the emphasis it places upon the aspirations of the French Revolution—Liberty, Equality, Fraternity. The civil and political human rights serve primarily to protect the liberty of the individual against the oppression of the nation state. The social welfare rights function mainly to reduce social inequalities and to assist the most deprived members of a society to live a more nearly normal human life. The solidarity rights are needed to protect vulnerable groups of people and to advance the unity and well-being of humanity in general.

It will be useful to have an example of this third generation of human rights in mind in order to enable us to discover what they have in common and to illustrate their problematic aspects. The rights of peoples are the best paradigms both because they are more firmly established in international law and because they are discussed more fully in the legal and philosophical literature.

The Right to Existence

Article 1 of the *Universal Declaration of the Rights of Peoples* asserts, "Every people has the right to existence." This is also the first peoples' right explicitly affirmed in the *African Charter on Human and Peoples' Rights.*[5] Although neither of these is a document issued by the United Nations, they can be taken to reaffirm its previous conventions on genocide. This may be why they do not spell out the specific content of this peoples' right.

In the *Convention on the Prevention and Punishment of the Crime of Genocide*, 1948, the General Assembly defined genocide in some detail:

> In the present Convention, genocide means any of the following acts committed with intent to destroy, in whole or in part, a national, ethnical, racial or religious group, as such: (a) Killing members of the group; (b) Causing serious bodily or mental harm to members of the group; (c) Deliberately inflicting on the group conditions of life calculated to bring about its physical destruction in whole or in part; (d) Imposing measures intended to prevent births within the group; (e) Forcibly transferring children of the group to another group.

When this *Convention* was adopted, the United Nations was no doubt motivated primarily by the Holocaust, the wholesale killing of Jews by the

Nazi regime; but today we might think first of the recent ethnic cleansings in what used to be Yugoslavia.

Presumably, then, the peoples' right to existence concerns its physical existence rather than its cultural identity; it is the right that others not act with intent to annihilate the group. Although genocide is most frequently committed by acts of killing a number of individual human beings, what makes it a violation of the peoples' right to existence is that these individual murders are done with intent to destroy the group as such. And the kinds of groups protected by this right are or include national, ethnical, racial, or religious groups.

The peoples' right to existence is a solidarity right not only because it is the right of a people rather than an individual person, but also because it holds primarily upon the international community. Because genocide is typically committed by military personnel on the command of, or at least with the acquiescence of, the political authorities, it is unrealistic to rely upon the individual nation states to prevent or punish it. Hence, the *Convention on Genocide* declares that "to liberate mankind from such an odious scourge, international co-operation is required." To this end, it recognizes the jurisdiction of international penal tribunals to adjudicate cases involving persons charged with genocide. The *Convention* asserts that genocide is a crime even when committed by constitutionally responsible rulers or public officials, and it imposes an obligation upon each state party to extradite such persons and not to refuse to do so—on the grounds that genocide is a political crime analogous to resistance to colonial rule. Finally, it obliges the competent organs of the United Nations to take such actions as they consider appropriate for the prevention and suppression of acts of genocide.

Legal Critique

Although there is often debate about the legal status of this or that particular third-generation human right, most jurists do not doubt that solidarity rights can be real human rights, for both advocates and opponents agree that they are emerging rights in international law. Disagreements between jurists concern primarily questions of whether to encourage or discourage this development and of how such rights could be institutionalized.

First, many jurists maintain that it is unnecessary to add a third category of solidarity rights to the first and second generations of human rights. To be sure, individual persons cannot enjoy their human rights in isolation from the groups of which they are members. But there is obviously a social dimension to most civil and political rights and to all economic, social, and cultural rights. These rights hold against one's state and impose obligations upon the United Nations and other international organizations. The civil right to life, for example, requires that one's state take measures to protect one's life, and the economic right to an adequate standard of living imposes a duty upon the United Nations and various international bodies to assist the developing countries to progress economically. Rather than introduce a third generation of human rights, it would be better to develop more fully the solidarity aspects implicit in the human rights of individuals.

Thus Article 22 of the *Universal Declaration of Human Rights* asserts, "Everyone, as a member of society, has the right to social security." And Article 27 of the *International Covenant on Civil and Political Rights* reads: "In those States in which ethnic, religious or linguistic minorities exist, persons belonging to such minorities shall not be denied the right, in community with other members of their group, to enjoy their own culture, to profess and practice their own religion, or to use their own language." There is no need to introduce rights of peoples as such because international law already recognizes that many of the human rights of individuals belong to them as members of social groups.

Other jurists reply that this individualistic approach to group rights does not go far enough. To be sure, it is individual persons who speak their own language to one another or participate in the culture of their community. But some rights essential to human flourishing cannot be exercised by individual persons, even as members of some social group. The right to self-determination can be exercised only by a people collectively. Although this right can be, and has been, exercised by means of a plebiscite, in which each member of the group votes, it is the aggregate outcome that determines the people's choice of its political status. No individual member of the minority has the right to a form of government different from that chosen by the majority. Similarly, the peoples' right to physical existence cannot be reduced to the individual rights to life of the members of the group. Why is genocide such a monstrous crime against humanity? It is not merely that so many individuals are destroyed; many lives are lost in any major war. The essence of genocide lies in the intention to destroy a racial, religious, or national group as a whole.

A second legal issue concerns this proliferation as such. Many jurists believe that it is undesirable to add an entire third generation of human rights to those previously established in international law. Any such inflation will devalue the currency of human rights. The more human rights there are the less weight each will carry, for the resources of the international community are very limited. It is especially unfortunate to introduce a new category of less urgent rights while such fundamental human rights as the rights to life, liberty, social security, and political participation are so widely violated. It would be better to concentrate on the more effective realization of the most necessary human rights rather than to burden our legal system with an additional set of rights that do not yet command widespread respect among the nation states, which must cooperate to secure any human right in international law.

Other jurists concede that it is a mistake to attempt to introduce impractical aspirations into human rights law; to do so would merely create unrealistic expectations and, when these expectations fail, lead to a general disillusionment with human rights. Nevertheless, they argue that it is not always possible to enforce the human rights of individuals without the legal recognition of peoples' rights. As long as the Jews remain a despised people in some states, it will not be possible to protect the right to life of Jewish individuals without international action to outlaw the genocide of the Jewish people. And the human right to enjoy one's own culture, in community with others, of individual American Indians or Australian Aborigines becomes empty unless the human right of indigenous peoples to preserve and develop their shared cultures is respected. Therefore, the introduction of a very few solidarity rights is desirable and can be accomplished without any devaluation of the entire currency of human rights.

A third objection of some international lawyers to the introduction of solidarity rights is the fear that they pose a threat to the human rights of individuals. Group rights will often conflict with individual rights, so that the protection of peoples' rights will sometimes require the violation of fundamental human rights of persons. The right of a people to preserve its own culture may well conflict with the right of parents to choose how their child shall be educated; for example, the right of the Amish people to preserve their religious tradition might conflict with the right of Amish parents to decide that their children would be better prepared for life in the United States by public schools than by schools in which the values of the Amish religious community are taught. Again, the right of an Indian tribe to preserve its own culture implies a claim over its traditional lands, for the two are inseparably connected; but this conflicts with the human right to property of those members of the Indian tribe that might purchase portions of that land and subsequently wish to sell it to someone other than another member of the tribe.

Other jurists reply that there will inevitably be conflicts between rights within any system of specific rights. Conflicts between civil rights or between civil rights and social welfare rights have been resolved by the gradual redefinition of each specific right to avoid future conflicts and, where this is impossible, by balancing one right against another in each particular case. Because no legal right is immutable or absolute, the conflict between group rights and individual rights is no more serious than the many conflicts between the human rights of individual persons. Moreover, the debate about individual rights versus collective rights becomes much less crucial once it is accepted that certain individual rights cannot be exercised in isolation from the community.

Moral Criticisms

In addition to the debates among jurists as to whether solidarity rights can and should become real human rights under international law, there are philosophical criticisms of the recent assertions of these rights considered as a new category of moral rights. For one thing, these group rights seem to be incompatible with the nature of human rights. Because human rights are rights one possesses merely as a human being—not by virtue of some special status, such as one's citizenship or moral virtue—they must be possessed equally by all human beings. Article 1 of the *Universal Declaration of Human Rights* asserts, "All human beings are born free and equal in dignity and rights." Then Article 2 asserts as a corollary: "Everyone is entitled to all the rights and freedoms set forth in this Declaration, without distinction of any kind, such as race, colour, sex, language, religion, political or other opinion, national or social origin, property, birth or other status." Thus the fundamental principle that human rights are universal and equal implies that any racial, religious, sexual, or similar discrimination is morally wrong.

This seems to exclude recognizing any basic moral rights of peoples. What defines any people is its culture, consisting in its distinctive language, religion, traditions, and such characteristics. Therefore, to admit special rights for a people would be to give the members of this limited community special privileges denied to other human beings. For example, to establish Spanish as a second language in the public schools in states such as California and Texas in order that Hispanics could preserve their traditional culture would be to discriminate against those Italian, Polish, and Russian immigrants, among others, who are denied equal treatment in this respect. This policy would seem to be discrimination on the basis of language or national origin, thereby a violation of human rights, and not a new sort of protection for human rights. Therefore, some argue that there cannot be a third generation of human rights because they would be inconsistent with the principle of the universality and equality of human rights.

In reply, others argue that solidarity rights need not confer special privileges upon any human being. Although it might be discriminatory to establish the Spanish language in our public schools, while excluding Italian, Polish and Russian, it does not necessarily follow that group rights are discriminatory. Genuine solidarity rights are universal; they are rights of *all* peoples and thereby beneficial for every member of every people. If any people has a right to preserve its language, so does every group; and if a state assists one ethnic community in this endeavor, it ought to give equal assistance to all the other ethnic communities within its territory. Also, far from inevitably perpetuating inequality, solidarity rights are sometimes necessary to preserve or promote equality. In a pluralistic society, some ethnic minorities may be so small that without special rights they would be swallowed up by the majority culture. Even in a democratic society, the equal universal rights of the members of a minority will often count for nothing against an overwhelming majority of voters indifferent or even antagonistic to the minority's special interests. Full equality for these human beings requires more than that they have human rights as individual members of some minority; the minorities to which they belong must have fundamental moral and legal rights as peoples.

The most fundamental criticism of recent declarations of peoples' rights is that a people is not the kind of being that could possibly possess any moral rights. When someone picks a flower, does she violate its moral right to life? Presumably not. This is not because the flower is not killed by her action; plants are simply not the kind of beings that could possess any moral rights at all. Why not? Why is it that normal adult human beings can and do possess moral rights but sticks, stones, and plants cannot? What qualifies some entities to be possible moral right-holders?

I have argued in *Real Rights* that only moral agents can possess moral rights. This is because according to my conception of a right, every right includes liberties and powers, and one exercises a liberty or power by acting in the appropriate manner. For example, one exercises one's liberty of free speech by public speaking or one exercises one's power of disposing of one's property by handing one's book to another while saying, "here, this is yours." Because it would be pointless and misleading to ascribe a liberty or a power to any being incapable of exercising either, moral theory should ascribe rights only to moral agents. Because I believe that groups, including peoples, are incapable of acting collectively, I deny that a people as such could have any moral rights.

Other moral philosophers disagree and try to explain how group action is possible. Thus Peter French, an important contributor to business ethics, has argued that corporations have an internal organizational decision procedure by virtue of which they can and do act. Even if this is true, it seems irrelevant to third generation human rights. A people is not a corporate body, not an organized group like a nation state or a private corporation. Vernon Van Dyke, a political scientist especially interested in the status of minorities, offers one of the most clear and accurate definitions of a people:

> Two definitions of a *people* show up in UNESCO's deliberations. According to one, a *people* is identified with a distinctive culture: those who share a given culture are a people. I will assume that a culture is distinguished by such characteristics as language, religion, and race, and more broadly by shared attitudes, customs and traditions. To qualify as a people, those sharing a culture should think of themselves as collectively possessing an enduring, separate identity, and they are likely to be predominantly of common descent.[6]

Those who assert solidarity rights typically believe that such a people has a human right to self-determination whether or not they are organized into a nation state or any other sort of corporate body.

The question then becomes whether only organized groups are capable of acting. Larry May, a moral philosopher who has defended the existence of group rights, argues that this is not so. He holds that the storming of the Bastille cannot be reduced to the individual actions of the members of the Paris mob of 1789. To be sure, this mob action consisted of the actions of the individual members of the group, but it also consisted of the concerted actions of these persons as a group. What enabled them to act collectively or "as one person" was their solidarity: their common reaction to the injustices that had been perpetrated upon the lower classes and their implicit agreement to take action against the perpetrators. Quite possibly this sort of explanation can be extended to apply to a people. They are capable of genuine group action by virtue of their solidarity, their thinking of themselves as collectively possessing an enduring, separate identity. Still, whether the actions of a mob can be reduced to the actions of its members and whether a people can really possess any solidarity like that of the Paris mob remain controversial questions.

Equally controversial is the question of what does qualify an entity to possess moral rights. One would expect Joel Feinberg, perhaps the most influential contemporary American moral and legal philosopher, to agree with me that only beings capable of action are possible right-holders. This is because Feinberg maintains both that to have a right is to be in a position to claim the performance of the correlative duty and that this claiming should be understood as the process or action of demanding something as one's due. But this seems to imply that tiny babies could not have any right to life or to be cared for by their parents, for they have not yet learned the language of claiming and have no conception of what might be due to them. Feinberg points out, however, that parents or guardians can claim the legal, and presumably the moral, rights of young children. Hence, a right-holder can be either someone capable of claiming or someone on behalf of whom a representative can make claims. Because claiming would be pointless were one not claiming something in one's interest, and because to act on behalf of someone is to act in the interests of that person, Feinberg concludes that it is having interests that qualifies an entity to be a genuine right-holder.

Jeremy Waldron, a philosopher on the law faculty of Columbia University, arrives at the same conclusion by a more direct route. Instead of accepting Feinberg's claim theory of rights, he adopts the interest theory of Joseph Raz, an Oxford jurist and philosopher. Raz defines a right as an interest-based reason sufficiently important to impose one or more duties upon others to promote, or at least not damage, that interest. For example, there is a human right to life because the interest one has in her own life is important enough to impose a duty both upon others not to kill one and upon one's state to protect one's life. On this basis, Waldron defends the reality of third generation human rights. An interest is something that is in the interest of someone, some component of that being's good. Now some public goods cannot be properly valued as merely goods for the individual members of the public. For example, when one enjoys the conviviality of a party, one is not merely enjoying oneself but is aware that others are enjoying similar pleasures. One's enjoyment is partly constituted by the enjoyment of others; indeed, one person's enjoyment of conviviality is unintelligible apart from the enjoyments of others. Therefore, conviviality is necessarily an essentially communal good. Examples of communal goods more relevant to a people include the value of a cultured or tolerant society or the value of a general respect for persons. Because values such as these can be interests of a people collectively, a people could have a moral or legal right to these sorts of collective goods.

Those who advocate third generation human rights frequently speak on the side of the angels: They champion morally worthy causes and seek to advance the freedom and welfare of human beings around the world. The question remains, however, whether these worthy aspirations can best be achieved by the appeal to a new generation of solidarity rights. Here the lawyer's doubt that there is any way to identify the person or persons legally empowered to claim or waive a people's right before an international court merges with the philosopher's doubt about whether a people as such is capable of exercising the power of claiming or waiving any right. Perhaps the proliferation of alleged moral rights has gone too far.

Even if peoples do have moral rights that can and should be recognized in international law, these probably should not be thought of as a third generation of human rights. A human right is by definition a right one possesses as a human being. Although a people is a cultural community of human beings, it is not itself a human being. At the very least, this distinction between individual and group rights should not be obscured in moral and political discourse.

Fragmentary Conclusions

The debates concerning the development of human rights continue undiminished. Nevertheless, it may be possible to draw a few relatively noncontroversial conclusions. Clearly there has been a proliferation of human rights in the five decades following the formation of the United Nations. This proliferation has taken two very different forms. There have been a number of attempts to introduce new human rights into international law. Where these have been successful, new human rights have actually been created. There have also been numerous assertions by moral reformers and moral philosophers of new human rights. But success in convincing others to agree with such an assertion does nothing to bring a new moral right into existence. This is because genuine moral rights, if they exist, are different from the conventional rights created by the moral code of a society. An alleged moral right is real only if there exist moral reasons sufficient to justify its assertion. Thus there have been both a proliferation of legal human rights and a proliferation of assertions of moral human rights.

Rather different considerations are relevant to these two strands in the proliferation of rights. Any attempt to introduce a new legal right should be evaluated on institutional and pragmatic grounds. Such an introduction will be successful only if the legally authoritative documents can be effectively applied by the relevant states parties and international bodies, especially in some court of human rights. The introduction of a new legal right is wise only if creating an additional human right is a useful method of advancing the cause of human freedom and welfare in some important way. Any assertion of a new moral right should be assessed more in terms of theory than of utility. Is the newly asserted human right a right in the sense defined by the most adequate theory of the nature of rights? And is the alleged possessor of the right a possible moral right-holder? As we have seen, these considerations are very complicated. It is no wonder that there is little agreement about whether these parallel strands in the proliferation of human rights are desirable or undesirable.

Notes

1. The most convenient place to find this and many other human rights texts is Ian Brownlie, ed., *Basic Documents on Human Rights*, 3d ed. (Oxford: Clarendon Press, 1992).

2. Robert Nozick, *Anarchy, State and Utopia* (New York: Basic Books, 1974), p. 92.

3. Nozick, *Anarchy*, p. 171.

4. Nozick, *Anarchy*, p. 30.

5. These and other related documents are reprinted in James Crawford, ed., *The Rights of Peoples* (Oxford: Clarendon Press, 1988).

6. Vernon Van Dyke, "The Cultural Rights of Peoples," *Universal Human Rights* 2 (1980): 2–3.

Suggestions for Further Reading

Brownlie, Ian. 1992. *Basic Documents on Human Rights*, 3d ed. Oxford: Clarendon Press. A convenient source for the most important texts.

Cranston, Maurice. 1967. "Human Rights, Real and Supposed." In *Political Theory and the Rights of Man*, ed. D. D. Raphael. Bloomington: Indiana University Press. This essay is a clear and powerful criticism of the alleged economic, social, and cultural human rights.

Crawford, James, ed. 1992. *The Rights of Peoples*. Oxford: Clarendon Press. An excellent collection of papers on the rights of peoples with selected relevant documents.

Feinberg, Joel. 1980. *Rights, Justice, and the Bounds of Liberty*. Princeton: Princeton University Press. See especially pages 143–158. The best explanation of the view that rights are claims.

French, Peter A. 1979. "The Corporation as a Moral Person." *American Philosophical Quarterly* 16, pp. 133–149. An influential argument to show that corporate bodies are capable of moral action.

Goodwin-Gill, Guy S. 1983. *The Refugee in International Law*. Oxford: Clarendon Press. Pages 101–123 give a clear and accurate description of the human right to asylum.

Hartney, Michael. 1991. "Some Confusions Concerning Collective Rights." *Canadian Journal of Law and Jurisprudence* 4, pp. 293–314. This article provides an illuminating discussion of theories of group rights.

Henkin, Louis. 1981. "International Human Rights as 'Rights.'" In *Human Rights*, ed. J. Roland Pennock and John Chapman. New York: New York University Press. Henkin responds to those who argue that human rights are not real human rights under international law.

Honoré, Tony. 1977. "Property, Title and Redistribution." In *Equality and Freedom: Past, Present and Future*, ed. Carl Wellman. Wiesbaden: Franz Steiner Verlag. A critique of Nozick's view that welfare rights would be inconsistent with the natural right to property.

Kymlicka, Will. 1989. *Liberalism, Community, and Culture*. Oxford: Clarendon Press. Pages 135–161 argue for the recognition of group rights of minorities.

Lyons, David. 1977. "Human Rights and the General Welfare." *Philosophy & Public Affairs* 6, pp. 113–129. Argues against the view that utilitarianism could not explain our fundamental moral rights.

Marks, Stephen P. 1981. "Emerging Human Rights: A New Generation for the 1980s?" *Rutgers Law Review* 33, pp. 435–452. An informative article on the new third generation human rights.

May, Larry. 1987. *The Morality of Groups*. Notre Dame Ind.: University of Notre Dame Press. See especially pages 31–57. An explanation of how unorganized groups can and do act collectively.

McCloskey, H. J. 1965. "Rights." *Philosophical Quarterly* 15, pp. 115–127. McCloskey explains and defends the view that rights are entitlements rather than claims.

Nozick, Robert. 1974. *Anarchy, State, and Utopia*. New York: Basic Books. Pages 26–53 reject the conceptual possibility and moral legitimacy of human rights to welfare benefits.

Raphael, D. D. 1967. "Human Rights, Old and New." In *Political Theory and the Rights of Man*, ed. D. D. Raphael. Bloomington: Indiana University Press. Raphael defends economic, social, and cultural human rights against the attack by Cranston.

Raz, Joseph. 1986. *The Morality of Freedom*. Oxford: Clarendon Press. See especially pages 165–192. A sophisticated explanation of the theory that rights are interest-based reasons sufficient to impose one or more duties.

Scheffler, Samuel. 1976. "Natural Rights, Equality, and the Minimal State." *Canadian Journal of Philosophy* 6, pp. 59–76. Rebuts Nozick's arguments against moral rights to welfare benefits.

Shue, Henry. 1980. *Basic Rights*. Princeton: Princeton University Press. See especially pages 35–64. Shue argues that any basic right implies three kinds of correlative duties.

Trubek, David M. 1984. "Economic, Social and Cultural Rights in the Third World: Human Rights Law and Human Needs Programs." In *Human Rights in International Law*, ed. Theodore Meron. Oxford: Clardendon Press. A clear informative account of second generation human rights.

Tuck, Richard. 1979. *Natural Rights Theories*. Cambridge: Cambridge University Press. Probably the best account of the historically important theories of natural rights.

Van Dyke, Vernon. 1980. "The Cultural Rights of Peoples." *Universal Human Rights* 2, pp. 1–21. A strong defense of the human rights of peoples.

Waldron, Jeremy. 1993. *Liberal Rights*. Cambridge: Cambridge University Press. Pages 339–369 argue that groups can possess some collective rights.

Wellman, Carl. 1995. *Real Rights*. New York: Oxford University Press. See especially pages 105–136. A controversial argument for the conclusion that only moral agents could possess either moral or legal rights.

3

New Civil Rights

Civil rights are those legal rights one possesses as a citizen, those rights the legal system confers upon all members of a society in contrast with those it confers upon some more limited class, such as persons licensed to operate motor vehicles, owners of real estate, or members of its police force. Paradigm examples recognized in most civilized societies are the legal rights to life, liberty, freedom of speech, or a fair trial. In a special and narrower sense engendered by the civil rights movement in the United States, civil rights are rights conferred by a legal system in order to secure the equality of all of its citizens. Paradigm examples of civil rights in this special sense are the rights not to be enslaved, to the equal protection of the laws, and to freedom from racial discrimination. Although these rights were introduced into U.S. law to eliminate the oppression of African-Americans by whites, they are not rights of African-Americans as blacks, but legal rights they possess as citizens. Hence, Hispanics or female citizens can also appeal to these civil rights to achieve equality with white males in our society.

Because civil rights are by definition one species of legal rights, they lack the ambiguous status of human rights, which are primarily fundamental moral rights that are often also legal rights recognized and protected in international law. Nevertheless, there is a considerable overlap between declarations of human rights and bills of civil rights. Although this does not imply that civil rights as such are also moral rights, it does indicate that they are often enacted into law in order to protect the analogous human rights.

Accordingly, this chapter will examine three new civil rights introduced into U.S. law by decisions of the Supreme Court. The chapter will examine the legal reasoning advanced by the judges and by the lawyers arguing against these decisions, as well as the alleged moral rights used to justify or oppose demands for these legal reforms. Our examination will reveal how deeply moral reasoning penetrates our legal system and how central the language of rights is to our political discourse.

The Civil Rights Movement

The civil rights movement consisted of a series of coordinated activities by individuals and groups to achieve full legal, political, and economic equality for African-Americans. Central to its struggle for racial equality were organizations such as the National Association for the Advancement of Colored People (NAACP), the Congress of Racial Equality (CORE), the Student Nonviolent Coordinating Committee (SNCC), and especially the Southern Christian Leadership Conference organized by Martin Luther King, Jr. Although white reformers tended to dominate the movement at first, the vast majority of its participants have been African-Americans, and they have increasingly assumed leadership in the movement. They have sought to achieve their goal of full racial equality primarily by political action designed to enact legislation and influence public policy, but an important complementary tactic has been to take legal action in both the state and federal courts. Because the civil rights movement was primarily, although not exclusively, a struggle by and for African-Americans, this chapter will focus on rights relevant to racial discrimination. Hence, issues concerning sexual discrimination will be postponed until the next chapter.

Civil rights especially relevant to racial equality have, since the Civil War, been introduced into our legal system in three ways—constitutional amendment, legislation, and judicial decision. Thus, the Thirteenth Amendment nullified slavery and involuntary servitude, the Fourteenth introduced the right to the equal protection of the laws, and the Fifteenth prohibited the denial of the right to vote "on account of race, color, or previous condition of servitude." A series of civil rights acts has introduced several more specific rights, such as the right to full and equal enjoyment of the facilities of inns and places of public amusement (1875) and the right to equal employment opportunity (1964). Essential to the full enjoyment of such civil rights has been their recognition and enforcement in the courts. For example, the Supreme Court declared in *Carter v. Texas* (1899) that the right of blacks to the equal protection of the laws is violated when blacks are excluded from serving as jurors solely because of their race, and in *Plessy v. Ferguson* (1896) it held that blacks are entitled to equal, even if separate, accommodations on railroad coaches.

The civil rights movement probably began about 1938 and has not yet ended. After the New Deal, civil rights lawyers began to win cases before the more liberal Supreme Court, and after the Second World War, African-

Americans who had served in the armed forces or worked in the defense plants began to take a more active, often militant, part in politics. The heyday of the movement lasted only from the legal victory in *Brown v. Board of Education* of 1954 to the assassination of Martin Luther King in 1968. Then a white backlash slowed, but never completely stopped, the movement in its attempt to achieve full equality for African-American citizens of the United States.

The primary goal of the civil rights movement originally was to secure for African-Americans those civil rights long enjoyed by white citizens, but it has relied increasingly on a second strategy of attempting to introduce new civil rights into U.S. law. The reason for this new strategy is mainly that its attempts to apply the old civil rights to African-Americans through the courts and to enforce them through new legislation were insufficient to achieve legal, economic, and social equality for African-Americans. Although the Supreme Court had declared in *Plessy v. Ferguson* that separate facilities for African-Americans in public transportation (and by implication in public accommodations and education) must be equal to those provided for whites, in fact African-American citizens continued to be restricted by law to markedly inferior railroad carriages, buses, inns, and schools. Similarly, laws requiring color-blind procedures in hiring and promotion did not result in genuinely equal employment opportunities for African-American workers. Hence, most civil rights activists demanded new rights to racial integration and affirmative action programs. What is important about the civil rights movement for our purposes is not its history or organization, but the nature and value of the new civil rights it produced.

Nonsegregated Public Education

The first major victory of the civil rights movement during its second phase was the decision of the United States Supreme Court in *Brown v. Board of Education of Topeka*. By declaring that state laws segregating the public schools on a racial basis are unconstitutional, the Court recognized the new civil right to nonsegregated education. Although the plaintiffs in this case were African-American children, the judicial reasoning applies, at least in part, to all persons subject to the jurisdiction of any state. Hence, this is a civil right, a right African-Americans possess simply as citizens. Its content is negative rather than positive. It could not consist in any claim to be provided with integrated education, for in some communities there may not exist residents of more than one race. It is a claim-right *not* to be denied admission to any public school on the basis of any law or public policy requiring or permitting racially segregated education.

Legal Reasoning

Chief Justice Warren delivered the opinion of the Supreme Court in *Brown*. The outline of his argument is as follows: Today education is perhaps the most important function of state governments because it is required to prepare a person for good citizenship and for success in life. Hence, there is a right to educational opportunity. The Equal Protection Clause forbids any state to "deny to any person within its jurisdiction the equal protection of the laws." Hence, where a state has undertaken to provide educational opportunity to anyone, it must make it available to all on equal terms. But racially segregated education is inherently unequal. Therefore, any state law or policy that requires or permits segregated education is invalid because it is unconstitutional. By implication it follows that there is a constitutional right to nonsegregated public education.

The crucial step in this judicial reasoning, and the one that introduced a new civil right into U.S. law, was the step that rejected the principle of separate but equal public facilities established in 1896 by *Plessy v. Ferguson*. Why was it constitutionally impermissible for the southern states to improve the schools to which they assigned African-Americans until these schools were as good as the ones to which they admitted only white persons? The answer of the Supreme Court was that separate educational facilities, especially when they are required or permitted by law, are inherently unequal because segregation itself has adverse effects on the education of African-American children.

One reason for this conclusion was expressed more fully in the previous opinions in *Sweatt v. Painter* and *McLaurin v. Oklahoma State Regents*. This reason is that any adequate education necessarily involves interaction—studying and discussion—among the pupils. Hence, to separate African-American pupils from white children, who compose 85 percent of the population, is to reduce their opportunity to learn what they need to know in order to perform their public responsibilities, pursue their careers, and live their lives. The other reason for desegregation, based upon several recent psychological studies of the harmful effects of racial discrimination on personality development, is that segregating African-American children, especially when it has the sanction of law, denotes the inferiority of their race and thereby engenders a sense of inferiority that affects the motivation of a child to learn. Segregated education is inherently unequal because it has a tendency to retard the educational and mental development of African-American children and to deprive them of some of the benefits they would receive in a racially integrated school system.

The legal decision in *Brown v. Board of Education* hinged on the proper interpretation of the Fourteenth Amendment. The segregationists had argued that the original purpose of the Equal Protection Clause was simply to ensure that the law treated the recently freed African-Americans equally as citizens; it applies only to their rights of citizenship, such as their rights to vote, to hold public office, and to speak freely in public debates. Therefore, it requires only political equality not social equality. Whether African-American and white persons are segregated or integrated in public transportation, accommodations, and schools is a purely social matter entirely within the police power of the states. Surely the United States Constitution does not require a white family to invite African-Americans to its dinner parties or a private association of white persons to admit African-Americans to its dances or other social events. Although the Supreme Court accepted this interpretation in *Plessy v. Ferguson* and therefore held that separate but equal public transportation is permissible, it rejected this view in *Brown*. It seems to have reinterpreted the Equal Protection Clause as requiring that a state must give equal protection to African-American and white persons regarding all legal rights, not merely the rights of citizens to participate in political processes by voting or holding public office.

The question then becomes whether the opportunity to attend a public school is a legal right or merely a legal privilege. You can hardly complain that your state has denied you equal protection of the law on the ground that it has located the nearest state park, in which you wish to hike, eight miles from your home but much nearer to the homes of other citizens. This is because having a public park at the most convenient distance is merely a privilege afforded to some but not a right required for all. Hence, Justice Warren needed to show that there is a right to education. Most segregationists did not challenge this claim; they argued instead that segregated schools do in fact give equal educational opportunity to black children.

At this point a second interpretation of the Equal Protection Clause becomes relevant. Civil rights lawyers argued that the original purpose of the Equal Protection Clause was to prohibit every form of discrimination by the states against African-Americans. In *Brown* the Supreme Court agreed and noted that this had been the accepted interpretation long before *Plessy*. Hence, any racial distinction in state law that treats African-Americans worse than it treats white persons is unconstitutional.

The legal issue then becomes whether state laws requiring or permitting racially segregated public schools do in fact treat African-American children adversely, worse than they treat white children. Segregationists argued that this is not the case. For one thing, these laws applied equally to both races; they excluded white children from the schools attended by African-Americans just as they excluded African-American children from schools attended by whites. Moreover, long experience in the southern states has shown that segregated schools are better for the children of both races; in particular, they are advantageous for African-American children because they need a simpler and more disciplined sort of education from that appropriate for white children. Justice Warren, speaking for the Court, rebutted the latter assertion by showing that segregated schools are harmful to African-American students. Justice Harlan, in dissenting to *Plessy*, had replied to the former argument by pointing out that the real purpose of state segregation laws is not so much to exclude whites from public facilities assigned to African-Americans as to exclude African-Americans from those afforded to whites.

At this point, lawyers for the southern states objected that the Equal Protection Clause could not have meant to prohibit all legal discriminations. Every legal rule is formulated in general terms and thus distinguishes between classes of persons. Hence, properly interpreted, the Equal Protection Clause excludes only arbitrary and unreasonable discriminations. It is not unconstitutional to deny the vote to children while permitting it to adults because children are incapable of either participating fully in political debate or understanding the issues decided by elections. Nor is it denying equal protection to mentally retarded children to assign them to separate classes in which they can receive special instruction because this is the most reasonable way to provide for their education. Similarly state laws that provide separate schools for African-American and white children do not deny equal protection because, far from drawing arbitrary distinctions, they are reasonable regulations justified by the legitimate state interests in preserving public peace and in promoting the effectiveness of public education. Under present conditions, mixing African-American and white children in the public schools would lead to disorder and even violence that would threaten harm to children of both races. And because African-American and white children have different levels of educational capacity and attainment, they can each benefit more fully from different sorts of instruction best provided in separate schools. Of course, civil rights lawyers argued that laws requiring or permitting segregated schools are not reasonably related to either legislative objective.

Moral Presuppositions

Let us put to one side the factual disagreements between the parties to this dispute and turn our attention to the moral presuppositions that lie behind their legal arguments. Aristotle, the ancient Greek philosopher whose theory of justice remains the starting point for most modern discussions, asserted that justice consists in equality. The different interpretations of the Equal Protection Clause reflect different conceptions of social justice as equal treatment by one's society.

A traditional reformulation is that equality consists in treating similar cases similarly. It would, for example, be unjust for a teacher to give one student an A and another a B for two philosophical papers that were equally well researched, clearly formulated, and imaginatively argued. This does not imply, however, that justice demands that a teacher should give equal academic credit to every student in the class. Justice also requires that the teacher give a lower grade to any student whose paper is substantially less well researched or more poorly written because justice also consists in treating dissimilar cases dissimilarly. Suppose, however, that a teacher gives lower grades to African-American students than to his white students merely because they are racially dissimilar, although their papers are equally good on all philosophical criteria. This would be unjust because racial differences are irrelevant to academic grading. Thus the philosophical problem is to find some principle by which one can determine which distinctions are relevant and which are irrelevant to just treatment in each case.

The simplest solution is the view that relevance is determined by moral reasoning. That a philosophical paper is less thoroughly researched is relevant to grading because it is a reason that justifies the action of awarding a lower grade; it is a consideration that implies that this action is, other things being equal, morally right. That the student is an African-American person is irrelevant because it is not a moral reason for giving him a lower grade, or a higher grade either for that matter. On this view of justice, the legal system of any just society will make only reasonable distinctions between classes of persons; that is to say, its laws will affect those subject to its jurisdiction differently only when the classifications employed are valid moral reasons for different treatment. The society is unjust whenever its laws discriminate arbitrarily between its citizens: when there is no moral reason to justify different treatment of them. This conception of social justice is presupposed by those who interpret the Equal Protection Clause as prohibiting state laws that are arbitrary or unreasonable.

Although William K. Frankena, a twentieth century moral philosopher, agrees that social justice requires equal treatment in some sense, he rejects the view that relevant distinctions are simply moral reasons that justify unequal treatment. Not every morally justifying reason is a justicizing reason; not every consideration that might make an action morally right makes it just. For example, a teacher might be justified in refraining from failing a student who does not deserve to pass if giving the student an F would probably cause her rich father to withdraw his offer to give the university 2 million dollars to provide financial assistance to needy students. Again, the fact that a student who had plagiarized in his paper has repented might make it morally right to forgive him, but this would be an act of mercy rather than of justice. How can one identify those moral reasons that are justicizing? These are specified by the principles of justice stated in the correct moral theory (and, of course, different moral theories might hold different principles). Other moral principles, such as the principles of benevolence or mercy, identify right-making or wrong-making reasons that are not just-making.

According to Frankena's theory, a just society is one that treats everyone equally except when there is some justicizing or just-making reason for unequal treatment. On the other hand, a society is unjust whenever its legal system treats some person or class of persons adversely, worse than other similarly situated individuals, without a justicizing reason. It is this conception of social justice that suggests that the Equal Protection Clause prohibits at least discrimination *against* African-American citizens.

A question that has long puzzled philosophers is why it is that there is a moral presumption in favor of equality. Why is it that unequal treatment always requires some special justification but that equal treatment normally does not? Gregory Vlastos, best known as an interpreter of the ethical theories of Plato and Aristotle, attempts to answer this question in his theory of social justice. He defines a just act as one that is prescribed exclusively by regard for the rights of all those whom it affects substantially. He then argues that a just society ought to treat all its members with regard for their human rights and that the human rights of one person are equal to those of any other person because human rights are grounded on the equal worth of all human beings. He suggests that this egalitarian conception of social justice is confirmed by the fact that the great historic movements for social justice have mainly concerned the demands for equal rights: struggles against slavery, political absolutism, the disenfranchisement of women, colonialism, and racial oppression. Those who interpret the Equal Protection Clause as requiring equal respect for all legal rights adopt an analogous conception of legal justice.

As Vlastos points out, his theory of justice makes the answer to the question of whether some action or institution is just depend upon the answer to the question "What are the rights of those who are substantially affected by it?" What alleged moral rights, then, might bear on the justice or injustice of laws requiring or permitting racially segregated public schools? (1) The *Universal Declaration of Human Rights* asserts that everyone has the right to education. If all human beings do have an equal human right to education and if, as Justice Warren argued in *Brown*, segregated public schools do not provide black students with an education equal to that of white students, then any law segregating public schools would seem to be socially unjust. (2) Many moral philosophers assert that there is a human right to equal opportunity. Justice Warren argued that segregated schools denied black children equal educational opportunity and also that educational opportunity is essential to their opportunity to succeed in life. Here, then, is another chain of reasoning from an alleged fundamental moral right to the injustice of laws providing for racially segregated public schools. (3) Ronald Dworkin, a contemporary philosopher of law, argues that the most fundamental of all moral rights, the one that ultimately justifies all constitutional rights, is the right to equal concern and respect.

Central to the judicial reasoning in *Brown* is the assertion that laws segregating public schools are usually interpreted as denoting the inferiority of African-Americans. If this is actually true, then those laws might well be unjust because they violate the human right of black children to be treated with equal respect.

Retrospective Assessment

Given the benefit of hindsight, one may wonder whether the Supreme Court was wise to create the right to racially nonsegregated public education in 1954. Ought it to have introduced this new civil right into U.S. law? Well, we have found a straightforward moral justification for its decision. The new civil right to nonsegregated public education was required by social justice because racially segregated schools fail to consider the equal human rights of many African-American children. This moral reasoning rests on the factual consideration asserted in the opinion of the Supreme Court that segregated education treats African-American students adversely, as well as on the conception of social justice defended by Gregory Vlastos and on an appeal to one or more of the human rights to education, equal opportunity, and equal respect.

But are any or all of these alleged human rights genuine? The *Universal Declaration of Human Rights* does not give any reasoning to justify its assertion that everyone has the right to education, and few if any of the moral philosophers who assume the existence of a fundamental moral right to equal opportunity even attempt to defend this assumption. It is not clear whether Ronald Dworkin simply postulates the right to be treated with equal respect or accepts it as necessary presupposition of the political theory implicit in the United States Constitution. Critics might well suspect that in assuming the existence of any of these human rights there is an unjustified proliferation of alleged moral rights.

One could give a moral justification for instituting this new civil right, without presupposing any of these dubious human rights, were one to accept William Frankena's conception of social justice. Although this does enable one to escape the burden of proof imposed upon those who assert the existence of some specific human right, it requires that one be able to specify those principles of justice that determine which differences are justicizing or just-making and which are not. Are the fundamental principles of justice any better known or easier to establish than assertions of human rights? Neither seems to be a very firm foundation for a conclusive moral argument. What is needed here is either a more persuasive theory of the grounds of moral rights or a more complete account of the principles of justice.

In 1954, civil rights lawyers proclaimed the decision in *Brown v. Board of Education* a great triumph for social justice. Even then, however, the

Supreme Court recognized that there would be many difficulties in giving practical effect to the new civil right to nonsegregated public education. Therefore, it restored the cases at issue to its docket and requested the various parties to present further arguments on how to desegregate the public schools in the affected states. The following year, in what came to be known as *Brown II*, it remanded the cases to the district courts and instructed them to "enter such orders and decrees consistent with this opinion as are necessary and proper to admit to public schools on a racially nondiscriminatory basis with all deliberate speed the parties to these cases."[1] The rest is history, and disillusioning history at that. The very best that can be said is that there has been much more deliberation than speed and that after four decades progress has been most disappointing.

Some are even more pessimistic and judge the decision in *Brown* a disaster. (1) It has proven far too costly. Vast sums have been spent on busing African-American children to formerly white schools and white children to predominantly black schools in a vain attempt to achieve integrated education for all. In addition to these financial expenses, there have been the vast amounts of time lost riding on buses that the children could have spent in more educational activities, and there have been lost opportunities for friendships and the emotional security that could have been provided by those neighborhood schools from which the bused children were taken. (2) Far from improving educational opportunity for African-American children, the effort to integrate public education has reduced the quality of education for all. It has diverted funds to busing that could have been better used to improve classroom instruction, introduced severe problems of discipline into the forcibly integrated schools, and lowered public support for the taxation desperately needed to support the schools. Worst of all, (3) attempts to integrate the public schools have been counterproductive because they have actually increased racial segregation. They have caused many white families to flee to the suburbs or to move to predominantly white school districts. More affluent white parents have removed their children from public schools and enrolled them in "safer" private schools. Many conclude that however enlightened one may originally have considered the judicial reasoning in *Brown v. Board of Education*, its legal conclusion must now be judged a failure in practice.

But should such merely practical considerations be allowed to defeat a moral requirement? Well, such considerations are not morally irrelevant because there was a causal link in the moral justification for introducing the new civil right to nonsegregated public education. The argument was that this new legal right was required in order to prevent or reduce the violation of fundamental human rights or the principles of justice. But if in fact the new civil right fails to prevent or at least greatly reduce such violations, then the moral argument for introducing it is undermined. And if it turns out that attempts to enforce this new civil right really are counterproductive because they increase the racial segregation that violates human rights and social justice, then the decision in *Brown* should be morally condemned. Whether this harsh moral verdict is appropriate depends in large measure upon how effectively our legal system can put the decision of the Supreme Court into practice.

A legal historian might say that these very harmful consequences have resulted not from enforcing the civil right to nonsegregated public education introduced in *Brown* but from later decisions of the federal courts that have misinterpreted this as implying a right to integrated public schools. It is one thing to declare state laws excluding black children from the public schools of their choice unconstitutional; it is quite another thing to require the states to restructure their educational systems in order to mix black and white children in every public school.

But was this shift from nonsegregated public education to integrated public schools a misinterpretation of the judicial reasoning in *Brown*? Probably not, because underlying this reasoning may well have been both the ideal of an integrated society and the history of our public schools as the great "melting pot" in which a series of immigrant minorities have been educated to be as American as all the other citizens of our land of opportunity. This attractive ideal, this vision of a shared culture, a common identity and civic fraternity, is a moral as well as a political ideal. Communitarians, who insist on the importance of a common culture and shared values in any society, argue that this sort of community is necessary both for the full development of the individual self and for the full social cooperation required for democratic institutions to function properly. Others point out that the traditional goal of the civil rights movement has been the integration of African-Americans into the mainstream of the society in which white citizens are in the majority.

More recently, however, many segments of the African-American community have begun to question this ideal. They fear that integration will amount to assimilation and the loss of their identity as African-Americans. This is one reason that they refer to themselves as African-Americans rather than as blacks and that their ideal is a pluralistic society in which they would be able to preserve their own culture and their distinctive personal identity. Some even assert the human right of every people to preserve and develop its culture. Of course, the predominantly white majority can also insist on its human right to preserve and develop the mainstream culture of our country. But are either African-Americans or "we the people of the United States" a people in the sense required to possess any right to preserve its own culture? Indeed, are such third-generation human rights really genuine moral rights at all? Once more, skeptical critics contend that the proliferation of alleged moral rights has gone too far.

There remains the question of how integrated or pluralistic the ideal society should be. Because any legal system reflects and in turn projects social ideals, we have here a third factor, in addition to social justice and practical considerations, that must be taken into account in deciding whether it was wise to introduce a new civil right to nonsegregated public education into U.S. law.

Interracial Marriage

One of the reasons that the southern states resisted so vigorously all attempts to enforce the new civil right to nonsegregated education was the widespread conviction that integrating the public schools would inevitably lead to miscegenation. This thesis was clearly stated in the 1956 essay by Herbert Ravenel Sass, a freelance author and Episcopalian, entitled "Mixed Schools and Mixed Blood":

> For the democratic public school is the most critical of those areas of activity where the South must and will at all costs maintain separation of the races. The South must do this because, although it is a nearly universal instinct, race preference is not active in the very young. Race preference (which the propagandists miscall race prejudice or hate) is one of those instincts which develop gradually as the mind develops and which, if taken in hand early enough, can be prevented from developing at all. . . .
>
> Many well-meaning persons have suddenly discovered that the tenets of the Christian religion and the profession of our democratic faith compel us to accept the risks of this hybridization. No one who will face up to the biological facts and really think the problem through can believe any such thing or see the partial suicide of the white race in America (and of the Negro race also) as anything other than a crime against both religion and civilization.[2]

The fact that the *Atlantic Monthly*, an intellectually reputable magazine, published this essay indicates that, although prejudiced, it cannot be discounted as completely irrational rhetoric.

The condemnation of miscegenation was by no means confined to the South. In 1952, thirty of the forty-eight states still had statutes making racial intermarriage unlawful. Although such laws had been increasingly challenged by the civil rights movement, both state and federal courts had almost without exception refused to declare them unconstitutional. The one exception was the 1948 decision of the Supreme Court of California in *Perez v. Lippold*, and even then three of the seven justices dissented. A Gallop Poll in late 1968 reported that seventy-two percent of American adults still disapproved of marriage between whites and nonwhites.

Nevertheless, the United States Supreme Court created a new civil right to interracial marriage in its 1967 decision *Loving v. Virginia*. The defining core of this right is the bilateral legal liberty of the individual citizen to marry or not marry a person of another race.[3] This liberty is not, of course, unlimited. The person one chooses to marry must be of marriageable age, not currently married to another, of the opposite sex, and not a close blood relative. This core liberty is protected at least by a legal immunity against state statutes prohibiting interracial marriage; that is to say, any state law that purports to render interracial marriages illegal is null and void because it is unconstitutional.

Legal Issues

The facts of the case were not at issue. In June 1958, two residents of Virginia, Mildred Jeter, an African-American woman, and Richard Loving, a white man, were married in the District of Columbia. Shortly after their marriage, they returned to Virginia and established their marital residence in Caroline County. On January 6, 1959, they were sentenced to one year in jail both for violating the Virginia statutes prohibiting marriage between any white and any colored person and for leaving the state to evade this law.

Chief Justice Warren delivered the opinion of the Court. He argued that these statutes violated the Equal Protection Clause of the Fourteenth Amendment. Virginia had interpreted that clause to rule out only arbitrary and unreasonable classifications, but the Court insisted on more stringent interpretations. For one thing, the Equal Protection Clause was clearly intended to exclude all discriminations against African-American citizens. Hence, any racial classification in the law is suspect and requires a very heavy burden of justification. Moreover, that clause applies with special force to the fundamental rights of the citizen. Because marriage is one of the basic civil rights, any statute that restricts the freedom to marry solely because of race violates the central meaning of the Equal Protection Clause.

Justice Warren also reasoned that state statutes that prohibit interracial marriages violate the Due Process Clause of the Fourteenth Amendment. This reads, "nor shall any state deprive any person of life, liberty, or property without due process of law." That this clause applies to the freedom to marry was unambiguously asserted in *Meyer v. Nebraska*:

> While this court has not attempted to define with exactness the liberty thus guaranteed, the term has received much consideration, and some of the included things have been definitely stated. Without doubt, it denotes not merely freedom from bodily restraint, but also the right of the individual to contract, to engage in any of the common occupations of life, to acquire useful knowledge, to marry, establish a home and bring up children, to worship God according to the dictates of his own conscience, and, generally, to enjoy those privileges long recognized at common law as essential to the orderly pursuit of happiness by free men.[4]

Therefore, the freedom to marry or not marry a person of another race resides with the individual and cannot be infringed by the state.

Virginia attempted to resist this conclusion by appealing to the Tenth Amendment that reserves to the states the police power: the right of a government to make laws necessary for the health, morals, and welfare of the people. It argued that because marriage has traditionally been subject to state regulation without federal intervention, the regulation of marriage should be left to exclusive state control. The Supreme Court granted that marriage is a social relation subject to the state's police power but denied that its power to regulate is unlimited. In particular, this power is circumscribed by the Fourteenth Amendment.

Just as the state's police power is not unlimited, so no individual right is absolute. Although any statute infringing a civil right must be subjected to the most rigid scrutiny and thus bear a very heavy burden of justification, it will be upheld if the court finds it necessary to some legitimate overriding state purpose. As one would expect, Virginia argued that its laws prohibiting interracial marriage were necessary to promote public morals and to preserve the racial integrity of its citizens. In *Reynolds v. United States* and later in *Mormon Church v. United States*, the Supreme Court had upheld state statutes prohibiting polygamy on the ground that polygamy is contrary both to the moral principles upon which our government rests and to the spirit of Christianity. Virginia argued that because interracial marriage is immoral and an interference with the will of God, the Court should uphold the laws prohibiting the marriage of white and colored persons on the same grounds. Again, the Supreme Court in *Buck v. Bell* had upheld on eugenic grounds a law authorizing the sterilization of feebleminded persons confined to state institutions, clearly an abridgment of the civil right to procreate. Because interracial marriages are biologically harmful, in that they tend to produce inferior offspring, Virginia's law prohibiting blood-mixing should be held to be constitutional. However, the opinion of the Supreme Court rejected both of these arguments and insisted that the individual does have a civil right to marry or not marry a person of another race.

Moral Arguments

As is so often true in civil rights cases, the legal issues in *Loving v. Virginia* reflect underlying moral views. The main official purpose of laws prohibiting interracial marriages was no doubt to preserve public morality. But why should it be thought that it is immoral for white and African-American persons to intermarry? Some judges, not all southern, and many sincere Christians believed that it is against the will of God. For reasons inscrutable to man, God created easily distinguishable races—white, black, yellow, and red—and placed them on separate continents. He also implanted in each race an instinctive sexual preference for members of one's own race. These undeniable facts prove that God has ordained the segregation of the races and that any blood-mixing is a violation of His will.

Other Christians rejected the view that the races of mankind are as fundamentally different as biological species: as different as cats and dogs, for example. God created all human beings in His image, so the members of all races are essentially the same. In the eyes of God and from the moral point of view, whether one is white or red or black makes no difference.

Recognizing that Christians are deeply divided among themselves and that not everyone accepts a religious morality, many argued that interracial marriage is immoral because it is unnatural. It should be morally condemned, and therefore legally prohibited, on much the same grounds as sodomy: copulation of a human being with an animal or anal intercourse between males. What are those grounds? Either that such acts are deviant, deviations from the natural purposes of sex and marriage, or that they are violations of the natural law, the self-evident moral rules known by natural reason. Such moral reasoning is unconvincing, however, both to those who are unable to find any purposes in nature once divine providence has been discounted and to those who do not see that interracial marriages are self-evidently wrong.

The least speculative arguments for the immorality of interracial marriage are based upon the harms it is believed to cause. Perhaps one can discount the marital stress and strain it imposes upon the couple themselves, because of their very different backgrounds and the racial prejudices of most other members of their society; it may be up to them whether to thus burden their lives and undertake a marriage that may well break under the strain. What is not morally permissible is to victimize others, especially one's children. Many citizens and some moral philosophers appealed to biological theory and argued that the children of interracial marriages will be defective because, although line breeding may generate a superior animal, crossbreeding tends to cause the deterioration of any species. Moreover, social psychology shows that their children will be rejected by members of both races and therefore will find it hard to develop any strong self-identity with which to resist the stress under which they must live. Interracial marriage is also immoral because of the harm it does to society by impairing peace and public order. It increases social tensions, exacerbates racial prejudices, and thus leads to violence, such as the terrorism of the Ku Klux Klan and even the lynching of innocent black citizens.

Moral philosophers often reject these considerations as irrelevant and reply that these harms do not count because they result from the immoral racial prejudices of persons other than the racially mixed couple that marry one another. But how can these harms, assuming that they are real, fail to count when they are suffered by innocent victims? Surely it is morally wrong to act in a manner that one knows will seriously injure others.

Perhaps not, if one is exercising a fundamental moral right. Article 16 of the *Universal Declaration of Human Rights* reads in part: "Men and women of full age, without any limitation due to race, nationality or religion, have the right to marry and to found a family. . . . Marriage shall be entered into only with the free and full consent of the intending spouses." The defining core of this alleged human right is the bilateral moral liberty of the adult human being to marry or not marry a consenting adult individual. This fundamental moral right presumably implies the moral right to marry a person of another race because its core liberty is without any limitation due to race. If real, this human right would constitute a moral justification for the decision of the Supreme Court to create the new civil right to interracial marriage.

But is it a real right? The *Universal Declaration* is an essentially political document, the product of discussion and compromise within UN committees and then debate in the General Assembly. It does not contain, nor do the deliberations that produced it contain, any articulate moral reasoning to justify its assertions. Although its preamble does refer to "the dignity and worth of the human person," it does not define these obscure terms or explain precisely how human dignity and worth constitute grounds of specific human rights, such as the right to marry and found a family. Nor is it obvious how any of the theories of the grounds of rights advocated by moral philosophers could firmly establish the existence of this alleged human right. Skeptics may wonder whether it is not one more example of the dogmatic and unhelpful proliferation of alleged moral rights.

Even granted that there really is a human right to marry or not marry another consenting adult, what are the limits of its core liberty? Does it imply that bigamy and even polygamy are morally permissible? Does it rule out all legal prohibitions against incestuous marriages? And on what grounds does it exclude limitations due to race, nationality, or religion without also excluding limitations due to sex? After all, the United Nations has repeatedly condemned sexual discrimination as well as racial discrimination. Some moral philosophers argue that state statutes rendering same-sex marriages—marriages of gay or lesbian couples—unlawful are just as discriminatory as those prohibiting interracial marriages. Asserting the existence of a human right to marry does little or nothing to settle the debate about whether it is morally permissible for white and African-American persons to marry, unless one knows where the boundaries of the liberty to marry another person lie. Unfortunately, theories of moral rights provide very little guidance on this matter. What, then, is gained by appealing to human rights to justify the institution of any civil right? Not much unless these deficiencies in the theory of rights can be overcome.

Preferential Admissions

Of all the legal and moral issues raised by the civil rights movement, the most controversial—and the ones most heatedly debated even today—concern preferential treatment for African-Americans (and members of other minorities) in affirmative action programs. Typical examples would be the policy of a predominantly white police department to hire equal numbers of African-Americans and whites until its racial composition matches that of its community, the decision of a corporation to promote African-Americans (even if somewhat less qualified) in order to provide role models for its African-American employees, and the attempt to compensate for educational disadvantage by adding twenty points to the SAT scores of black applicants in the admission procedures of a highly selective private university. What makes any such preferential treatment legally suspect and morally problematic is the fact that it seems to constitute reverse discrimination. If racial discrimination against African-Americans is normally illegal and immoral, why is not racial discrimination against whites equally so?

This question has given rise to a large number of hard cases: court cases in which there is no clearly correct judicial decision. In order to simplify our discussion, let us limit our attention to those involving preferential treatment in the admissions procedures of colleges and universities. Some indication of how difficult the legal issues are is given by the fact that the Supreme Court was unwilling to decide these issues in *De Funis v. Odegaard*, the first test case it accepted for its docket, and that it was unable to agree on an opinion of the Court in *University of California Regents v. Bakke*, a second test case it could no longer evade.

The Bakke *Case*

Nevertheless, in *Bakke* a sharply divided Court did recognize a civil right to preferential admissions. This is not the claim-right of African-Americans to be treated preferentially in admissions procedures, but the liberty-right of academic institutions to use race in its admissions programs in a manner that favors minority applicants. Its defining core is the legal liberty of colleges and universities to consider the race of a minority applicant as one reason among others in deciding which candidates to admit. This liberty is limited, however; an institution may not adopt any racial quotas or set aside any places for African-American or minority candidates only.

Allan Bakke was a white male who was twice denied admission to the medical school of the University of California at Davis, even though applicants with much lower entrance examination scores were admitted under its special admissions program in which only disadvantaged members of certain minority races were considered for sixteen of the places. He alleged that he had been a victim of reverse discrimination (discrimination against members of the white majority rather than the usual discrimination by whites against African-Americans) and took legal action on the grounds that the university's admissions program violated both Title VI of the Civil Rights Act of 1964 and the Equal Protection Clause of the Fourteenth Amendment.

Without considering the constitutional issue, four members of the Supreme Court (Justices Stevens, Burger, Stewart, and Rehnquist) were of the opinion that Bakke had been the victim of illegal racial discrimination in violation of the Civil Rights Act of 1964. Section 601 provides: "No person in the United States shall, on the ground of race, color, or national origin, be excluded from participation in, be denied the benefits of, or be subjected to discrimination under any program or activity receiving Federal financial assistance." When asked to define the word "discrimination" as used in the bill, Hubert Humphrey, the Senate floor manager, explained that it means "a distinction in treatment . . . given to different individuals because of their different race."[5] Although Congress enacted this legislation with the problem of discrimination against African-Americans in mind, the solution provided by this legislation is much broader and prohibits discrimination against any person on the ground of race. Because Bakke had been excluded from the medical school of the University of California at Davis, a program that receives considerable federal financial assistance, and treated differently from African-American applicants because of his race, he had been the victim of illegal reverse racial discrimination.

Four other members of the Court (Justices Brennan, White, Marshall, and Blackmun) were of the opinion that Bakke had not been illegally denied admission to the medical school of the University of California at Davis. They agreed with Justice Powell that Title VI goes no further in prohibiting the use of race than the Equal Protection Clause of the Fourteenth Amendment. Hence, their reasoning hinged, not on the Civil Rights Act of 1964, but on the relevance of equal protection to racial discrimination. Given their interpretation, the Equal Protection Clause does not require color-blindness; it does not render racial classifications per se invalid.

Still, the Equal Protection Clause does require that any statute that restricts a fundamental right or that contains a suspect classification be subjected to strict scrutiny. The former requirement is irrelevant here because no fundamental right is involved. Bakke had no right to be admitted or even, as the California Supreme Court suggested, to be considered for admission on nonracial qualifications only. The legal issue is simply one of racial discrimination, the use of a racial distinction that disadvantages some person or persons. A statute enacted for ostensibly benign purposes may in fact prove malign if it stigmatizes any group or singles out those least well represented in the political process to bear the brunt of an otherwise benign program. However, Alan Bakke was not stigmatized by the admissions program at Davis; it recognized that he was fully qualified for the study of medicine. Nor did its program in rejecting a white male single out those least well represented in the political process to bear any wrongful burden. The racial discrimination of the Davis Medical School was benign because it was used for the purpose of remedying the disadvantages suffered by a racial minority due to past discrimination.

It does not follow that even benign discrimination is legally innocent, for every racial distinction in the law is suspect. Any state statute using racial classifications is valid only if it is substantially related to some important governmental purpose. The Davis admissions program survives this test of strict scrutiny. Its purpose was to solve the substantial and chronic under-representation of minorities in medicine, and this could not be remedied without racial preferences in admitting applicants to medical schools.

So far we have a judicial stalemate and no decision of the case before the Supreme Court. Justice Powell wrote the decisive opinion in which he explained why he agreed in part with one set of colleagues and in part with the others. The legislative history of the Civil Rights Act of 1964 shows that Title VI was meant to prohibit only unconstitutional racial discrimination. Although the Fourteenth Amendment was designed to end discrimination against African-Americans, discrimination against white citizens also violates the Equal Protection Clause because this clause applies to "any person" within the jurisdiction of a state. Therefore even preferential treatment enacted to remedy past discrimination against African-American citizens, however benign, is a denial of equal protection because racial classifications in the law are always suspect. Hence, racial discrimination is legally permissible only if it can survive strict scrutiny, demonstrating that it is necessary for some substantial state purpose.

The only substantial purposes alleged by the University of California at Davis were improving the delivery of health-care services to communities now underserved and attaining a diverse student body. But the use of racial quotas to exclude white applicants from consideration for a specified number of places in each entering class is not necessary for either purpose. Hence, Alan Bakke had been subjected to illegal reverse racial discrimination. On the other hand, the state purpose of achieving a diverse student body does require some consideration of race, among a number of other factors, so that academic institutions do have a legal right to give some kinds of preferential treatment to African-American applicants in their admissions programs. Therefore, Justice Powell together with Justices Brennan, White, Marshall, and Blackmun constituted a bare majority of the Supreme Court, and this majority recognized a new civil right, a limited right to preferential admissions.

Because there is no appeal from a decision of the United States Supreme Court, the legal issue is settled, at least until the applicable federal law is revised. This leaves open, however, the moral questions at issue here. Granted that U.S. academic institutions do have a legal right to give preference to African-Americans in their admissions procedures, do they have any analogous moral right? Many citizens and not a few moral philosophers argue that this new civil right is unjust, and hence ought to be abolished, and that meanwhile it is morally impermissible for any academic institution to exercise this merely legal liberty to engage in reverse discrimination. Whatever the Supreme Court may say, it is morally wrong to engage in any form of racial discrimination.

Racial Discrimination

The definition of racial discrimination is not very controversial. Almost everyone agrees that it consists in treating the members of some race differently in a prejudicial or unjust manner. However, there seem to be different interpretations of this definition implicit but not clearly articulated in debates about the morality of racial discrimination. To borrow a distinction from the theory of justice, although there is only one concept of racial discrimination, there are three different conceptions of its nature.[6] It is no accident that these are closely analogous to the three interpretations of the Equal Protection Clause contested in *Brown v. Board of Education,* since both reflect similar presupposed conceptions of justice.

The first conception is that racial discrimination consists in any different treatment of the members of some race motivated by racial prejudice. Prejudice is usually taken to be an attitude of favor or disfavor, especially malice or hatred, without any rational justification. But one's motivation seems more relevant to the moral character of the agent than to the moral wrongness of his or her action.

After all, one can do the right thing for the wrong reason, as when a student refrains from cheating out of the fear of getting caught. And granted that making distinctions without any reason is arbitrary, what is morally wrong with acting arbitrarily? Moreover, this conception of racial discrimination seems far too narrow because unprejudiced actions often have an unfair impact upon the members of some race. If our department chairperson recruits new faculty members through the "old boy network," by inviting the predominantly white male faculty of the most prestigious philosophy departments to recommend candidates, this will tend to exclude African-American candidates unfairly, not because our chairperson has any dislike or hatred of African-Americans but because the "old boys" hold faculty positions in universities that have very few African-American graduate students or faculty members.

The recent recognition of this so-called institutional discrimination has led to the introduction of a second conception of racial discrimination. Racial discrimination consists in the adverse treatment of similarly situated members of some race without any sufficient just-making or justicizing reason. This conception promises an explanation of what is morally wrong with racial discrimination; namely, it is adverse treatment, whereby the victim is treated worse than other similarly situated persons. Discrimination is morally wrong because it is harmful, or at least less beneficial than the act one ought to do. Still, not all adverse treatment is unjust. It is not unfair for me to give birthday presents to my children but to refrain from giving them to the children of our neighbors, since the children of other parents are not similarly situated to my own. However, should my son enroll in my philosophy course, it would be unjust for me to disallow late work from some students while giving my son an extension without any justicizing reason, since all students in my course are similarly situated.

What determines whether some class of persons, for example children living in my neighborhood or students enrolled in my course, are similarly situated regarding some sort of treatment? A tempting answer is that persons are similarly situated when they have an equal right to be treated in some specific manner. This suggests a third conception of racial discrimination. Racial discrimination consists in any different treatment of the members of some race that prevents or impairs their equal exercise or enjoyment of their human rights. For example, Article 1 of the UN *Convention on the Elimination of All Forms of Racial Discrimination* reads:

> In this convention the term "racial discrimination" shall mean any distinction, exclusion, restriction or preference based on race, colour, descent, or national or ethnic origin which has the purpose or effect of nullifying or impairing the recognition, enjoyment or exercise on an equal footing, of human rights and fundamental freedoms in the political, social, cultural or any other field of public life.

Although this definition may be appropriate to the human rights document in which it occurs, it seems too narrow for the purposes of moral philosophy.

Why is it only fundamental human rights that determine when persons are similarly situated? Surely any adverse treatment of the members of some race having the same moral or legal right to be treated in some manner is also racial discrimination, at least if there is no justicizing reason for the different treatment. It may even be that persons can be similarly situated when no right of any sort is at stake. Suppose that one gives less candy to African-American children than to white children who come trick-or-treating on Halloween. Is not this racial discrimination even though none of the children can claim any right to be given candy?

It seems, therefore, that for our present purposes, the best conception of racial discrimination is the second one. Racial discrimination consists in the adverse treatment of the members of some race who are similarly situated without any sufficient justicizing reason. The third conception can then be accepted as describing one species of this more generic injustice.

The Reverse Discrimination Debate

Now Bakke could, and many moral philosophers would, argue that giving preferential treatment to African-American applicants in the admissions procedures of a college or university is morally wrong because it is reverse discrimination. It is the reverse of the more usual form of racial discrimination in two respects: It is discrimination in favor of rather than against African-Americans, and it remedies or at least compensates for the serious injuries they have suffered because of past discrimination against them. Still, it is itself a form of racial discrimination and as such is morally impermissible.

There are three ways one might try to rebut this reasoning. First, one could argue that preferential treatment of African-American applicants is not racial discrimination in the morally relevant sense. Racial discrimination, properly interpreted, consists in adverse treatment of the members of some race who are similarly situated without a sufficient justicizing reason. But giving preferential treatment to African-American applicants is not treating them adversely, quite the opposite; it is treating them better, not worse, than white applicants to the college or university. This answer is surely unavailing. Because the terms "better" and "worse" are comparative, to treat African-American applicants better than white applicants is necessarily to treat white applicants worse than African-American applicants. Hence, although preferential treatment of African-American applicants may not be discrimination against them, it presumably is racial discrimination against whites. This was precisely Bakke's complaint.

Or one might deny that this sort of adverse treatment constitutes racial discrimination because white and African-American applicants are not similarly situated. A white applicant has no more right, or even moral claim, to be admitted by an academic institution than an African-American trick-or-treater has to be given candy. This reply is, of course, very controversial. Some maintain that African-American and white applicants are similarly situated *as applicants* and that each applicant has a moral right to be considered on the basis of his or her academic qualifications only. Because one's race is irrelevant to one's ability to pursue any program of studies, it is racial discrimination to use one's race as a criterion for admission into or rejection from any college or university. Even if the existence of this alleged moral right is not granted, rejecting a white applicant while accepting a less well qualified African-American applicant does seem to be racial discrimination.

One might, however, deny that this sort of adverse treatment constitutes racial discrimination because it is required by a justicizing reason, a reason specified by a fundamental principle of justice. The obvious justification for reverse discrimination is that it reverses or makes amends for the gross injustices inflicted upon African-Americans throughout the history of our society. Hence, every African-American applicant has a moral right to a remedy for the wrongs he or she has suffered. Given the seriousness of these wrongful injuries, it is not unjust to reject some white applicant who has probably benefited from rather than suffered from past racial discrimination in our society.

Almost all moral philosophers accept the principle of remedial justice, but many doubt that it is applicable to programs of preferential admission such as the one of the University of California at Davis. No doubt anyone who has been wrongfully injured has a right to a remedy. But against whom does this claim-right hold? The generally accepted principle of remedial justice is that one who has been wrongfully injured has a right to be compensated or made whole by the party who has acted wrongfully. Thus the correlative duty falls upon the party who has acted unjustly, and only upon that party.

Now granted that any African-American applicant accepted under the program of preferential admission at Davis has repeatedly suffered from serious racial discrimination in the past, no one alleges that he or she has been wrongfully injured by the University of California at Davis or by any white applicant, such as Alan Bakke, who may happen to be rejected because of the preferential treatment given to black applicants. To be sure, the state of California may have discriminated against the African-American applicant by its failure to assure that the primary and secondary schools in predominantly African-American neighborhoods were equal to those provided for most white children. If so, California does owe the African-American applicant some appropriate remedy. But preferential admission to one of its universities is not a morally appropriate remedy because it places the unfair burden of compensating for the injustice perpetrated by society as a whole upon a very few citizens: those rejected white applicants who are innocent victims of its program of preferential admission for African-American citizens.

Let us grant, but only for the sake of the argument, that preferential treatment for African-American applicants is reverse racial discrimination against white applicants. Still, the moral debate is not over. A second rebuttal is that this sort of racial discrimination is not morally wrong. Why is racial discrimination against African-Americans morally wrong, indeed a very serious moral wrong? This is because it does great injury to its victims. Although each individual act of racial discrimination may seem only a little wrong, such actions have a serious cumulative effect because each takes place in the context of pervasive and persistent racial discrimination in our society. As a consequence, racial discrimination against African-Americans is extremely harmful in at least two ways.

For one thing, it stigmatizes African-Americans as inferior to whites. It expresses the lack of respect of white Americans for African-Americans and thereby undermines the self-respect of those subject to almost continual racial discrimination. For another thing, it biases our social institutions so that they subordinate African-American citizens to whites. To be sure, subordination is not slavery. But it does impose very real economic and political disadvantages that greatly reduce the well-being of African-Americans. Any discrimination in education is especially serious both because it is here that the stereotypes central to the attitudes of whites toward African-Americans, and of African-Americans toward themselves, are formed and because in our society education is crucial to equal economic and political opportunity.

Preferential treatment for African-American applicants, even if it were reverse discrimination, still might not be morally wrong because it is not harmful in either of these ways. It does not express any lack of respect for the white applicants rejected for admission; in fact, it recognizes that they possess the qualifications needed for the academic programs to which they applied. Nor should it undermine the self-respect of those reluctantly denied admission because the number of available places in each entering class is limited. Also, it does not subordinate white Americans, who constitute the political majority and the economically advantaged, to African-Americans. If anything, it tends to equalize the place of African-American and white citizens in our society. Therefore, if it is racial discrimination, it is benign discrimination and morally permissible.

But should one either ignore the harms imposed on those white applicants rejected because African-American applicants were given preferential treatment in the admissions procedures or deny that it is unfair to discriminate against white applicants, albeit with the most benign intentions? Even if reverse discrimination is less wrong than the past discrimination against African-Americans, it is still racial discrimination and as such is morally wrong.

At this point a third rebuttal becomes relevant. Although preferential treatment for African-American applicants may be prima facie morally wrong, wrong unless there is some stronger contrary consideration, it may be morally justified by some overriding moral reason. What morally relevant consideration could possibly outweigh the injustice of preferential admissions? Some moral philosophers argue plausibly that the incidental injustice to rejected white applicants can be justified by a consideration of the fundamental moral right to equal opportunity. Of course, Alan Bakke can and did complain that he was denied an equal opportunity to continue his education at the University of California at Davis because of the preferential treatment given to African-American applicants in its admissions procedures.

This may be true, but it is only a very small part of the entire picture. The human right to equal opportunity is the right to be provided with an equal opportunity to succeed in one's life as a whole and to enjoy the wealth and happiness one thus earns. Because of the very persistent and pervasive racial discrimination in our society, every African-American applicant to a college or university will have much less opportunity overall than any white applicant. Giving some preferential treatment to African-American applicants tends to equalize the opportunity of African-Americans without greatly reducing the opportunity of any white applicant. Therefore, some conclude that the fundamental moral right to equal opportunity implies the moral right of academic institutions, in the United States at this time in our history, to give preferential treatment to African-American applicants in their admissions procedures.

Other Considerations

Although Ronald Dworkin does not appeal to the alleged moral right to equal opportunity, he does give a similar argument to explain why De Funis, and by implication Bakke, has no case. He distinguishes between a right to equal treatment and a right to be treated as an equal. He denies that Bakke has any legal or moral right to equal treatment, any right to be treated in the same way as African-American applicants. Hence, Bakke has no moral or legal complaint merely because he was not treated in the same manner as African-American applicants to the University of California at Davis.

What every citizen does have is a right to treatment as an equal, a fundamental moral right to be treated with equal concern and respect. The traditional racial discrimination against African-American citizens is morally wrong and a violation of the Equal Protection Clause because it fails to be as concerned for the interests of African-Americans as for those of white Americans and treats African-American citizens as inferior to and undeserving of equal respect with white citizens. However, giving preferential treatment to African-American applicants in the admissions procedures of an academic institution, although it may be detrimental to the interests of some white applicants, does not violate their right to be treated with equal concern and respect. As long as the institution considers the interests of those rejected to be as important as the interests of others affected by its decisions and does not reject any applicant because it considers him or her to be inferior as a person, it has not violated the right to equal concern.

Those who do not wish to appeal to any alleged moral right to equal opportunity or to equal concern and respect could argue that the modest harm done to white applicants rejected by any preferential admissions program is outweighed by important public goods such programs will achieve. For example, giving preferential treatment to African-American applicants to the medical school of the University of California at Davis will improve public education by increasing the diversity of its student body. It will also improve public health in those predominantly African-American neighborhoods now underserved by physicians. And in the long run, such preferential treatment will reduce the exceedingly harmful racial tensions in our society both by decreasing the frustration and anger of African-Americans who feel that they are unjustly denied opportunity to participate fully in our society and by providing role models to motivate African-American youths to develop their talents to the point where they will no longer need any preferential treatment.

This utilitarian argument can be challenged on either factual or moral grounds. Some social scientists deny that these important public goods will in fact be achieved by programs of preferential admissions. Admitting less qualified African-American applicants to each entering class will reduce rather than increase the quality of public education in our colleges and universities. Rejecting better qualified white applicants may generate a backlash that will exacerbate racial tensions, not reduce them. And the value of African-American role models will be undermined by the suspicion that they would not have succeeded without being given an unfair advantage to offset their academic inferiority.

Also, many educational and social reformers suggest that there are other and less unjust ways to achieve these admittedly important social goals. And some moral philosophers will reject this appeal to public goods on the ground that mere utility cannot morally outweigh injustice. No matter how expedient programs of preferential admissions may be, the value of an end can never, from the moral point of view, justify using an immoral means to achieve it.

It will probably be as difficult for moral philosophers and conscientious American citizens to reach any consensus on whether giving preferential treatment to African-American applicants is reverse discrimination (and, if so, on whether it is morally wrong) as it has been for the justices of the United States Supreme Court to agree on the analogous legal issues. Fortunately, such consensus is not necessary for our present purposes. What we want to know is whether these moral debates reveal any proliferation of asserted moral rights and, if so, whether these alleged rights are real.

Many of those who debate the morality of academic programs of preferential admissions, both those who argue that they treat white applicants unjustly and those who argue that they are required by social justice, appeal to the fundamental moral right to equal opportunity. The belief that every citizen has a right to equal opportunity is hardly novel: It surely motivated the creation of the Equal Employment Opportunity Commission in

1964 and explains much of the appeal of other aspects of the civil rights movement. Still, the widespread appeal to this alleged right is relatively recent and remains controversial. It was not asserted in any of the traditional declarations of natural rights, and I have been unable to find any mention of it in any of the more recent human rights documents. Even more controversial and less widely accepted is Ronald Dworkin's assertion that every citizen has a fundamental moral right to equal concern and respect.

One of the most common and plausible of the arguments against programs that give preferential treatment to black applicants to a college or university is that they violate the moral right of each white applicant to be considered on the basis of his or her academic qualifications only. But do applicants have any such right? The existence of this alleged moral right appears self-evident to many moral philosophers and highly dubious to many others.

Finally, there are some moral philosophers who, after reflecting critically upon the debates reported above together with other considerations, conclude that African-American applicants to colleges and universities in the United States possess at this time in our history a moral claim-right to be given preferential treatment in admission procedures. If this is true, then it is not only morally permissible but morally required for academic institutions in our country to give preferential treatment to black applicants. But is it true? And is there any evidence to support this conclusion sufficient to convince those critics to whom it appears clearly false?

Tentative Conclusions

What can we learn about the proliferation of rights from our study of the civil rights movement? First, the Supreme Court has contributed to the proliferation of legal rights. In its recent decisions, it has recognized the new civil rights to nonsegregated public education, to interracial marriage, and to preferential admissions. Because these decisions serve as precedents binding upon the lower federal courts and all state courts, these three civil rights have now been added to those previously existing in the law of the United States.

Second, alleged moral rights, especially human rights, have played an important role in these legal developments. For one thing, the moral convictions of those who believe in these rights have motivated many of them to join the civil rights movement and to support those who have appealed to the courts to vindicate what they take to be their moral rights. For another, these alleged moral rights have been advanced as reasons to accept or reject judicial reasoning to justify the creation of new civil rights. The civil rights cases we have studied show the legal relevance of moral rights, especially fundamental human rights. Recall the interpretations we encountered of both the Equal

Protection and Due Process Clauses and of the moral terms, such as "discrimination," used in the Civil Rights Act of 1964. It is not surprising, then, that the moral debates in the political arena, as well as the arguments heard by our courts, often presuppose the existence of fundamental moral rights. In the cases we have studied, these include the human rights to education and to marry and found a family and the fundamental moral rights to a remedy, to equal opportunity, and to equal concern and respect.

Third, some of these alleged moral rights are new. This is not to say that the publications of a moral philosopher or the speeches of a moral reformer can create new moral rights in anything like the way in which the decisions of the Supreme Court can and sometimes do create new legal rights. What are new are the assertions of moral rights not previously believed to exist—or, in many cases, not even thought of before. In this sense, there has also been a proliferation of alleged moral rights. Thus assertions that the fundamental moral rights to equal opportunity, to found a family, and to equal concern and respect exist have only recently become common in moral philosophy and political debate.

Has the recent creation of the new civil rights to nonsegregated public education, to interracial marriage, and to preferential admissions improved our legal system? Any reasonable answer needs to consider each right individually and to distinguish the ways in which each might improve the law of our land. (1) These new civil rights might be thought to have settled previously unresolved legal issues. One of the most important functions of any legal system is to settle disputes between the members of society. Otherwise these conflicts can, and when bitter will, lead to violence and harm to innocent as well as guilty parties. The decision in *Loving* seems to have been entirely successful in this regard; very few are now inclined to challenge the legal right of interracial couples to marry. Although the right to nonsegregated public education recognized in *Brown* is today widely accepted, disputes about its limits continue to be fought out in court cases concerning forced busing and the very costly financing of attempts to integrate the schools in our metropolitan areas. And *Bakke* has probably settled very little, both because in that decision the Supreme Court failed to draw the line between legally permissible and impermissible forms of preferential treatment for African-American and other minority applicants and because vigorous efforts to overturn that controversial decision continue.

Also (2) the introduction of these new civil rights might be thought to have helped to solve some urgent social problems. For example, to the degree that *Brown v. Board of Education* has led to the integration of our primary and secondary schools, it probably has improved the education of African-Americans and thereby increased their opportunities for finding and holding jobs. If so, to some extent this integration has helped to reduce the excessive unemployment in our country and to increase the number of taxpayers who contribute to holding down the staggering deficit in our federal budget. Similarly, programs of preferential admission to colleges and universities in the United States may have somewhat increased the number of African-American physicians and lawyers and thereby improved the medical and legal services to those living in the predominantly African-American urban cores of our major metropolitan areas. And perhaps the recognition of all three new civil rights has helped to reduce the racial tensions in our society that always hinder social cooperation and that all too often cause destructive violence. One must leave the verification or refutation of these claims to social scientists.

Finally (3) the introduction of these new civil rights might have made our legal system, and thereby our society, more just. Whether this is true will depend in part upon whether creating and maintaining a legal right is always, or even usually, the best way to protect or enhance the analogous or related moral right. This will not be the case when the new civil right is either very ineffective or counterproductive. Many argue that the law cannot remove the injustices arising from racial discrimination in our society because it cannot change the hearts and minds of those who discriminate. Only education in our homes, schools, and churches can effectively eradicate this moral evil. Others point to the flight of the more affluent whites from neighborhoods in which the schools have been integrated, thereby increasing rather than reducing racial segregation in our public schools, as an example of the way in which creating a new civil right can aggravate the injustice it was intended to eradicate.

Whether the creation of these three new civil rights has made our legal system more just also depends upon whether the alleged moral rights at stake are real. There are two philosophical problems that arise from any appeal to a fundamental moral right to justify the introduction of a new civil right. First, how can one know whether the presupposed right really exists? The existence of the declared human welfare right to education or the alleged moral right to equal concern and respect remains controversial. Second, and worse yet, there does not seem to be any rational method by which to resolve such moral disagreements.

Even when the existence of the presupposed moral right is accepted, how can one define its precise content? Granted that there is a fundamental moral right to a remedy, moral philosophers disagree about whether this applies to groups as well as individuals. Only if it does apply to groups, is it clear that one can infer that white Americans as the dominant class in our society owe each and every African-American, however fortunate his or her individual circumstances, a remedy for the past racial discrimination of our predominantly white society against African-Americans generally. Even granted that there is a human right to marry and found a family, its limits remain in dispute. Hardly anyone admits that the creation of a civil right permitting polygamy would make our legal system more just, and only some argue that the introduction of a legal right permitting gay or lesbian marriages is required by the human right to marry.

The persistence of such controversies does not show that appealing to these alleged moral rights is misguided, but it does leave any moral conclusions drawn from them open to doubt. Therefore, there can be reasonable disagreement about whether the recent proliferation of new civil rights has improved our legal system.

Notes

1. *Brown v. Board of Education of Topeka*, 349 US 294, 301 (1955).

2. Herbert Ravenel Sass, "Mixed Schools and Mixed Blood," *Atlantic Monthly* 195 (November 1956), pp. 48–49.

3. A bilateral liberty is a liberty to do or refrain from doing some specific action as one chooses.

4. *Meyer v. Nebraska*, 262 US 390, 399 (1922).

5. Quoted in *University of California Regents v. Bakke* 438 US 265, 415 (1978).

6. There must be some one concept of justice, for otherwise the word "justice" would be ambiguous, so that philosophers who advance various theories of "justice" would be talking about different things, not disagreeing about one and the same subject. At the same time, philosophers must have different conceptions of justice, different interpretations of this concept, because they conceive of the nature of justice very differently.

Suggestions for Further Reading

Aristotle (fourth century B.C.), *Nicomachean Ethics*. Book 5, pp. 1129a–1138c. A classic and most influential theory of justice.

Bardolph, Richard, ed. 1970. *The Civil Rights Record*. New York: Thomas Crowell Company. A useful collection of relevant documents.

Blackstone, William T., and Robert Heslep, eds. 1977. *Social Justice and Preferential Treatment*. Athens: University of Georgia Press. This book contains illuminating essays concerning both social justice and its relevance to the preferential treatment debates.

Boxill, Bernard R. 1992. *Blacks and Social Justice*. Lanham Md.: Rowman and Littlefield. A judicious and well-argued book relevant to issues of racial discrimination in the United States.

Brown v. Board of Education of Topeka. 1954. 347 US 483. The landmark case holding that racially segregated public schools are unconstitutional.

Brown v. Board of Education of Topeka. 1955. 349 US 294. So-called *Brown II*, which ordered the states to end segregation in their public schools with all deliberate speed.

Cohen, Carl. 1979. "Why Racial Preference Is Illegal and Immoral." *Commentary* 67 (June), pp. 40–52. One of the strongest arguments against preferential admissions programs in colleges or universities.

Dworkin, Ronald. 1977. *Taking Rights Seriously*. Cambridge Mass.: Harvard University Press. See especially pages 223–239. Dworkin argues that De Funis, and by implication Bakke, has no basis upon which to argue that preferential admissions programs are either illegal or immoral.

Frankena, William K. 1962. "The Concept of Social Justice." In *Social Justice*, ed. Richard B. Brandt. Englewood Cliffs N.J.: Prentice-Hall. Frankena argues that social justice is adverse treatment without a justicizing reason.

Fullinwider, Robert K. 1980. *The Reverse Discrimination Controversy*. Totowa, N.J.: Rowman and Littlefield. Both a report and an assessment of the main arguments for and against reverse discrimination.

Graglia, Lino A. 1976. *Disaster By Decree*. Ithaca: Cornell University Press. A vehement denunciation of the decision in *Brown v. Board of Education* together with supporting factual information.

Gross, Barry R., ed. 1977. *Reverse Discrimination*. Buffalo N.Y.: Prometheus Books. Another collection of important essays for and against reverse discrimination.

Harris, John. 1989. In *Children, Parents and Politics*, ed. Geoffrey Scarre. Cambridge: Cambridge University Press. An excellent discussion of the human right to found a family.

Loving v. Virginia. 1967. 388 US 1. The landmark case holding that state statutes prohibiting interracial marriages are unconstitutional.

Meyer v. Nebraska. 1922. 262 US 390. An early case in which the Supreme Court declared that the right to marry falls within the constitutional right to liberty.

Newby, I. A. 1965. *Jim Crow's Defense*. Baton Rouge: Louisiana University Press. A very clear and plausible account of the reasons for racial segregation in the South.

Plessy v. Ferguson. 1896. 163 US 537. The case upholding state laws prescribing separate but equal facilities in public transportation and accommodation, and presumably in education.

Sass, Herbert Ravenel. 1956. "Mixed Schools and Mixed Blood." *Atlantic Monthly* 198 (November), pp. 45–49. Sass argues that public schools must be segregated in order to prevent the miscegenation that would harm both white and black southerners.

Sickels, Robert J. 1972. *Race, Marriage and the Law*. Albuquerque: University of New Mexico Press. A clear accurate account of U.S. law relevant to marriage, especially interracial marriages.

University of California Regents v. Bakke. 1978. 438 US 265. A rather ambiguous decision declaring racial quotas unconstitutional but upholding the right of academic institutions to consider race as one factor in admitting applicants.

Vlastos, Gregory. 1962. "Justice and Equality." In *Social Justice*, ed. Richard B. Brandt. Englewood Cliffs N.J.: Prentice-Hall. Vlastos argues that social justice requires treating all persons with respect for their equal human rights.

Wasserstrom, Richard. 1976. "The University and the Case for Preferential Treatment." *American Philosophical Quarterly* 13, pp. 165–170. An imaginative and very influential argument for the permissibility of preferential treatment by colleges and universities.

4

Women's Rights and Feminist Theory

Until late in the nineteenth century, before a woman married, she was under the complete control of her father, and then when she did marry, she became for all legal purposes one person with her husband. Thus she had few if any rights to acquire, own, or dispose of property, much less to obtain credit in her own name. Of course she had no right to vote or to serve on juries, for her father or husband could and did speak for the entire family.

Although there were a few advocates of women's rights earlier, the first wave of the women's movement did not become effective until the first three decades of the twentieth century. At the core of this movement were the suffragettes who championed extending the right to vote, long enjoyed by males, to females. Others sought to obtain equal property rights for women. There were also women, sometimes supported by male allies, who attempted to overcome the legal and social restrictions that excluded women from many occupations and from the education required to enter the professions. Only in 1920 did the Nineteenth Amendment declare that "the right of citizens of the United States to vote shall not be denied or abridged by the United States or by any State on account of sex." During the same period, there were similar women's rights movements in the United Kingdom and on the Continent.

The second wave of the women's movement began after the Second World War and has become increasingly active from about 1960 until the present. Originally, its strategy was the same as that of the first wave: to obtain for women the same old legal rights enjoyed by men. Gradually, however, women began to claim new moral rights and, in some cases, to achieve new legal rights. In this way, the women's movement parallels the civil rights movement.

This parallel is no accident. Just as many African-Americans had left the South to work in the northern defense industries during the Second World War, so many women had moved into industrial and even service jobs left empty by the men inducted into the armed services. Most of these women did not, as had been expected, leave the labor market after 1945. Moreover, many women, both white and African-American, became involved in the civil rights movement itself. They then extended both their commitment to social reform and their skill in leadership to the struggle to obtain civil and economic rights for women.

At first their enthusiasm for the pursuit of women's rights, primarily through political action and petitions to courts of law, was virtually unbounded. But their limited success gradually led to considerable disillusion. Moreover, some of the recent developments in feminist theory have suggested that their struggle for legal rights has been misguided. These suggestions range from the view that our legal system is an instrument used by males to oppress females, through the thesis that rights are too individualistic to remedy wrongs suffered by women as a group, to the rejection of the morality of rights and justice in favor of the morality of care and responsibilities.

This chapter will examine some of the new legal rights introduced to benefit women and some of the alleged moral rights used to justify demands for social reform by the women's rights movement. Reflection upon feminist theory will require us to reconsider the nature and value of rights and enable us to reach a more reasonable conclusion as to whether the recent proliferation of legal rights and alleged moral rights has been beneficial or harmful.

The Right to Equal Pay

Although increasing numbers of women moved into the labor market during and after the Second World War and many of them worked side by side with men, their remuneration was markedly less. Naturally, high on the agenda of the second wave of the women's movement was the attempt to rectify this gross injustice. In response, Congress passed the Equal Pay Act of 1963. Its crucial section reads in part: "No employer . . . shall discriminate . . . between employees on the basis of sex by paying wages to employees . . . at a rate less than the rate at which he pays wages to employees of the opposite sex . . . for equal work on jobs the performance of which requires equal skill, effort, and responsibility, and which are performed under similar working conditions." Although the act contains exceptions for seniority systems, merit systems, systems measuring quantity or quality of work, and differentials based on factors other than sex, it does apply to large numbers of working women.

This law confers on women employees a new legal right to equal pay. Its defining core is a negative legal claim against one's employer not to be paid less than employees of the opposite sex on the basis of one's sex. It is a women's right, not in the sense that it is a right possessed only by women, but in the sense that women are, and are intended to be, its primary beneficiaries. Hence, this new right constitutes an achievement in the struggle of women for rights, in this case a right to remuneration, equal to those already enjoyed by men.

Formal Versus Real Equality

Feminists, sometimes influenced by Marxism, frequently distinguish between formal and real equality. Although the law may take on the form of sexual equality, it continues to serve the interests of those with power, in this case male employers. As a consequence, they argue, the enactment of an equal legal right leaves virtually untouched the injustice it pretends to eliminate.

This theory seems confirmed by the experience of women after 1963. Even though the Department of Labor was successful in achieving wage parity in a considerable number of early court cases, the gross disparity between women's wages and those of men increased rather than diminished. This can be explained in large measure by sexual segregation in employment. More women than men are still employed in certain occupations, such as elementary teaching, nursing, and secretarial work; even today relatively few women are university professors, physicians, or executives. Therefore, the legal right to equal pay for equal work is unavailing for the large numbers of women who continue to be excluded from performing the same kind of work for which men receive much higher pay. Also, women are typically unable to compete with men for the more demanding and higher paid positions because of their domestic obligations as wives and mothers. Clearly, new legal rights can achieve little or nothing to equalize wages in the absence of much more basic social changes in employment patterns and in family roles. Some feminists infer that the appeal to women's rights will be inevitably futile and should be abandoned; others conclude only that the women's movement must define the rights it strives to achieve more carefully.

Although the women's movement welcomed the passage of the Equal Pay Act of 1963, it is worthy of note that it would have preferred another formulation. The bill first proposed by the Kennedy administration stated in part: "No employer ... shall discriminate ... between employees on the basis of sex by paying wages to any employee at a rate less than the rate at which he pays wages to any employee of the opposite sex for work of comparable character on jobs the performance of which requires comparable skills." Representative Saint George, incidentally a woman, objected to the "comparable work" language and offered an amendment, subsequently accepted, which limited equal pay claims to those "for equal work on jobs, the performance of which requires equal skills." Representative Goodell, a sponsor of the act, explained that this change was intended to make it clear that the jobs involved must be virtually identical, either very much alike or closely related to each other. The Senate also explicitly rejected the language of comparable work and accepted the bill reformulated in terms of equal work.

Why did Congress deliberately avoid creating any legal right to equal pay for comparable work? The legislative history of the act reveals that it did not wish to interfere with the efficient economic mechanisms of supply and demand by authorizing any federal agency or any court of law to compare the jobs of very different kinds of workers—such as a female nurse and a male orderly in a hospital, or a male working on the assembly line and a female secretary working in the office of a factory. Many women engaged in political action would conjecture that this was because legislators are mostly men influenced by the predominantly male leaders of business, industry, and the labor unions. This suggests that the attempt to achieve real sexual equality by the enactment of equal rights will have very limited, if any, success.

More recently some segments of the women's movement have gone beyond demanding equal pay for work requiring comparable skills and have campaigned for laws requiring equal pay for work of comparable worth. Elizabeth Fox-Genovese, a historian with a special interest in women's studies, has asserted that "comparable worth forces us to confront the difficult truth that our society has not been willing to pay for much of what it claims to value. We have not placed a high monetary value on the various activities, traditionally associated with women, that concern nurture, personal service, and many forms of education."[1] She goes on to suggest that comparable worth cannot be defended on conventional individualistic grounds. As one might have expected, given the economic and political power of those who oppose this reform, the many attempts to introduce a right to equal pay for work of comparable worth have been ineffective.

Individual Rights and Social Value

Some feminists believe that the theory of individual rights excludes any recognition of social responsibilities or of value to society. Elizabeth Wolgast, a political philosopher and a feminist, argues that the theory of natural rights that has shaped our conception of moral and legal rights presupposes a social atomism. The self that possesses any right is assumed to be an autonomous individual entirely independent of society and pursuing his own self-interest. If this assumption of self-interest is correct, then the theory of fundamental human rights would justify a laissez-faire marketplace in which workers compete for jobs and the price of labor is determined by the economic laws of supply and demand without any social intervention. Because both employers and employees are assumed to be motivated purely by self-interest, there is no room in this theory of rights even to conceive of a moral right to equal pay for work of comparable worth to society. It seems, therefore, that the appeal to equal rights is theoretically incapable of overcoming the social injustice of wage discrimination against women.

Martha Minow, a professor of law at Harvard University, denies that rights presuppose autonomy in the sense of an independent self unencumbered by social relations. Quite the contrary, rights presuppose that the community is willing for the individual to make claims and to participate in the process of defining and redefining personal boundaries. Hence, the autonomy presupposed by individual rights is essentially relational and social. Some other feminists believe that although the traditional concept of rights presupposes an individual right-holder, it also assumes a social context within which the possessor of any right could appeal to society to recognize her right and protect it against other individuals who might violate it.

On balance, the development of rights theory reveals that although some theories of natural rights—such as that of Thomas Hobbes, a seventeenth-century political philosopher who maintained that individuals are essentially selfish—do presuppose that the right-holder is a self-interested individual entirely independent of society, there are other and equally plausible theories that recognize that rights presuppose a social context. Therefore, there is no inherent contradiction in the very concept of a right to equal pay for work of comparable social worth. On the other hand, it is not at all clear what sorts of reasons could ground this moral right, and there would be practical problems in enforcing any such legal right because every proposed measure of the social worth of very different kinds of labor is highly controversial.

The Right to Equal Employment Opportunity

Discrimination against women regarding employment takes many forms in addition to the payment of lower wages for equal work. A firm may hire a male rather than a much more qualified female applicant for a position or, when business declines, dismiss a female rather than a male worker. It is a common employment practice to exclude women from some of the more desirable positions and also to give preferential treatment to males in promotion. Congress tried to remedy these and similar forms of injustice in the Civil Rights Act of 1964.

Title VII concerns equal employment opportunity and Section 703 (a) reads:

> It shall be an unlawful employment practice for an employer—(1) to fail or refuse to hire or to discharge any individual or otherwise to discriminate against any individual with respect to his compensation, terms, conditions, or privileges of employment, because of such individual's race, color, religion, sex, or national origin; or (2) to limit, segregate, or classify his employees in any way which would deprive or tend to deprive any individual of employment opportunities or otherwise adversely affect his status as an employee, because of such individual's race, color, religion, sex, or national origin.

Although The Civil Rights Act of 1964 was intended primarily to address racial discrimination, our present concern is with its application to women.

Title VII confers on women a legal right to equal employment opportunity. This is not a positive right to be provided with a job or even with any opportunity to obtain and hold a job, but a negative right not to be denied equal employment opportunity. Its defining core is a legal claim of each individual woman not to be discriminated against by any employer in any of the ways specified in the act. The act also created an Equal Employment Opportunity Commission authorized to hear and settle disputes concerning alleged violations of Title VII. If no acceptable settlement can be achieved, a suit can be brought before a federal court. Is this new right an effective remedy for the unjust treatment of women regarding employment?

Racial and Sexual Discrimination

Some feminists believe that a right to equal employment opportunity is and will remain an inadequate remedy because it misconceives the problem that needs to be remedied. The Civil Rights Act of 1964 was primarily designed to eliminate, or at least greatly reduce, racial discrimination against African-Americans. Very late in the debate, however, a southern member of Congress, probably in an effort to discredit the bill, offered an amendment to insert "sex" into Title VII. To his consternation, the bill as amended was enacted into law. In this way a statutory remedy for racial discrimination was extended to deal with sexual discrimination. This presupposes that these two sorts of injustice are fundamentally the same. The word "sexism," coined on the model of the word "racism," assumes this also.

But does justice require that sexual differences be treated in the same way that racial differences ought to be treated? Elizabeth Wolgast argues that this is not so. Because differences of race such as skin color or hair texture are relatively superficial, a society ought not to distinguish between black and white citizens for legal purposes. This implies that the rights of African-Americans ought to be equal to the rights of white Americans. Indeed, racial differences are not even biologically fundamental so that interbreeding could assimilate what are now thought to be distinct races of human beings. Hence, the moral ideal of social assimilation of the races is at least plausible.

Not all sexual differences are similarly superficial. In particular, the fact that only women can become pregnant, carry a fetus to term, and deliver a child is not something that biology or modern technology can now or will in the foreseeable future be able to change. This difference between the sexes is fundamental to the nature, situation, and self-image of every woman. Hence, legal distinctions between females and males are not always arbitrary and unjust. In fact, the reproductive function of women ought to shape the social institutions of the ideal society because it has an important impact both on the needs of women and on the need of society to fix responsibility for caring for the children they bear.

It follows that conferring on women equal rights, that is, the same rights as those enjoyed by men, will not always achieve social justice. The unjust treatment of women is not always similar to racial discrimination; it sometimes arises from a failure or refusal to discriminate between their needs and the very different needs of the men who control the legislatures and the courts. Because the new legal right to equal employment opportunity confers one and the same right on men and women, it cannot do justice to those special needs of women that arise from their exclusive reproductive function and its social implications.

This claim does not repudiate completely the struggle for equal rights. For many purposes, sexual differences are biologically superficial and irrelevant to the proper social roles of men and women. Hence, women ought to enjoy the same rights to vote, run for public office, serve on juries, own property, and have credit in their own names as men. Quite likely they ought also to possess a legal right to equal employment opportunity. Nevertheless, additional remedies will be required to achieve complete justice for women even regarding employment.

One would hope, however, that the new legal right to equal employment opportunity would at least greatly reduce the forms of sexually discriminatory employment practice that it renders unlawful. Yet empirical evidence indicates that this right has not achieved even this modest goal of the women's movement. It is still the case that employers often hire males in preference to better qualified female applicants, dismiss women at the same time they retain men who have performed no better on the job, and promote women employees more slowly than they advance men to higher or better paying positions in their establishments. Although some women have benefited to some extent from Title VII of the Civil Rights Act of 1964, most women still enjoy significantly less employment opportunity than similarly situated men. Why is this so?

Individual Rights and Group Wrongs

Some feminists explain that no right could possibly be adequate to remedy the unjust treatment of women. Rights, in theory and in practice, are paradigmatically rights of individuals. Thus, women's rights are taken to be rights of each and every individual woman, not rights of women as a group. Note that Title VII makes it an unlawful employment practice "to fail or refuse to hire or to discharge any individual, or otherwise to discriminate against any individual." Carol Smart, a British sociologist who specializes in criminology, points to a general problem with any feminist appeal to rights. In case of violation, it is up to the individual to claim her right in court and prove that it has been violated. Hence, even when many individuals may have benefited from taking legal action, the vast majority will have gained very little, if anything. Although individual women are the victims of wrongful sexual discrimination, they are discriminated against because they are women; they are treated not on their individual merits, but in terms of their group membership. Hence, no appeal to individual rights can ever adequately remedy the sexual discrimination against women as a group.

Carol Smart argues that this is a problem with rights as they are often formulated to deal with social wrongs. She does not conclude that the women's movement should abandon the struggle for women's rights. Instead, she cautions us both to expect only partial remedies for injustice from legislation conferring new individual rights and to supplement this approach with other solutions to the many social problems of women in our society.

The Right to Maternity Leave

In spite of the enactment of Title VII, the employment opportunities of women continued to be adversely affected by the fact that they, but not the men with whom they competed for jobs and promotions, can become pregnant. Many private firms and even government agencies treated pregnancy differently from other conditions that render an employee temporarily incapable of working. Women were often fired when they became pregnant, and even if they retained their positions, their medical expenses were seldom covered under the employer's health benefits plan; and they sometimes returned to work having lost their seniority. The women's movement contended that these practices constituted sexual discrimination against women, but the courts divided on this issue.

Therefore, Congress passed the Pregnancy Discrimination Act of 1978. This amended Section 703 of Title VII of the Civil Rights Act of 1964 to specify: "women affected by pregnancy, childbirth, or related medical conditions shall be treated the same for all employment-related purposes, including receipt of benefits under fringe benefit programs, as other persons not so affected but similar in their ability or inability to work." In practice, this confers on women a conditional right, a new legal right to maternity leave with the same fringe benefits that men receive if, but only if, the firm has a system of disability leaves with benefits.

In the following year, the United Nations went even further. Article 11.2 of the *Convention on the Elimination of All Forms of Discrimination Against Women* declares: "In order to prevent discrimination against women on the grounds of marriage or maternity and to ensure their effective right to work, States Parties shall take the appropriate measures . . . to introduce maternity leave with pay or with comparable social benefits without loss of former employment, seniority or social allowances." Thus, the United Nations asserted that women ought to have an unconditional legal right to maternity leave with pay and without penalty.

Equal Versus Special Rights

Although these two formulations would require similar employment practices, they define the right conferred on women in very different terms. The Pregnancy Discrimination Act conceives of it as the right of women to be treated the same as men by any system of disability leave. Its purpose is to give women an equal right to leaves when they are temporarily incapable of working. Although men and women may be unable to work because of very different medical conditions—only men develop prostate cancer and only women become pregnant—both can and should enjoy the same right to disability leaves with the same benefits. The UN *Convention* conceives of the right more specifically as a special legal right that only women could possess and not as a universal right of all employees, since no man is capable of becoming pregnant and giving birth to a child. Feminists disagree about which conception is preferable.

The women's movement has traditionally struggled for equal rights; its goal has been for women to enjoy the same rights as those that men enjoy. Although Elizabeth Wolgast agrees that women ought to possess some equal rights, such as the same rights to vote and to own property that men possess, she argues that women ought also to possess some special rights, some rights that only women can or even could possess. She argues that thinking of a woman's right to a maternity leave as an equal right to a disability leave distorts our moral and legal reasoning.

Wolgast asks us to consider, for example, the California program of medical benefits that covered prostatectomies but not pregnancy. How, then, should a women argue for a right to a maternity leave by appealing to equal rights? It would be a very odd way of talking to begin by assuming that she has an equal right to medical treatment for prostate cancer should she ever become a man. A reasonable and equitable system of medical insurance ought to cover some disabilities that pertain to both sexes and some that pertain to only one sex. To ensure the latter, our society ought to enact special rights, some rights that only males possess and others that are specifically women's rights. The attempt to ground any right to maternity leave upon equal rights will necessarily ignore the special needs of pregnant women, needs that are inevitably different from those of men who never do or could become pregnant.

Wendy Williams, a jurist with a special interest in women's rights, rejects this appeal to special rights and defends the right of women to equal treatment when they become pregnant. The equal rights approach is part of a larger feminist strategy of getting the law out of the business of reinforcing traditional sex-based family roles. To argue for a special right for maternity leave is to suggest that women are essentially different from men and that their "natural" function is to bear and rear children; to argue for this special right is thereby to evoke this harmful ideology. Moreover, to appeal to a right for a special disability leave for a woman while she is temporarily pregnant is to separate pregnancy from long-term childrearing and thus to close the important possibility of redefining the male role to include the more general role of parenting one's children. Finally, asserting some special right that only a woman could possess will be perceived by the males who dominate legislation and the courts as reverse discrimination and thus generate a backlash that will victimize women. The most effective strategy for the women's movement is to fight for equal legal rights but at the same time to seek more fundamental solutions for social injustice outside the legislature and the courtroom.

Justice or Care

Both the United States Congress and the United Nations invoke a right to maternity leave as necessary to prevent the injustice of sexual discrimination against employed women. But some feminists argue that the women's movement ought to ground its demand for maternity leave on needs rather than rights. Carol Gilligan, a Harvard psychologist who has done empirical research on the moral development of children, found that although most boys approach moral problems from the perspective of justice, girls tend to approach them from the perspective of care. The morality of justice judges the conflicting claims of autonomous selves in terms of equal rights and abstract moral principles; the morality of care responds to the perception of need within the concrete context of personal relationships. Gilligan explains the underlying reasons for these two perspectives: "Since everyone is vulnerable both to oppression and to abandonment, two moral visions—one of justice and one of care—recur in human experience. The moral injunctions, not to act unfairly toward others, and not to turn away from someone in need, capture these different concerns."[2] Accordingly, some feminists argue for maternity leave from the care perspective and ground their demand upon the needs of women employees for respite from work during the last stage of pregnancy, for a period to recover from the labor of delivering a baby, and for the time to care for their newborn child.

Other feminists defend an approach in terms of rights. Martha Minow grants that there is something lacking in any conception of rights that speaks only of autonomy rather than needs. But she points out:

> There is something too valuable in the aspiration of rights, and something too neglectful of the power embedded in assertions of another's need, to abandon the rhetoric of rights. That is why I join in the effort to reclaim and reinvent rights. Whether and how to use words to constrain power are questions that should be answered by those with less of it. For this task, rights rhetoric is remarkably well suited. It enables a devastating, if rhetorical, exposure of and challenge to hierarchies of power.[3]

Therefore, although rights should be reinterpreted in terms of personal relationships and individual needs, they are the appropriate instrument for women to use to reform the employment practices of the men who now dominate business and industry.

Two questions emerge from these feminist debates. One is practical: What is the best strategy for women to use to achieve maternity leaves that fully meet their needs? The options seem to be: striving for equal legal rights, working for special legal rights, or making their needs apparent to employers and the public. The other is more theoretical: What moral foundation best justifies the demand for adequate maternity leaves? If one opts for the morality of justice, then one must decide whether justice requires equal rights or special rights. If one appeals to the morality of care, one must decide who is responsible for meeting the needs of pregnant workers and exactly what kinds of care are morally appropriate. The discussions to date leave these hard questions undecided.

The Right to Abortion

For more than two-thirds of the twentieth century, it was a crime for a physician to perform an abortion or for a woman to obtain one except to save the life of the mother. As part of a larger campaign for reproductive freedom, some women's organizations sought to have the state statutes prohibiting abortion declared unconstitutional. Not until 1973 did the Supreme Court do so in *Roe v. Wade*: "This right of privacy, whether it be founded in the Fourteenth Amendment's concept of personal liberty and restrictions upon state action, as we feel it is, or, as the District Court determined, in the Ninth Amendment's reservation of rights to the people, is broad enough to encompass a woman's decision whether or not to terminate her pregnancy."[4] Thus, Justice Blackmun, delivering the opinion of the Court, inferred a legal right to abortion from the constitutional right to privacy.

This is emphatically not an equal right; it is clearly a special women's right. It is the right of the individual pregnant woman to make the abortion decision, and the father of her unborn child has no legal say in the matter at all. The right to abortion is not a claim-right to be provided with an abortion or even with the funds to obtain one. It is the bilateral liberty-right of the mother to terminate her pregnancy by obtaining an abortion or not to do so as she chooses. Her constitutional right is not, however, without limits. The state may regulate abortion during the second trimester to protect the health of the mother or even prohibit abortion during the third trimester to protect the life of the fetus. Should women rejoice in this new legal right?

Political Discourse

Not all women have. Today pro-choice women and men are pitted in vehement debate and political struggle against pro-life men and women over the abortion issue. Each side appeals to a right that it regards as absolute and decisive because it assumes that a basic moral right necessarily outweighs every other consideration in moral deliberation and political debate. Mary Ann Glendon, a political scientist active in promoting women's rights, argues that this illusion of absoluteness promoted by our rights talk is extremely harmful: "the rhetoric of absoluteness increases the likelihood of conflict and inhibits the sort of dialogue that is increasingly necessary in a pluralistic society. . . . Claims of absoluteness have the further ill effect that they tend to downgrade rights into mere expressions of unbounded desires and wants."[5] Glendon's criticism of rights talk, one of the most crucial objections to the proliferation of rights, seems to be confirmed by the uncompromising attitude of those on both sides of the current abortion controversy. The result of their appeal to conflicting rights has been a political stalemate that has generated both disrespect for the law and even violence.

Others believe that the problem does not lie in the language of rights but in its abuse by those who pretend to appeal to a moral right when they are actually expressing only their moral prejudices and blind passions. Properly understood, rights tend toward reason and dialogue rather than dogmatic pronouncements, for to claim a right is to demand something on the basis of some ground, some reason why one's demand ought to be recognized. Hence, the appeal to conflicting rights will, at least among reasonable parties, lead to rational discussion in the light of the grounds or morally relevant considerations advanced by both parties. Only when all the reasons lie on one side of an issue, as is clearly not the case regarding abortion, will the appeal to rights rule out a compromise acceptable to all members of the community.

The Right to Privacy

Some feminists believe that the legal right to abortion was misconceived in *Roe v. Wade* because of the shortsighted reasoning of the Supreme Court. Justice Blackmun derived the woman's right to terminate her pregnancy from her constitutional right to privacy: "The Constitution does not explicitly mention any right of privacy. In a line of decisions however, . . . the court has recognized that a right of personal privacy, or a guarantee of certain areas or zones of privacy, does exist under the Constitution."[6] Justice Blackmun goes on to explain that these decisions make it clear that this right extends at least to activities relating to marriage, procreation, and family relationships.

Although almost all feminists welcome the reproductive freedom thus derived, many believe that the right to privacy also has unacceptable implications. Elizabeth Fox-Genovese argues:

> It is not easy to reconcile the defense of women's right to abortion on the grounds of privacy with sustained attempts on the part of the women's movement to break down other aspects of what was traditionally viewed as the privacy of the family. Most of us applaud the state's growing willingness to help to protect women and children against sexual or physical abuse by husbands and fathers. But only very recently would all interference between a man and a wife have been viewed as an invasion of privacy. In effect, the defense of a woman's right to abortion as a matter of privacy represents a decisive reinforcement of the extreme individualistic view of society as composed of atomized individuals. More frighteningly, by implicitly identifying reproduction as a woman's individual right, it dismisses men's claims and dissolves their responsibilities to the next generation.[7]

This passage contains two criticisms of viewing the right to abortion as a privacy right.

First, this view draws the line between the public and the private spheres in a way that is dangerous for women and children. Traditionally we have assumed that the public sphere concerns the political and economic institutions of society and should be regulated by law; on the other hand, marriage, reproduction, and the family are zones of privacy that ought to be governed by personal decisions and ought not to be intruded upon by the law. As a consequence, many fathers and husbands are and presumably ought to be left unrestrained and free to continue their activities of child abuse, wife battering, and marital rape. Surely this is unacceptable to any feminist and ought to be rejected by any fair-minded and caring male, even a male who does not consider himself a feminist.

Second, this way of defining the right to abortion takes the abortion decision to be a purely private one, one that belongs to the pregnant woman alone. Just as it is wrong for anyone else to read one's private correspondence without one's permission, so the abortion decision is taken to be no business of anyone else, not even the father of the unborn child. But if the father has no responsibility for making the decision as to whether a child will be born, why should he be imagined to have any responsibility of child support, much less a responsibility to care for any child its mother decides not to abort? Thus the family, and more generally society as a whole, is reduced to a collection of isolated individuals, each with his or her completely independent life. This totally neglects the fact that the abortion decision involves concerns of the entire community, such as who shall suffer the consequences of the crimes of rape or incest, who will care for unwanted children or pay child support for children born to impoverished mothers, and who will provide the kind of arrangements for rearing children that will be most likely to produce responsible citizens rather than adults incapable of productive work and destined, perhaps, for a life of crime.

Nevertheless, Alison Jaggar, a feminist and political philosopher, defends the right of the pregnant woman to make the abortion decision. She rests her case on two moral principles. The first is that the right to life is a right to a full human life and to whatever means are necessary to achieve this; the second is that decisions should be made by those, and only those, who are importantly affected by them. She grants that the father has some claim to decide whether or not his unborn child shall be born because his life would be affected by the birth of a child. But in our society, it is understood that the primary responsibility for raising the child belongs to the mother and that the father has considerable choice as to how far his life is affected by the birth of a child. He is never subjected to the dangers of pregnancy and childbirth, and he can often evade even his minimal legal obligation to provide child support. Because it is the life of the mother, rather than that of the father, that is most importantly affected by the abortion decision, she has the right to decide whether or not to terminate her pregnancy.

Jaggar also recognizes that society has a considerable stake in the abortion decision. But she argues:

In this society, each woman is primarily responsible for her own support, for the medical expenses she will incur during pregnancy and childbirth and for providing her child with both its material and emotional needs. Because of this situation, women's lives are enormously affected by the birth of their children, whereas the community as a whole is affected only slightly. Moreover, because of this situation, each woman finds that she, rather than the state, is the primary protector of her child's right to life.[8]

Therefore, each woman has the sole moral right to determine whether or not, in her case, abortion is justified. This right is not derived from any right to her own body or from her right to privacy. It is a contingent right rather than a universal one, a right resulting from women's situation in our society.

Unfortunately, the general public remains bitterly divided over whether the introduction of this new right to abortion into our legal system was a humane expansion of the liberty of women or an inhumane invitation to murder unborn children. At best this continuing struggle between the pro-choice and pro-life movements distorts politics by diverting attention away from many of our urgent social problems; at worst it leads to violence, including the bombing of abortion clinics and the murder of physicians who perform abortions.

There seems to be no theoretical resolution or even assistance at hand. One problem concerns whether the human fetus is the kind of being that could possess any moral rights, even the human right to life. The fetus surely does not possess moral agency and probably does not, at least during the first two trimesters, have any interests—the two qualifications most often held to be necessary to be a moral right-holder. On the other hand, many believe that its potential agency or future interests are sufficient to qualify it as a right-holder. Another problem concerns the grounds of moral rights. What reason or reasons are there to justify the claim that a pregnant woman does have a moral right to abort her unborn child? Although philosophers have proposed a number of theories of the grounds of rights, none of these theories has been solidly established and very few are defined with enough precision to enable one to derive any very specific right. Therefore reasonable disagreement over a woman's right to abortion remains.

The Right Not to Be Raped

Rape is both a tort and a crime.[9] It is a tort because it is a violation of the victim's common law right to the bodily integrity or security of her person; it is a crime because all fifty states have statutes prohibiting rape. Therefore, women now have, as they have had for many decades, a legal right not to be raped. Still, the women's movement has long been and still is struggling to redefine this right. One problem with its traditional definition, and the one on which we will focus here, is the marital rape exemption or spousal rape immunity by virtue of which a husband does not commit rape even if he compels his wife to submit to sexual intercourse by the most brutal force or even the threat of death.

The common law origin of this marital exemption is found in the explanation of the seventeenth-century English jurist Lord Hale: "But the husband cannot be guilty of a rape committed by himself upon his lawful wife, for by their mutual marital consent and contract the wife hath given up herself in this kind unto her husband, which she cannot retract."[10] In other words, because a women consents to have sexual intercourse with her husband when she marries, and because the marital contract remains in force as long as they both shall live, she has consented to every subsequent act of marital intercourse.

This doctrine was judicially recognized in the United States as early as 1857 and has influenced the definitions of rape under criminal law in all the states. As late as 1985, Section 213.1 of the *Model Penal Code*, a code of criminal law that the American Law Institute adopted and recommended for enactment throughout the United States, included a marital exemption in its definition: "*Rape*. A male who has sexual intercourse with a female not his wife is guilty of rape if . . . he compels her to submit by force or by threat of imminent death, serious bodily injury, extreme pain or kidnapping." Over the past ten or fifteen years the courts and state legislatures have been modifying or even eliminating this spousal immunity.

What we have, at least as of 1995, is a new legal right in the making, a right already existing in some states and taking shape in most others. It is the right of a married woman not to be raped by her husband. Although its defining core varies from state to state, it typically includes a wife's legal claim holding against her husband that he not compel her to submit to sexual intercourse by force or the threat of force and not impair her resistance by employing drugs or intoxicants. Should we encourage the development of this new legal right?

Efficacy

Although very few feminists would oppose the right not to be raped by one's husband, some would deny that it will be at all effective in significantly reducing, much less eliminating, marital rape. This is both because substantive and procedural law are formulated in essentially masculine terms and because those who administer and apply the law are predominantly men. Hence, the law is a most inappropriate instrument for women to use in their efforts to overcome male oppression and to achieve justice. Although this is true of the law in general, it is most evident in the law concerning rape.

Catherine MacKinnon, a professor of law best known for her feminist jurisprudence influenced by Marxism, expresses this viewpoint most clearly.

> As a beginning, I propose that the state is male in the feminist sense. The law sees and treats women the way men see and treat women. . . . Substantively, the way the male point of view frames an experience is the way it is framed by state policy. To the extent possession is the point of sex, rape is sex with a woman who is not yours, unless the act is so as to make her yours.[11]

Thus, rape is defined in terms of penetration, however slight, by the penis into the vagina, as though thrusting the penis into the vagina is what sex is all about and as if even the grossest intrusions into other openings of the female body, or the use of other tools, do not matter. Whether the woman in fact consented to sexual intercourse is ignored by the law because the fact that the victim knew the rapist or that she had previously allowed him sexual liberties is taken as proof of consent to even the most brutal intercourse. While previous convictions for sexual crimes by the rapist are not permissible evidence of his guilt, reports of the sexual history of the victim are admitted as evidence of her consent on this occasion. Although the courts presume that sexual intercourse between cohabitants or social companions is consensual, women experience rape most often by men they know. Consequently, most women get the message that the law against rape is virtually unenforceable as applied to them.

From this examination of the law of rape, MacKinnon infers a discouraging conclusion:

> Attempts to reform and enforce rape laws, for example, have tended to build on the model of the deviant perpetrator and the violent act, as if the fact that rape is a crime means that society is against it, so law enforcement would reduce or delegitimize it. . . . Even if it were effective in jailing men who do little different from what nondeviant men do regularly, how would such an approach alter women's rapability? Unconfronted are *why* women are raped and the role of the state in that. Similarly, applying laws against battery to husbands, although it can mean life itself, has largely failed to address, as part of the strategy for state intervention, the conditions that produce men who systematically express themselves violently toward women, women whose resistance is disabled, and the role of the state in this dynamic.[12]

MacKinnon concludes that the women's movement should abandon its hope of achieving any real reform by introducing new legal rights and should turn its efforts to much more radical changes in our society and, especially, in the underlying viewpoint that frames our legal institutions.

Carol Smart believes that this conclusion is too radical. She grants that the form of law is not gender-neutral, as many liberal feminists imagine, and that the content of legislation and its implementation may be oppressive of women. At the same time, she rejects any jurisprudence, like that of MacKinnon, that attempts to account for everything in relation to one mode of explanation. One of the lessons of history is that legal reform is always partial and incomplete:

> The idea of the uneven development of law is an important one. It allows for an analysis of law that recognizes the distinctions between law-as-legislation and the effects of law, or law-in-practice. It rejects completely any concept of law as a unity which simply progresses, regresses or reappears as a cycle of history to repeat itself. It perceives law as operating on a number of dimensions at the same time. Law is not identified as a simple tool of patriarchy or capitalism. To analyze law in this way creates the possibility of seeing law both as a means of 'liberation' and, at the same time, as a means of the reproduction of an oppressive social order.[13]

Accordingly, the women's movement should continue to struggle for legal reform, including the introduction of new women's rights, while recognizing the limitations of these efforts and supplementing them with attempts to bring about more fundamental changes in our social institutions.

The Value of Rights

Many feminists are suspicious of rights, at least as men conceive of them. Joel Feinberg, a moral philosopher and philosopher of law who advocates a claim theory of rights, argues that what would be lacking in any society without rights and what gives rights their special value is the activity of claiming: "Even if there are conceivable circumstances in which one would admit rights diffidently, there is no doubt that their characteristic use, and that for which they are distinctively well suited, is to be claimed, demanded, affirmed, insisted upon."[14] Apparently upon this legalistic conception of rights, the essential function of any right is to enable the rightholder to impose demands upon some adversary as one does in a court of law.

It is because Elizabeth Wolgast accepts some such view of rights that she is reluctant to protect the interests of members of the family by giving them rights. For a child or a wife to press his or her claim against a parent or a husband would be to threaten their close relationship. She writes:

> A defender of atomism or individualism might argue that any alternative will be a theory that supports some form of natural domination by some over others, and this conclusion is anathema. But a more rational answer is that an alternative model is needed for understanding marriages and families, as well as communities of other kinds. We need a model that allows for organic connections, some more fundamental than others, among people, connections of dependency and interdependency of many kinds.[15]

She proposes a model conceived in terms of responsibilities rather than rights.

Some feminists find a suitable model in the work of Carol Gilligan. They believe that although the morality of justice and rights is necessary to regulate the interactions of strangers, the morality of care is more appropriate for the family because demanding one's rights is destructive of our most valuable intimate relationships.

This concern for the intimacies of marriage is not limited to feminists; the state of New York used it to defend its spousal immunity against rape. In *People v. Liberta*, Judge Wachtler rejects this argument:

> The first of these recent rationales, which is stressed by the People in this case, is that the marital exemption protects against governmental intrusion into marital privacy and promotes reconciliation of the spouses, and thus that the elimination of the exemption would be disruptive to marriages. . . . Clearly, it is the violent act of rape and not the subsequent attempt of the wife to seek protection through the criminal justice system which "disrupts" a marriage. . . . Moreover, if the marriage has already reached the point where intercourse is accomplished by violent assault it is doubtful that there is anything left to reconcile.[16]

In short, by the time a wife has occasion to claim her right not to be raped by her husband, there no longer exists any intimate relationship worth preserving.

Martha Minow does not agree with Elizabeth Wolgast that legal rights presuppose a social atomism:

> When the system assigns rights to individuals, it actually sets in place patterns of relationships, for legal rights are interdependent and mutually defining. They arise in the context of relationships among people who are themselves interdependent and mutually defining. In this sense, every right is no more than a claim limited by the possible claim of others.[17]

Therefore, she rejects the view that to introduce rights into what should be purely private family relationships is inevitably damaging.

Minow wishes to reconceive rights as the language of a continuing process in which the right-holder and duty-bearer attempt a reasonable resolution of their conflicting interests by appealing to the standards of a wider community, standards that are themselves subject to change in the light of an ongoing community discourse:

> To believe that rights, when claimed and recognized, create conflict and adversarial relations between children and adults is to presume that there would otherwise be community and shared interests. I suggest instead that legal language translates but does not initiate conflict. . . . Although the language of rights, on its surface, says little of community or convention, those who exer-

cise rights signal and strengthen their relation to a community. Those who claim rights implicitly agree to abide by the community's response and to accord similar regard to the claims of others. In a deeper sense, those claiming rights implicitly invest themselves in a larger community, even in the act of seeking to change it.[18]

Viewed in this way, rights can be seen as a means of reconciliation and improvement within personal relationships rather than as necessarily destructive of marital and other intimacies.

There is probably some truth on both sides of this debate within feminist theory. Ideally, there would be no need for anyone to claim her rights against other members of her family because those who genuinely care for one will more than respect one's rights. Moreover, one who demands her rights reveals a lack of trust that tends to undermine loving relationships. At the same time, aggressive impulse or calculated self-interest sometimes motivate those family members who ought to care for one, and at such times one needs rights to challenge those who wish to mistreat one. Under such circumstances, to claim one's rights does not create conflict and may even minimize it because to claim a right is implicitly to appeal to its grounds and thereby to initiate a consideration of the relevant legal or moral reasons. This appeal at least provides an opportunity for some kind of a reasonable resolution of the conflict, something much better than demanding satisfaction by an appeal to brute force. On balance, this new legal right of a wife not to be raped by her husband seems both necessary as an imperfect protection against a great harm to her person and desirable as a means that might occasionally salvage an intimate relationship at the breaking point.

Conclusion

As one would expect, debates concerning the recent proliferation of women's rights remain unresolved on both the theoretical and practical level. Feminists, and moral philosophers or philosophers of law both sympathetic to and critical of their viewpoints, are involved in an ongoing attempt to come to a better understanding of the nature of rights and of the contexts in which they are appropriate. Those in women's movements and their allies continue to try new tactics and to disagree about what strategy will be most effective in accomplishing their goals. Although it is too early to draw any firm conclusions, let us hazard a few provisional hypotheses.

First, although rights do not presuppose any social atomism, contemporary theory of rights remains predominantly individualistic. With the exception of organizations such as political states or private corporations, only individuals are usually thought to be right-holders. This raises the question as to whether discrimination against groups or entire classes of individuals could possibly be eliminated by the introduction of any new legal right or challenged by the assertion of any new moral right. Some theorists regard this as a reason to modify rights theory to recognize group rights, such as rights of African-Americans or of women in general. To justify this move, however, one would need to define the qualifications necessary for the possession of a right with care and then show that groups, at least some kinds of groups, do in fact possess these qualifications. Recent attempts to accomplish this remain controversial.

Second, both feminists and their critics disagree among themselves about whether justice requires special rights as well as equal rights. The civil rights movement and the women's rights movement began by struggling for equal rights; their goal was the enjoyment of the same rights that white males already enjoyed. The theoretical and practical advantage of this strategy was that it enabled them to appeal to moral principles and legal rights accepted by those in power.

But this appeal to equal rights all too often seemed inapplicable to the special circumstances of women and the children for whom they cared. Hence, the women's movement has added several special women's rights to its agenda. Many men charge that this is to demand special privileges that impose an unjust burden on males. For example, affirmative action programs in employment both deny male applicants jobs for which they are better qualified than the females hired and subsequently prevent the fair promotion of males on the basis of merit. The theoretical and practical complexities revealed in the *Bakke* case apply to any special employment rights for women just as much as to special educational rights for African-Americans. What is lacking to resolve this debate is a theory of the grounds of rights adequate to distinguish between merely alleged moral rights and real rights. In the absence of such a theory, it appears that the arguments for a few special rights are at least plausible.

Third, experience has shown clearly that one must distinguish between formal equality and real equality. Although legislation may appear not to discriminate against women, and the courts may apply procedures that are on their face sexually neutral, the way our legal institutions actually function is often unfair to women. Moreover, much of the injustice women suffer in our society is imposed by social institutions that are regarded as private and thus beyond legal regulation. For example, the social roles of wife or mother continue to impose far greater burdens on women than men bear. Most basically, our conceptions of ourselves as males or females serve as rationales for the mistreatment of women by individual men and for the continuing oppression of women by our social institutions. Very wisely, few feminists infer that the women's movement should abandon its attempts at reform by striving for legal rights. Still, it is obvious that much more will be required to achieve social justice for women as a group or to protect individual women from wrongful treatment. Many nonlegal institutions must be radically modified and our ways of thinking must be changed fundamentally before women can be fully liberated.

Fourth, it is not merely legal rights that have their limits in the struggle for an ideal society; moral rights also have limited applicability. There is more to morality than rights. Part of this is probably articulated in the morality of care revealed by the research of Carol Gilligan and developed by other feminists. But much more moral theory is required to explain both those moral duties not grounded on or correlative with rights and the entire range of values, both individual and social, that underlie moral reasons in general. This is not to deny the importance of moral rights, much less to reject their significance entirely. It is to imply that any adequate moral ideal for our society must depend upon other considerations in addition to the recognition of moral rights, old or new.

Notes

1. Elizabeth Fox-Genovese, *Feminism Without Illusions* (Chapel Hill: University of North Carolina Press, 1991), p. 77.

2. Carol Gilligan, "Moral Orientation and Moral Development," in *Women and Moral Theory*, eds. Eva Feder Kittay and Diana T. Meyers (Totowa N.J.: Rowman and Littlefield, 1987), p. 20.

3. Martha Minow, *Making All the Difference* (Ithaca: Cornell University Press, 1990), p. 307.

4. *Roe v. Wade*, 410 US 113, 153.

5. Mary Ann Glendon, *Rights Talk* (New York: Free Press, 1991), pp. 44–45.

6. *Roe*, 152.

7. Fox-Genovese, *Feminism Without Illusions*, p. 83.

8. Alison Jaggar, "Abortion and a Woman's Right to Decide," in *Women and Philosophy*, ed. Marx Wartofsky and Carol Gould (New York: Putnam, 1976), p. 356.

9. A tort is any wrongful act, damage, or injury done willingly, negligently, or in circumstances imposing strict liability (but not a breach of contract) for which the party wronged can sue for damages; a crime is any act committed or omitted in violation of a law forbidding or commanding it for which punishment can be imposed upon conviction.

10. Sir Matthew Hale, *Historia Placitorum Coronae: The History of the Pleas of the Crown*, vol. 1, ed. P. R. Glazebrook (1736; reprint, London: Professional Book Limited, 1971), p. 629.

11. Catherine A. MacKinnon, "Feminism, Marxism, Method, and the State: Toward Feminist Jurisprudence," *Signs* 8 (1983), p. 644.

12. MacKinnon, "Feminism," p. 643.

13. Carol Smart, *Law, Crime and Sexuality* (London: Sage Publications, 1995), p. 154.

14. Joel Feinberg, *Rights, Justice, and the Bounds of Liberty* (Princeton: Princeton University Press, 1980), p. 151.

15. Elizabeth H. Wolgast, *Equality and the Rights of Women* (Ithaca: Cornell University Press, 1980), p. 147.

16. *People v. Liberta*, 474 NE2d 567, 574.

17. Minow, *Making*, p. 277.

18. Minow, *Making*, pp. 291, 294.

Suggestions for Further Reading

Brown, Emily. 1995–96. "Changing the Marital Rape Exemption: I Am Chattel (?!); Hear Me Roar." *American Journal of Trial Advocacy* 19, pp. 657–671. Brown argues strongly for abolishing the marital rape exemption.

Feinberg, Joel. 1980. *Rights, Justice, and the Bounds of Liberty*. Princeton: Princeton University Press. See especially pages 143–158. The best formulation of the theory that both legal and moral rights are claims.

Fox-Genovese, Elizabeth. 1991. *Feminism Without Illusions*. Chapel Hill: University of North Carolina Press. See especially pages 55–86. Fox-Genovese argues against any atomistic conception of women's rights and for viewing their rights as deriving from a conception of individuals as responsible and interdependent members of society.

Gilligan, Carol. 1987. "Moral Orientation and Moral Development." In *Women and Moral Theory*, eds. Eva Feder Kittay and Diana T. Meyers. Totowa, N.J.: Rowman and Littlefield. A brief but clear explanation of the difference between the ethics of justice and the ethics of care.

Glendon, Mary Ann. 1991. *Rights Talk*. New York: Free Press. Glendon condemns the atomism, abstractness, and absolutism of the language of rights as currently used in political discourse and advocates reforming rights talk to recognize individual responsibility and the importance of social solidarity.

Hilf, Michael Gary. 1980. "Marital Privacy and Spousal Rape." *New England Law Review* 16, pp. 31–44. Hilf defends the spousal rape immunity as necessary to protect the more important interest in marital privacy.

Jaggar, Alison. 1976. "Abortion and a Woman's Right to Decide." In *Women and Philosophy*, eds. Marx Wartofsky and Carol Gould. New York: Putnam. A clear argument to show why the pregnant woman, rather than the biological father or society, has a right to decide whether to terminate her pregnancy.

MacKinnon, Catherine A. 1983. "Feminism, Marxism, Method, and the State: Toward Feminist Jurisprudence." *Signs* 8, pp. 635–658. MacKinnon argues that feminists should not rely on legal rights because the legal system is an instrument by which males exercise oppressive power over females.

McGlen, Nancy E. and Karen O'Connor. 1983. *Women's Rights: The Struggle for Equality in the Nineteenth and Twentieth Centuries*. New York: Praeger. See especially pages 149–195 and 271–312. A very clear and informative overview of the women's rights movement.

Minow, Martha. 1990. *Making All the Difference*. Ithaca: Cornell University Press. See especially pages 267–311. Minow argues that rights should be reinterpreted as features of relationships open to renegotiation within a community in order to respect the differences of groups within a pluralistic society.

People v. Liberta. 474 NE2d 567. An especially interesting set of opinions in a case concerning a spousal exemption clause in the definition of rape.

Roe v. Wade. 410 US 113. The landmark case creating the constitutional right of a pregnant woman to have an abortion if she so chooses.

Smart, Carol. 1989. *Feminism and the Power of Law*. London: Routledge. See especially pages 146–185. Smart argues that legal rights have some limited power to advance the cause of women.

_____. 1995. *Law Crime and Sexuality*. London: Sage Publications. See especially pages 138–159. An informed intelligent discussion of feminist jurisprudence and the best political strategy for feminists to use.

Williams, Wendy W. 1985. "Equality's Riddle: Pregnancy and the Equal Treatment/Special Treatment Debate." *New York University Review of Law and Social Change* 13, pp. 325–380. Williams argues that equality for women will be better achieved by rights equal to those of men rather than special rights for women only.

Wolgast, Elizabeth H. 1980. *Equality and the Rights of Women*. Ithaca: Cornell University Press. See especially pages 18–36 and 77–102. Wolgast argues that women need some equal rights together with some special rights.

_____. 1987. *The Grammar of Justice*. Ithaca: Cornell University Press. See especially pages 28–49. A brief, clear argument to show that the appeal to rights is sometimes inappropriate and ineffective either in meeting the needs of women or children or in achieving social justice.

Young, Iris Marion. 1990. *Justice and the Politics of Difference*. Princeton: Princeton University Press. See especially pages 156–191. Young argues for an ideal of respecting sexual, racial and ethnic differences in political discourse and political action.

5

Animal Rights and Environmental Ethics

The achievements of the civil rights movement and the women's rights movement have inspired an animal rights movement. We human beings have forced animals to perform hard labor for us, have used them as sources of raw materials like leather or fur, and have even killed and eaten them at our pleasure. But if human slavery is unjust, what right do we have to enslave nonhuman animals? How could the exploitation of our fellow animals—for human beings are also animals—be morally justified when the exploitation of humans is morally wrong? And is not eating the flesh of nonhuman animals as grossly immoral as cannibalism?

But there is a difference between cannibalism and eating the meat of non-human animals. According to the *Oxford English Dictionary*, cannibalism is "the practice of eating (the flesh of) members of one's own species." We do not dine on human flesh; we eat only the flesh of other species of animals. To some vegetarians this explanation seems like human arrogance and mere prejudice. The distinction between human and nonhuman animals no more justifies eating meat than did either the assertion of the slave-owner that he did not enslave whites but only Negroes or the explanation of the factory-owner that he did not exploit male breadwinners but only women laborers. Discrimination against other species of animals is morally wrong for precisely the same reason that discrimination against the members of another race or against women is immoral: It is adverse or harmful treatment based on a morally irrelevant distinction. Those who find racism and sexism morally repugnant ought to object equally to speciesism: the adverse treatment of members of another species without a justifying reason.

Many theologians reject this analogy between racism or sexism and our traditional treatment of nonhuman animals. God created all human beings in his image, but he created plants and nonhuman animals for the use of humans. Most moral philosophers reply that what makes racism and sexism morally wrong is primarily that they violate the fundamental human rights of their victims. Obviously, nonhuman animals have no human rights, and presumably they have no moral rights at all. Therefore, there is nothing wrong with forcing them to work for us, using them as resources, or even killing and eating them.

At this point the issue is joined. Article 3 of the *Universal Declaration of Human Rights* asserts, "Everyone has the right to life, liberty, and security of person." It may be true by definition that nonhuman animals possess no human rights, but this leaves open the question of whether they have equally fundamental moral rights to life, liberty, and security. Although philosophers traditionally rejected this suggestion as preposterous, it is now the subject of serious debate.

Let us begin by examining some of the arguments about three recently alleged moral rights of nonhuman animals. We will discover that debates about whether animals really do have any moral rights depend in part upon the more fundamental question of whether animals are the kind of beings that could possibly possess any moral rights at all. Subsequently, we will move on to consider both whether our conclusions regarding alleged moral rights apply equally to legal rights and whether the strategy of the animal rights movement ought to be adopted by environmentalists.

The Right to Life

James Rachels, a contemporary moral philosopher, asserts that nonhuman animals do have a moral right to life. His argument can be stated simply, although his underlying reasoning is rather complicated. If an individual has a life, then that individual has a moral right to life. Many nonhuman animals have a life. Therefore, many nonhuman animals have a moral right to life.

Rachels assumes that humans, at least normal adult humans, have a fundamental moral right to life. But what qualifies one for the right to life? What characteristic of the normal adult explains why he or she possesses a moral right to life? It is that a human being has a life. To have a life is not merely to be alive. Plants are alive, but they do not have lives. A life is a process that involves both goal-directed activities and projects that may succeed or fail and memories of what one has done in the past and what has befallen one. A life is a complex of experiences and activities that have a developmental unity, and it requires forward-looking and backward-looking attitudes. The concept of a life is a biographical not a biological concept. Biological life is morally important only because it is a necessary condition of having a biographical life. It is the fact that a human being has a biographical life that makes killing a human being wrong.

Hedonism, the theory that the only intrinsically good thing is pleasure, seems to imply that death is not an evil, because when one is dead, one no longer feels any pain; actually, death is a great evil because it frustrates one's hopes and prevents one from completing the projects that give meaning and value to one's life. To kill a human being is normally to harm that person grievously because it prevents the realization of all those goods that could otherwise have greatly enhanced the intrinsic value of his or her life. It is precisely in order to avoid this harm that one normally has a duty not to kill any human being.

But not every wrong act is the violation of a right. This is so only when (1) it is wrong to treat an individual in this manner for the sake of that individual, (2) when that individual or someone speaking for that individual may protest if treated in this way, and (3) when it is permissible for third parties to intervene to compel the wrongdoer to stop mistreating the individual. Rachels suggests that the evil of prematurely ending an individual's life makes these three conditions true, at least in the case of a normal adult human being: (1) It is primarily the individual killed who suffers the harm done because it is that person's life that is deprived of the goods it could have realized. (2) Hence, that individual or someone speaking for that individual has a special standing to protest this injury. And (3) the harm inflicted by being killed is so great that third parties are permitted to intervene to prevent it whenever possible.

Now Rachels argues that many nonhuman animals also have lives. At least baboons, dogs, wolves, and many members of the higher species of nonhuman animals are intelligent, live together in families and other social groups, and have forward-looking and backward-looking attitudes. Although their lives may be less rich and complex than ours, each of them does have a life in the biographical sense. Therefore, killing such animals is morally wrong for the same reason that killing a human being is morally wrong, and it is a violation of a moral right of the individual animal for the very same reasons that murder is a violation of a fundamental human right. Thus, the same reasoning that establishes the human right to life shows that many nonhuman animals also have a fundamental moral right to life.

H. J. McCloskey, who defines a right as an entitlement, finds this argument unconvincing. It is not merely having a life but having autonomy over one's life that gives a human being the moral right to life. Autonomy, the ability of self-determination concerning one's life, consists in the full capacity for rational decision and action, including moral choice. One's autonomy is one's most precious possession, and it gives one a property right in and to oneself. Autonomy is morally basic, in part, because of the immense worth of free existence, but it is also required for the possession of moral rights because the right-holder must exercise her capacities for self-determination and moral action in exercising her rights. Rachels correctly recognizes that there is a duty not to kill a human being, because death eliminates potentialities for great goods. Nevertheless, these are only supporting considerations when it comes to the human right to life. This right, like other moral rights, presupposes full autonomy.

Accordingly, the reasoning that establishes the human right to life has three foundations. First, this reasoning rests upon the presupposition of the capacity for autonomous existence of the normal human being. Second, it presupposes that respect for this autonomy or capacity for self-governance gives the individual moral rights over his own existence. Third, this reasoning presupposes that the most basic of these rights is the fundamental moral right to liberty. Now to kill a person or not assist her to live is to fail to respect her autonomous existence, for under normal circumstances no human being would freely choose death. Hence, a human right to life is implied by the fundamental human right to liberty.

Because Rachels's reasoning ignores autonomy, McCloskey argues that it fails to explain fully why the normal adult human being has a right to life. Moreover, the full explanation cannot be extended to nonhuman animals. Although many animals may have a life, even the higher animals lack autonomy. As far as the scientific study of animals goes, it does not reveal any nonhuman animals with the capacity to make rational decisions, much less moral choices, concerning their lives. Therefore, they are incapable of possessing either the fundamental moral right to liberty or the right to life this would imply.

The Right to Liberty

Of course James Rachels might, as indeed he did, assert that animals do have a right to liberty. Once more, his argument is simple to state but more difficult to explain in full. Human beings do have a moral right to liberty. There is no relevant difference between humans and other animals that would justify us in granting this right to humans while denying a similar right to animals. Therefore, the moral right to liberty is possessed by nonhuman animals as well as human beings.

Rachels defines the right to liberty as the right to be able to do as one pleases without being subject to external constraints on one's actions. Now what justifies us in granting this moral right to human beings? First, one has a moral right not to be deprived of any intrinsic goods that one is capable of enjoying—such as the good of liberty. Second, one has a basic right not to have one's interests needlessly harmed. A variety of other human interests, interests other than the interest in liberty for its own sake, are harmed if one's freedom is unduly restricted. These include one's interests in pursuing one's projects and achieving one's goals.

Now both of these justifications apply to nonhuman animals. Just as human beings enjoy being able to act without any external constraints, so nonhuman animals enjoy being able to act in one way rather than another. Constraints on one's ability to act are frustrating in and of themselves for humans and animals alike. And just as other human interests are harmed by the undue restriction of freedom, so various interests of many other species of animals are harmed by the loss of freedom. For example, wild animals do not fare at all well in captivity. They become frantic at first and then listless and inactive; they often fail to reproduce in zoos, and when they do, their offspring die sooner in captivity than in their natural habitats. The plight of animals confined to very small cages for the purposes of experimentation or of battery-raised chickens unable to walk about or even flap their wings is even worse.

Thus the grounds of the moral right to liberty apply equally to many nonhuman animals. Therefore, whatever differences there may be between human beings and other species of animals, such as the alleged lack of moral agency or lesser rationality, are irrelevant to this right and do not justify us in denying the right to liberty of nonhuman animals.

H. L. A. Hart, a recent Oxford professor of jurisprudence, maintains that a moral code, like the Ten Commandments, that consists merely in prohibitions and prescriptions would impose duties but confer no rights. This is because moral rights belong to that special branch of morality that is concerned to determine how one person's freedom may be limited by another's, and thus rights reflect those moral principles governing the proper distribution of freedom. Therefore, the various general and special moral rights are all grounded on the fundamental natural right to freedom, what is now called the human right to liberty. Thus the ascription of moral rights to human beings presupposes that any adult human being capable of choice has (1) a claim against others not to use coercion or restraint against her except to hinder coercion and restraint and (2) a liberty of acting in any way that is not coercing or restraining or designed to injure others. Because this fundamental moral right to liberty presupposes the capacity for choice—including the ability to conceive of alternative actions and choosing one rather than the other in the light of practical reasons—Hart infers that those who ascribe moral rights to animals are using the expression "a right" in an idle and misleading manner. Everything they wish to assert could be said more simply and clearly in the language of duties.

No doubt Rachels would object that Hart has begged the question by defining the right to liberty as the right of "any adult human being capable of choice."[1] And Rachels could go on to argue that some nonhuman animals are also capable of rational choice and thereby qualified to possess many moral rights, including the fundamental right to liberty. More likely, he would deny that the capacity for choice is required for the possession of moral rights. After all, what does rationality have to do with the value of liberty? Whether or not they are capable of rational choice, nonhuman animals are harmed when their freedom is severely restricted. To avoid begging the question of animal rights, one should define freedom as being able to do as one pleases rather than as being capable of acting as one chooses.

Hart believes that Rachels's conception of freedom fails to capture what we mean when we assert the human right to liberty. Suppose that a slave prefers working for her master and being cared for rather than bearing the responsibilities involved in choosing what to do, where to live, and how to feed and clothe herself. Luckily, she does what she pleases when she plants, tends, and picks cotton, although she has no choice in the matter: She is required to obey her master and would be cruelly punished were she to choose otherwise. She is surely not enjoying the human right to liberty. To have a liberty to do something, in the sense that is relevant to moral rights, requires that one also have a liberty not to act in that manner. Hence, the capacity for choice is presupposed by any liberty-right and especially by the fundamental natural right to liberty.

But is the capacity for rational choice also required for the possession of the claim-right not to be coerced or restrained? This is the crucial disagreement between Rachels and Hart. The argument Rachels states to prove that nonhuman animals have the moral right to liberty assumes first that one has a moral right not to be deprived of any intrinsic goods which one is capable of enjoying, and second that one has a basic right not to have any of one's interests harmed. Now why does he assume that these are basic moral rights? The reason is rooted in his conception of a right. To have a right is either to be the beneficiary of the performance of the correlative duty or, on a bad day, to be harmed by the nonperformance of that duty. Hence, if a wild animal is harmed by being caged in a zoo, and if this harm is great enough to impose a duty not to deny the animal its freedom in this way, then it follows that the animal has a right not to be so treated.

Hart rejects this beneficiary theory of rights. Suppose Able contracts with Baker that, in return for being paid twenty dollars, Baker will feed and exercise his dog while Able is away from home for a few days. Now Able's dog will benefit if Baker performs his contractual duty and will be harmed if Baker fails to do his duty. But it is Able, the one who contracted with Baker and has agreed to pay Baker for his services, who possesses the correlative right. This is shown by the fact that it is Able who is in a position to release Baker from that duty, if he so chooses, and who has the power to claim remedy or compensation in the event that he returns to find that Baker has failed to fulfill his contractual obligation. In short, to possess a right is not to benefit from the performance of a duty but to be in a position to control the corresponding duty by either insisting upon its performance or releasing the duty-bearer as one chooses. Accordingly, moral claim-rights presuppose the capacity for rational choice just as liberty-rights do. Because nonhuman animals lack this capacity, it is empty rhetoric to assert that animals have any moral right to liberty analogous to the fundamental moral right to liberty that any adult human being possesses.

The Right Not to Be Tortured

James Rachels rejects the assumption, widely accepted among moral philosophers, that there is some one property that is relevant to the possession of every right. Consider, for example, rights as different as the right to freedom of worship and the right not to be tortured. Only a being with the capacity to worship could have the former right; it would be idle to ascribe the right to freedom of worship to any being without the capacity to have religious beliefs and to participate in a form of life in which worship has some place. Hence, it seems senseless to think that rabbits could have any such right. Nevertheless, a rabbit might have a right not to be tortured, for the capacity to worship has nothing to do with this very different right.

What, then, is relevant to the moral right not to be tortured? Well, what is it that makes the cruel treatment of anyone morally wrong? It is the suffering, the pain, and the agony inflicted upon the victim. The characteristic that qualifies human beings for the right not to be tortured is their capacity to suffer. Because many nonhuman animals also have the capacity to suffer, to feel moderate and even acute pain, they are equally qualified to possess the right not to be tortured. That is, it is morally wrong to treat animals cruelly for the very same reason that it is wrong to torture any human being.

To be sure, not every wrong action is the violation of a right. This requires, among other things, both that the action is objectionable for the victim's own sake and that the right-holder may protest, in a special way, if he or she is treated wrongly. Now what makes the cruel treatment of any animal morally wrong is primarily the suffering it causes the animal itself and not some indirect consequence, such as its tendency to make the agent more inhumane; and because the primary injury is done to the mistreated animal, the animal is in a special position to protest, through some spokesperson, the wrong done to it. Accordingly, nonhuman animals that have the capacity to suffer have a moral right not to be tortured.

It is this second requirement—that the right-holder may protest, in a special way, if he or she is treated wrongly—that suggests to some moral philosophers that nonhuman animals have no moral right not to be tortured. The defining core of this human right is not some liberty, such as the liberty of worshipping as one wishes, but a claim that others not torture one, that they not cause one any unnecessary suffering. Therefore, the "special way" in which the right-holder may protest is not merely to complain of having been wronged but also to claim remedy from the wrong-doer. Now to claim remedy is to demand it as due to one, to insist that one is entitled to compensation for the injury done to one. But only a being capable of understanding the grounds of the right not to be tortured—and, thus, the reason why one is entitled to a remedy—could claim remedy in this special way. Nonhuman animals do not have any conception of either moral reasons or of how these could ground moral rights, such as the right not to be tortured. Because this renders animals quite incapable of claiming in the morally relevant sense, it would be empty and misleading rhetoric to ascribe any claim-right not to be tortured to them. Because, as Rachels himself admits, more than the capacity to suffer is required for the possession of the moral right not to be tortured, no nonhuman animal has any such right.

Possible Right-Holders

Up to this point, the debate has concerned the general question, "What moral rights, if any, do animals possess?" Gradually, moral philosophers became aware that there is a much more fundamental question that needs to be answered first: "Are nonhuman animals capable of possessing any moral rights at all?" Presumably normal adult human beings do have moral rights, and almost certainly sticks and stones have none. It is not that rocks, even precious gems, are unworthy of moral rights; they are simply not the sorts of things to which it would make sense to ascribe rights. Between our paradigms of right-holders and those kinds of beings that are obviously incapable of possessing rights, there are various borderline cases—newborn infants, human fetuses, irreversibly comatose patients, brain-damaged adults, and nonhuman animals. Before we argue about whether animals *do* have the rights to life, liberty, or not to be tortured, we should decide whether animals are the kind of being that *could* have moral rights. Well, what does qualify one to be a possible right-holders?

Interests

Joel Feinberg, who defines a right as a claim, argues that all and only beings with interests are capable of possessing rights. His argument begins with his theory of the nature of a right. He agrees with H. L. A. Hart that rights cannot be defined merely in terms of duties because there is something distinctive about a right that is lost in any reduction of rights to duties. He describes Nowheresville, a world in which there are values, moral virtues, right or wrong actions, and even duties but in which no one has any rights. What would be missing in such a world? He maintains that there could be no claiming in Nowheresville. Suppose, for example, that a promisor were to have a duty to do what he has promised but that the promisee had no right that he do so. If the promisor breaks his promise, then he will have acted wrongly and failed to fulfill his moral obligation, but this will be merely a matter between himself and his conscience, or perhaps his God. The promisee will have no standing either to claim performance of his duty or to claim remedy in the event of nonperformance.

To claim is to demand something as one's due, to insist on the performance of a duty to one as something to which one is entitled. Thus, it differs both from petitioning or begging for a favor from someone and from ordering someone to do as one wishes or suffer the threatened consequences. Because moral rights make claiming possible, they contribute to one's self-respect by enabling one to stand upon one's rights and face others as their equal and not as one who must beg them to do their duties. Feinberg concludes that a right is a valid claim. A legal right is a claim justified by the rules of some legal system; a moral right is a claim justified by the moral principles of an enlightened conscience.

But if a right is a valid claim, then it would seem that only a being capable of claiming, of demanding the performance of some duty as something to which one is entitled, could be said to possess a right. Thus, Joel Feinberg's conception of the nature of rights seems to imply that newborn infants—who are incapable of claiming because they lack any understanding of what would entitle them to something and cannot speak or write at all—could not be right-holders. Nevertheless, Feinberg insists that even newborn babies do have legal and moral rights. How is this possible? It is because adults, their parents or guardians, can make claims in their name. Hence, not only beings who are capable of claiming their own rights but also beings who can be represented by other spokespersons can possess rights.

The question then arises as to what kinds of beings are capable of being represented by others? Could someone, for example, claim the right to life of a beautiful wildflower by demanding that it not be picked? Presumably not. But why not? The reason is that a mere plant has no interest in life; the wildflower does not care whether it remains alive or dies. Only beings that have, or at least are capable of having, interests are possible right-holders because to act for someone is to represent that individual's interests. Parents or guardians can claim an infant's right to life or to adequate nutrition because even neonates have interests in such things. Now, non-human animals, at least the higher animals, similarly have interests in such things as adequate food and not being treated cruelly. Therefore, many nonhuman animals could possess moral rights, rights that they are not capable of claiming for themselves but that human beings could claim as their representatives.

Two serious criticisms have been made of this argument that animals are possible right-holders. Both ordinary language and the law distinguish between two different sorts of representation. To act *in* behalf of someone is to act in the interest of or for the benefit of that party; to act *on* behalf of someone is to act as the agent of or as a substitute for that party. Thus one party can represent either the interests of or the will of some second party. Now claiming is an activity, an expression of the will of the right-holder. If, as Feinberg maintains, claiming is what is definitive of and valuable about rights, then one would expect that any representative must be acting for a right-holder in the sense of acting as a substitute agent representing the will of the right-holder, rather than as someone acting in the interests of the right-holder. Hence, it is agency, having a will, rather than having interests that qualifies one to be a right-holder.

The other, and more common, criticism is that nonhuman animals cannot possess rights, even on Feinberg's own theory, because they are incapable of having any interests. Ordinary language distinguishes two senses of "an interest." In one sense, an interest is something in which one takes an interest, something that one desires or wants; in another sense, an interest is something that is in one's interest, something that is good for one or a component in one's well-being. Although Feinberg uses the expression in the latter sense when he asserts that it is having interests that qualifies a being to possess rights, he also asserts that interests are compounded out of desires or aims, both of which presuppose something like belief. This explains why inanimate objects or even plants cannot have any interests. Some moral philosophers insist that nonhuman animals are also incapable of desiring or aiming at the things that are good for them, either because they lack the ability to conceptualize these values or the linguistic abilities involved in having beliefs.

Neither of these two criticisms is decisive, however, because each rests on premises that are open to question.

Agency

Although H. J. McCloskey originally agreed with Joel Feinberg that it is the capacity to have interests that makes some being a possible right-holder, he later changed his mind. Moral rights have two essential aspects. They are entitlements that confer upon their possessors liberties to do, demand, or enjoy something and impose upon others duties to refrain from interference or sometimes to assist the right-holder. It is this active aspect of rights that explains why they cannot be reduced to mere duties. Probably the most important feature of the language of rights, and that which distinguishes it from the language of duties, is the reference to exercising, claiming, forgoing, or waiving one's rights. McCloskey concludes that a basic presupposition of the ascription of any right is the capacity or potential capacity for action. Where something is not the kind of being that is normally capable of action, we withhold the language of rights and confine ourselves to talk of duties regarding it.

At first glance, it might seem that the possessor of some rights need not have the capacity for action. All that seems necessary for the creditor to enjoy her right to be repaid is for the debtor to repay the debt, while the creditor remains the passive recipient. But even here, the creditor does act by accepting repayment and could have acted by either canceling the debt or, in the case of a reluctant debtor, demanding repayment. Therefore, only a being with the actual or potential capacity for self-determination and moral autonomy could possess a moral right. Although the higher species of animals may have some rudimentary capacity for action, they lack the practical reason and moral judgment that McCloskey believes necessary for genuine moral autonomy. Therefore, no nonhuman animal could possess a moral right.

An advocate of animals rights could, and many do, try to show that it is the capacity to have interests rather than the capacity for action that qualifies one to be a moral right-holder. But Robert Elliot takes a different tack. He recognizes that it would be empty rhetoric to ascribe a right to any being incapable of exercising it. What he denies, however, is that only a being with the capacities for practical reason and moral judgment can exercise their rights. Consider the human right to life. McCloskey is correct when he insists that in addition to imposing upon others the duty not to kill one, it also confers upon the right-holder moral liberties such as the liberty of defending one's life. Now a human being exercises her right to life not only when she rationally chooses to resist an attacker but also when she fights back instinctively and without rational deliberation. Similarly, many animals, and not merely those of the highest species, defend their lives by resisting attack. Thus many species of animals are capable of action in a sense robust enough to constitute the exercise of a moral right. In this way, Elliot rebuts McCloskey's argument that animals could not be moral right-holders.

Although Martin Golding, a moral philosopher and philosopher of law, does not go as far as asserting that nonhuman animals actually possess any moral rights, he does suggest that this might be so. He traces one strand in the history of rights theory—running at least from William Blackstone through Jeremy Bentham to H. L. A. Hart—according to which rights give some special standing to the will of the right-holder or confer some limited sovereignty upon her. For example, the creditor has the option of whether to insist on payment or to cancel the debt. Such option-rights do presuppose that the right-holder is an autonomous moral agent. Golding insists, however, that these are not the only rights; there are also welfare-rights to the goods of life recognized by the social ideal of one's community, for example, a child's right to an education, to adequate nutrition, and to protection from harm. What justifies us in classifying these as rights in the same sense that option-rights are rights is that both can be claimed, for claiming is central to the language of rights. But, as the case of newborn infants shows, welfare-rights presuppose only the capacity to enjoy goods or suffer from the lack of them; such rights do not presuppose necessarily moral autonomy. Thus, if nonhuman animals possess any rights, they are presumably welfare-rights rather than option-rights. At the very least, McCloskey's reasoning does not exclude this possibility.

Having a Life

The moral philosopher who is most closely associated with the animal rights movement is probably Tom Regan. Although he has developed a variety of arguments in support of animal rights over the past few years, the gist of his reasoning has remained fairly constant. He has consistently argued that at least some species of animals are capable of possessing certain basic moral rights. His model for a basic right is a human right such as the right to life or the right not to be tortured. These are rights the normal adult possesses because of the kind of being he or she is, not because of any voluntary transaction or because of some role in society. These are equal universal rights, rights normally possessed equally by all human beings. And they are the ground of our moral obligations to treat others with respect, not mere reflections of some duty independently grounded. Regan does not, of course, formulate his argument in terms of human rights because he wishes to show that nonhuman animals could possess similar moral rights.

In the critical phase of his reasoning, he refutes the main arguments of those who deny that animals could have any moral rights simply because they lack the qualification necessary to be a possible moral right-holder. Various moral philosophers appeal to different qualifications. The most common are self-consciousness, practical rationality, moral agency, or having desires—in a strong sense that presupposes a language in which one can formulate the object of one's desire. Regan points out that human babies and severely mentally limited adults also lack these qualifications. But very young and mentally limited human beings do have such basic rights as the right to life and the right not to be tortured. Therefore, these proposed criteria for being a possible right-holder must be rejected. Accordingly, the usual arguments for concluding that nonhuman animals could not have any moral rights fail.

In the constructive phase of his reasoning, Regan tries to justify the thesis that at least some animals could have basic moral rights. He begins with what Kant called a transcendental argument, an argument from some acknowledged fact to the presuppositions necessary to explain it. Regan accepts it as true that all human beings, including babies and the severely mentally enfeebled, have basic moral rights. Now, what is it about the nature of these beings that could possibly explain why it is that they have moral rights? Well, it must be something that explains why it is always wrong to treat them merely as a means and why respect for them requires us to treat them always as ends-in-themselves. This obviously cannot be their instrumental value, their value to us in achieving our own goals in life. Nor can it be the intrinsic value of their experiences—for this would lead to act-utilitarianism, the theory that what one ought to do is always that act that maximizes the amount of value in the universe, and that would justify us in harming one individual to achieve a greater value for another. Basic moral rights presuppose that each right-holder has inherent value, a very special value in himself or herself that commands our respect. Hence, the most fundamental of all moral rights is the basic right to be treated with respect, that is, to be treated neither merely as a means having instrumental value nor merely as a receptacle for intrinsically good experiences, but as an individual who may not be treated in any manner that is unjust to his or her own nature.

This poses the question of what it is in one's nature that gives one inherent value? Regan suggests that it is being a subject of a life; it is having a life that is better or worse for the being whose life it is. This suggestion explains why sticks and stones are not possible right-holders. It does not matter to them whether they are broken up or left intact. But many species of nonhuman animals do have a life. My cat's life is better when I feed her well, and a dog's life is worse when he is beaten. And the life of a deer goes well when it can roam freely where there is plenty of vegetation, and it is worse for the deer to be wounded or killed by a hunter. If, then, it is being a subject of a life that gives inherent value to human beings, some species of nonhuman animals also have inherent value. And if it is having inherent values that explains why human beings are capable of having basic moral rights, then some animals are also possible moral right-holders.

This reasoning rests on the premise that human beings, including babies and the severely mentally enfeebled, have basic moral rights, such as the right to life and the right not to be tortured. Why does Tom Regan believe that this is so? It is because he believes that it is morally wrong to kill babies or to treat the feebleminded cruelly and that such acts are wrong for a very special reason. Our duties not to kill babies or to treat the feebleminded cruelly are not indirect duties, duties owed to someone else, such as the parent or guardian, who might also be harmed by our actions. Nor are they duties owed directly to these individual babies or severely enfeebled persons because of the pleasures they would lose or the pains they would suffer; were this so we could justify such actions if our enjoyment in mistreating them was greater than their loss or pain. Rather, we have direct duties to these human beings required by our respect for their inherent value. This part of Regan's case for animal rights rests both on what he accepts as clear cases of moral judgments and on his theoretical framework, which explains why such actions are morally wrong in the way that they clearly are. Accordingly, anyone who also recognizes that we have direct duties of justice to babies and the feebleminded not to mistreat them in these ways must either agree with Regan that some nonhuman animals could possess basic moral rights or explain why such actions are morally wrong without appealing to the moral rights of babies and the severely mentally enfeebled.

Although morally enlightened and theoretically subtle, this line of reasoning is not beyond question. In its critical phase, it rests squarely on the premise that babies and the severely mentally enfeebled do possess basic moral rights. Some moral philosophers, especially those who adopt a will theory of rights, deny this assumption. They need not insist that the ascription of rights to beings incapable of choice and action is meaningless; the expression "a right" is used in many ways, some of which are probably applicable to animals. But if all one means by asserting that animals have moral rights is that it is morally wrong to mistreat animals, then this use of "a right" is theoretically redundant and a mere rhetorical gesture, because one can assert this more clearly in the simpler language of duties regarding animals. Babies and the very feebleminded are incapable of possessing any moral rights, in the sense of the term that captures what is distinctive and most important about rights. Although, to be sure, only a minority of moral philosophers deny the premise that these marginal human beings do have basic moral rights.

More often questioned is Tom Regan's proposal that it is as the subject of a life that a being has inherent value and thereby qualifies as a moral rightholder. The crucial problem here is specifying the psychological capacities that make one a subject of a life. Regan suggests that these capacities involve beliefs and desires; perception, memory, and a sense of the future, including one's own future; an emotional life, together with feelings of pleasure and pain; preferences and welfare-interests; and the ability to initiate action in pursuit of one's desires and goals. Those who are skeptical of animal rights argue that even the higher species of animals lack many of these capacities and, therefore, could not possess any basic moral rights even on Regan's own theory. Advocates of animal rights argue that this subject-of-a-life criterion is too restrictive because at best it excludes all but the very highest species of animals from the class of possible right-holders.

Presuppositions in the Debate

Three kinds of premises are used in the arguments that make up the debate over whether nonhuman animals could have any moral rights. One consists of assumptions about the nature of a moral right. Although the question is often asked whether it is meaningful to ascribe moral rights to animals, this is not the real issue. Those who assert that animals have the moral rights to life and not to be treated cruelly may mean only that it is morally wrong to kill animals unnecessarily or that we have a duty to treat them humanely. No one seriously doubts that such statements are linguistically proper. The philosophically important disagreement concerns which conception of a moral right would enable one to construct the most illuminating moral theory and to formulate clearly the most important moral decisions we must make concerning our treatment of animals. Those who adopt a will theory of rights, a theory according to which a right gives some special standing to the choice and the action of the right-holder, are tempted to deny that nonhuman animals possess the psychological capacities required to possess rights. On the other hand, advocates of animal rights often adopt either an interest theory of rights, a theory that construes rights as giving protection to the interests of the right-holder, or some other theory of rights that does not require practical reason and moral autonomy to qualify one to possess moral rights.

A second kind of premise used in the debate consists in the appeal to test cases. Just as a scientific theory is disconfirmed if it implies predictions that turn out to be false, so a moral theory must be rejected if it implies moral judgments that are false or unacceptable. Some moral philosophers, for example, reject the theory that what makes an act morally right or wrong is its utility, because this theory implies that we ought to punish innocent persons whenever this would be useful. Similarly, Tom Regan argues that theories holding that one must be self-conscious or fully rational in order to possess any moral rights must be rejected because they imply that babies and severely mentally enfeebled adults can have no rights to life or not to be tortured. He is here appealing to what are usually called our moral intuitions, meaning simply our firm pretheoretical moral judgments. Of course, a moral judgment that seems clearly correct to one person may appear false or at least doubtful to another. Thus it will often remain uncertain whether some theory of moral rights has been refuted by an appeal to test cases.

The third kind of presupposition made in the debate about whether animals are possible right-holders concerns animal psychology. Here the appeal is often to recent scientific research into the mental capacities of nonhuman animals and equally often to our everyday experience of interacting with them. Thus, those who assume a will theory of rights may disagree about whether animals have moral rights because they disagree about whether animals have the psychological capacities required for action in the morally relevant sense. Again, those who accept an interest theory of rights must then investigate the question of whether nonhuman animals have or could have interests. Regan asserts that some animals satisfy his subject-of-a-life criterion because he believes that they have a rich psychological life, including desires, beliefs, preferences, aims, and the ability to initiate action to pursue their goals. Even those who accept his conception of moral rights and agree with his moral judgments that babies and the feebleminded have basic rights may reject his case for animal rights because they doubt that even the higher species of animals have the psychological capacities he ascribes to them.

The debate over whether nonhuman animals could possess any moral rights is very complex. Disagreement continues concerning each of the three kinds of premises taken for granted by the disputants. Moral philosophers propose and defend very different theories of the nature of moral rights. Although most are willing to test their theories against clear cases of moral judgments, they disagree about whether their theories actually imply any unacceptable judgments. And typically, advocates of animal rights believe that nonhuman animals have a richer psychological life than do those who insist that only human beings are possible moral right-holders.

Legal Rights

We have been examining the debates concerning whether nonhuman animals *do* have any moral rights and, more fundamentally, whether they *could* have any moral rights. But legal rights are different. While moral rights are natural in the sense that their existence is independent of either human opinions or social institutions, legal rights are artificial creations of human lawmaking activities. Accordingly, debates regarding the legal rights of animals pose somewhat different questions.

Actual Rights?

First, do nonhuman animals have any legal rights? It might well be that some legal systems do confer rights on animals while others do not. Let us, therefore, limit our discussion to whether animals have any rights under U.S. law. In *Animals, Property and the Law*, Gary L. Francione, a Rutgers University law professor, has argued that they do not.

Crucial to his case is the legal distinction between persons and property. Legal persons are subjects of legal duties or legal rights; legal properties may be objects of such duties or rights but are not themselves duty-bearers or right-holders. The owner of a walking stick, for example, has the right to use it to steady herself while hiking and even the right to destroy it in a campfire, as well as the duty not to use it to batter her child; but the stick has neither a right not to be destroyed nor a duty not to injure children. Now an examination of both federal and state law in the United States shows that nonhuman animals are regarded as property. Domestic animals are the property of individual persons or sometimes corporate bodies; wild animals are the property of the state or the public. Also, the law adopts the liberal conception of property according to which the owner has wide discretion regarding the possession, use, and disposition of the objects she owns. Hence, animals have no legal rights against abuse by their owners.

Abuse or harm by anyone other than the owner is the violation of a right. If Baker hires a team of horses from Abel to pull his plow and, after working them until they are exhausted Baker beats them so harshly that he injures them, he can be sued for compensation; and if Abel then takes his horses to a veterinarian who exacerbates their injuries by his improper treatment, Abel can sue for medical malpractice. But, and this is the telling point, the measure of wrong done in both cases is the difference between the market value of the animals before and after their mistreatment; any pain the horses may have suffered or any lasting disabilities they may suffer in the future do not count at all. This fact shows that what the law recognizes and enforces are the property rights of their owner, not any right of the animals themselves.

There are, as one would expect, those who disagree with Francione. They point to various federal and state statutes prohibiting cruelty to animals. Thus, hunters are prohibited from using specified traps that inflict excessive pain upon wild animals, farmers are required to treat their animals humanely, and those who conduct scientific experiments upon animals are prohibited from causing unnecessary suffering. Surely, many argue, these and similar statutes confer legal rights upon nonhuman animals, at least the right not to be treated cruelly.

Francione disagrees. (1) No legal right is absolute and unlimited. Thus, one would expect the rights to use and dispose of property to be regulated by statutes. But these are merely limits to one's property rights, not rights-conferring laws. Just as an ordinance prohibiting the owner of a landmark home from modifying its appearance without permission of some public authority does not confer upon the building any right not to be modified, so anti-cruelty statutes merely limit the ways in which animals may be treated without conferring upon the animals any rights not to be mistreated.

(2) One might argue that anti-cruelty statutes do confer rights because they protect the interests of the animals not to be subject to inhumane treatment or not to be caused unnecessary suffering. But how do they do this? Presumably by requiring that the interests of the owners or others be balanced against the interests of the animals themselves. By an examination of a number of court cases, Francione tries to show that this requirement is illusory. Time and again, relatively trivial human interests are held to outweigh even the most serious interests of nonhuman animals. This is because these human interests are taken to be interests in exercising property rights, while the interests of the animals are interests unsupported by any conflict-

ing right. The point or purpose of a legal right is to rule out its violation merely because to do so would be beneficial; but no matter how much suffering they impose, our practices of using animals are judged to be legally justified whenever they are thought to be socially useful.

(3) Any asserted legal right is real only when someone has standing to take legal action to enforce it. Of course, nonhuman animals could not themselves petition any court to remedy any violation of their rights, but in theory it would be possible for a legal system to recognize some human being as acting for an animal. However, U.S. law does not admit this possibility. The leading case here is *Sierra Club v. Morton*. When the United States Forest Service approved the construction of a huge ski resort in an area designated by Congress as a national game refuge, the Sierra Club took legal action to stop the project. It claimed that it had standing because its concern with environmental matters made it a representative of the public. The Supreme Court rejected this claim on the grounds that a petitioner must himself be among the injured. Although this holding does not rule out the possibility of some individual or organization taking legal action to prevent the mistreatment of animals, it does show that the legally protected interest must be that of the petitioner, not that of the animals themselves. Thus it would be a misinterpretation of the law to assert that it recognizes any animal rights. Whatever may be true in other legal systems, nonhuman animals do not now have any legal rights in the United States.

Possible Rights?

The second question to ask is whether nonhuman animals *could* have any legal rights. Whether or not animals are possible *moral* right-holders, are they possible *legal* right-holders? The legal positivist, one who holds that the law is whatever the legally recognized authorities posit or pronounce, can easily answer this question. Because the law is whatever a constitution, legislature, or court says it is, if any of these authoritative sources of law say that animals have rights, then animals can and do have legal rights. True enough. But this leaves open the question of how any such constitutional clause, statute, or judicial opinion is best interpreted. Is the law using the expression "a right" in a misleading sense or in the sense that it should be used in the most adequate philosophy of law?

Although Gary Francione denies that animals now possess any rights under U.S. law, he asserts that such rights could be introduced into our legal system. He recognizes, however, that both his denial and his assertion depend on one's conception of a right. Therefore, he rebuts the most common arguments of those who maintain that animals are not possible legal right-holders.

Someone like H. L. A. Hart, who holds that an option or choice is at the core of every right, may insist that only beings capable of choice could possess any legal or moral right. Because nonhuman animals lack the practical reason and autonomy required to choose between alternative actions, they are incapable of possessing any sort of right. Francione rejects this argument on the ground that there are human beings, for example babies, who are incapable of rational choice but who do have legal rights.

Many advocates of animal rights reject the choice theory of rights and conceive of a right as a protected interest. They reason that because the law could protect the interests of nonhuman animals, animals could possess legal rights. R. G. Frey, a contemporary utilitarian, has responded by arguing that animals are not possible right-holders, even on the interest theory of rights, because they are incapable of having any interests. To have an interest in something one must be capable of wanting or desiring it. This is possible only if one is able to conceive of the object of one's interest, and this in turn requires one to possess a language in which one can describe what it is one wants or desires. Because animals lack the required linguistic abilities, they cannot have any interests. Francione believes that this reasoning is highly implausible unless one is using the term "an interest" in an unduly restricted sense. In the sense presupposed by the interest theory of rights, nonhuman animals can and do have interests.

Nevertheless, Francione admits that although having interests may be a necessary condition for possessing any legal right, it is not a sufficient condition. In addition, it must be possible, as the claim theory of rights suggests, to take legal action to enforce one's right. Some argue that animals cannot have any legal rights because they are incapable of claiming them before a court. Francione responds, as did Joel Feinberg, that babies and the mentally incompetent can and do have legal rights, rights that others claim in their name. Because it would be quite possible for a legal system to appoint guardians to represent the legally protected interests of nonhuman animals, animals are possible legal right-holders.

Legal Reform?

The third question is whether, if nonhuman animals are possible legal right-holders, they should have any legal rights? Specifically, ought we to introduce some animal rights into the legal system of the United States? At this point, the advocates of animal rights often quote a passage from Jeremy Bentham's *An Introduction to the Principles of Morals and Legislation*:

> The day has been, I grieve to say in many places it is not yet past, in which the greater part of the species, under the denomination of slaves, have been treated by the law exactly upon the same footing, as, in England for example, the inferior races of animals are still. The day *may* come, when the rest of the animal creation may acquire those rights which never could have been withholden

from them but by the hand of tyranny. The French have already discovered that the blackness of the skin is no reason why a human being should be abandoned without redress to the caprice of a tormentor. It may come one day to be recognized, that the number of legs, the villosity of the skin, or the termination of the *os sacrum*, are reasons equally insufficient for abandoning a sensitive being to the same fate? What else is it that should trace the insuperable line? Is it the faculty of reason, or, perhaps, the faculty of discourse? But a full-grown horse or dog, is beyond comparison a more rational, as well as a more conversible animal, than an infant of a day, or a week, or even a month, old. But suppose the case were otherwise, what would it avail? The question is not, Can they *reason*? nor, Can they *talk*? but, Can they *suffer*?[2]

Although Bentham denied the existence of any natural rights, he makes here a fervent plea for conferring upon animals at least the legal right not to be treated cruelly.

Many argue that it is unnecessary to add any such right to our legal system because nonhuman animals are already protected by both federal and state anti-cruelty statutes. These require that owners treat their animals humanely and prohibit anyone from causing unnecessary suffering to wild or domesticated animals. Those who advocate animal rights reply that these statutes are inadequate; they continually fail to prevent many gross abuses of animals.

Recent statistics of the U.S. government report that at least 20 to 25 million animals are subjected to scientific experimentation each year and that probably as many as 1 million experience unrelieved pain or distress. Much larger numbers of animals annually suffer physiological injury, psychological distress, or prolonged pain imposed by the current practices of factory farming in the United States. Over 5 billion chickens are killed for food each year. The vast majority of these are raised in cramped cages with no chance to exercise their natural impulses to walk about or even to scratch and peck the ground. Under these circumstances, they frequently peck each other unless they are debeaked. Although this was sometimes done with a blow-torch in the past, it is now typically done with a hot or cold knife that always causes severe pain and often leaves the birds with lasting injuries. The most efficient, and therefore the most common, way to raise calves for veal is both to confine them in stalls too small to enable them to groom themselves or to lie down and to raise the temperature so that they will consume larger amounts of dry feed. Most of the calves suffer from digestive disorders; many develop stomach ulcers and chronic diarrhea. Because normal qualities of iron would give a rosy color to their flesh, the calves are deliberately caused to suffer from anemia. Although ten to fifteen percent die during this process, the high price restaurants are willing to pay for very pale veal make this agricultural industry profitable. In the face of such facts, how can it be alleged that giving animals the legal right not to be treated cruelly is unnecessary?

But what reasons do we have to believe that a legal right not to be treated cruelly would be more effective than the legal duties imposed by the anti-cruelty statutes now established in U.S. law? (1) These existing legal duties have an ambiguous status because it is not clear whether they are direct duties owed to animals or indirect duties owed to their owners or the public. Because our legal tradition has considered nonhuman animals to be property, the courts tend to regard the rationale for these statutes to be the human interests animals serve. But to confer legal rights upon animals would be to recognize the interests of the animals themselves as the basis for these rights and to make it explicit that the duties implied by these rights are direct duties to the animals whose interests they protect. Skeptics reply that the courts currently interpret anti-cruelty laws as requiring that human interests be balanced against the animal interest in humane treatment, so that nothing would be achieved by adding a legal right not to be treated cruelly.

(2) The law does not give all recognized interests equal weight. Interests supported by a right count more heavily in the process of balancing conflicting interests against each other. This is why human interests inevitably win out over the interests of nonhuman animals when they conflict. Hence, adding a legal right of animals not to be treated cruelly would make their interest in not being mistreated more resistant to being outweighed by the more trivial human interests that now prevail in our courts. Perhaps, but how much more resistant? Remember that it is human beings who administer and enforce the law; nonhuman animals are merely subject to but never agents in our legal system. How probable is it that legal officials, all of whom are human beings, will interpret animal rights in any way that requires the real sacrifice of human interests? They are hardly impartial judges when human interests conflict with the interests of nonhuman animals.

(3) This is precisely why we need to add animal rights to our legal system. U.S. law both reflects and reinforces the ignorance of and prejudice against animals that is pervasive in our society. Now, conferring rights upon those frequently subject to unfair treatment gives them, or their representatives, standing to challenge this injustice and the prejudices that support it. This is why extending civil rights to African-Americans and recognizing women's rights have benefited African-Americans and women and why conferring at least the legal right not to be treated cruelly would be similarly beneficial for animals. The opponent of animal rights can here point to a crucial difference. African-Americans and female citizens are able to claim their own rights before state and federal courts, but nonhuman animals lack the psychological capacities required for them to articulate and demand their rights. To be sure, their rights could be claimed by human representatives acting for them. But would these human beings have both the insight into the lives of nonhuman animals required to articulate what

is really in their best interests and the objectivity needed to avoid all prejudice for or against animals? The case for adding animal rights to U.S. law remains contested.

Environmental Rights

Does the animal rights movement provide a useful model for environmentalists, those who are concerned about and dedicated to protecting the environment? The basic strategy of those who advocate animal rights has been to extend the range of rights from human to nonhuman animals, both by showing that nonhuman animals can and do possess moral rights and by taking political and legal action to confer legal rights upon animals. Would a similar strategy be helpful for environmental ethics and law?

Moral Rights

Some environmentalists argue that the reasoning used to establish the moral rights of nonhuman animals can be used to establish the moral rights of all living beings. They often cite two influential papers in which Kenneth E. Goodpaster, a contemporary moral philosopher, has defended the view that everything that is alive is morally considerable. Because every living being is worthy of our respect, we ought to consider the interests of everything that is alive in deciding what we ought morally to do. Although Goodpaster denies that being considerable is or implies having rights in the narrow sense quite properly adopted by most moral philosophers, others have taken his reasoning to justify the ascription of moral environmental rights.

Goodpaster begins negatively by rebutting the considerations advanced in support of more restrictive criteria. We should not hold that being rational, or even being potentially rational, is necessary for moral considerability, because we recognize that it is morally wrong to mistreat babies and incurable imbeciles. Nor is it sufficient to widen the scope of moral relevance to include only sentient beings, those capable of feeling pleasure or pain. We ought to recognize that the wanton destruction of plants does matter morally even though our actions do not cause them to suffer pain, and we ought to be suspicious of the hedonism that implies that only pleasure and pain have intrinsic value or disvalue.

Goodpaster then goes on to argue positively that the reasoning Joel Feinberg uses to show that animals can and do have moral rights can be extended to show that all living beings are worthy of moral consideration. Feinberg gives two reasons for holding that all and only beings capable of having interests are possible moral right-holders: (1) a right-holder must be capable of being represented and it is impossible to represent a being that has no interests, and (2) a right-holder must be capable of being a benefi-ciary in his own person, and a being without interests, having no good of its own, is incapable of being benefited. Goodpaster accepts these two rea-sons but rejects Feinberg's insistence that interests presuppose desires, wants, or aims. Living organisms like plants also have interests that can be represented, for example the interest of a tree in water, an interest that would be denied by tightly enclosing the tree in asphalt when paving a new parking lot. And plants such as flowers or vegetables are benefited when their needs for sun, water, and nourishment are met. Perhaps, then, the rea-soning Feinberg used to establish the moral rights of nonhuman animals could be extended to establish the moral rights of all living beings.

But would this line of reasoning go far enough to show that all the envi-ronmental entities we ought to protect have rights? Is it applicable not merely to individual plants but to species of animals and plants, to rivers and lakes, and to the atmosphere? Perhaps it is. Goodpaster suggests that ecological systems, and even the biosystem as a whole, satisfy the definition of a living system: one that remains in a persistent state of low entropy by sustaining metabolic processes for accumulating energy and by maintaining an equilibrium through homeostatic feedback processes. If ecological sys-tems really are alive, then they, and through them their components, might be shown to possess environmental rights.

Other environmentalists reason more along the lines of Tom Regan than of Joel Feinberg to extend moral rights from human beings and nonhuman animals to all living beings. Some of them use, but go beyond, arguments most clearly presented by the moral philosopher Paul W. Taylor. His point of departure is Kantian moral theories grounded on respect for persons. These theories distinguish between ends-for-us that have value merely be-cause we desire or take an interest in them and ends-in-themselves that have a value completely independent of our inclinations. Our moral duties presuppose ends-in-themselves because only such objective ends could im-pose categorical imperatives upon us, commands that are binding whether or not we desire to obey.

Moreover, Kant believed that only human beings are ends-in-themselves because only they possess a practical rationality and moral agency that commands our respect independent of our interests. Therefore, the funda-mental moral principle is that one ought always to treat human beings as ends-in-themselves and never as means only, and this principle implies that all human beings possess fundamental moral rights.

But some persons are more rational than others. How, then, can one ex-plain the equality of human rights? Here Taylor appeals to the distinction Gregory Vlastos makes in his recent essay on egalitarian justice between merit and inherent worth. The concept of merit is a grading concept involv-ing the ranking of objects on some dimension of value relative to some end or purpose. For example, the lightness of a metal is a merit when one is building airplanes, but a demerit when one is making an anchor. Similarly, quickness of mind, strength of body, and even moral virtue are standards of merit. But human rights are not grounded upon relative values like these; they are grounded on the equal inherent worth of all human beings. What makes every human being an end-in-himself possessing inherent worth is that his or her freedom and welfare are intrinsically good—not merely instrumentally good for other persons but of value to himself or herself. And because the intrinsic values each person enjoys are as good *for her* as the intrinsic values any other person enjoys are *for him*, all human beings have equal inherent value.

Taylor, like Regan, argues that all traditional Kantian theories are inadequate because they arbitrarily limit our moral concern to human beings. To imagine that only human beings have inherent worth is to adopt without justification a human-centered viewpoint of nature. Taylor argues that a life-centered viewpoint is less prejudiced and much more reasonable. The human species is only one natural species sharing a common relationship to the earth. Seen from an evolutionary point of view, our arrival on the earth is very recent and our emergence as a new species is of no particular importance to the entire scheme of things. The well-being of humans is dependent upon the ecological soundness and health of many plant and animal communities, while their well-being does not depend very much upon us—except for our ability to destroy the environment upon which every species depends. Moreover, modern science shows that the natural world is an organic system consisting of a unified web of interconnected organisms living in a shared physical environment. Surely it is presumptuous of us to imagine that we human beings are at the center of the universe; it is much more reasonable to adopt a life-centered viewpoint that respects all of nature as having equal importance.

Once we take a life-centered point of view, we will recognize that all living beings have inherent worth. The inherent worth of members of the human species depends on the fact that their freedom and welfare have intrinsic value for them, not merely instrumental value for others. This is why all human beings are ends-in-themselves, commanding our moral respect. But science reveals that every organism is a teleological center of life with its own good or bad fortunes. Thus each kind of living being has its own good, and the enjoyment of this good has intrinsic value for that organism. It follows, by the same logic that implies the inherent worth of human beings, that the members of every biological species have inherent worth also.

Perhaps, but many moral philosophers will insist that human beings have a greater inherent value than do members of the lower species. But why judge human beings to be any higher than nonhuman animals or plants? Well, humans are rational whereas nonhuman animals either lack reason or possess it in an inferior degree; human beings are conscious and self-conscious whereas plants lack any awareness of their environments or of themselves. True enough, replies Taylor, but these are merely standards of merit irrelevant to inherent worth. Practical reason is instrumentally good for solving many of the problems we face, and human consciousness probably developed during our evolution in order to enable us to survive and prosper by avoiding danger and satisfying our needs. Notice, however, that other species have other merits. The cheetah can run much faster than any human being, and the eagle has much better eyesight. Why, then, are these species not higher than the human species? From their point of view, these merits are of much greater value than ours, for they enable them to capture prey and sustain their very lives. This shows that merit consists in instrumental value relative to one's species. Mere prejudice would judge that the human species is higher than other biological species because its members possess some human merit in a higher degree than do other forms of life. When one adopts an objective life-centered viewpoint one recognizes that all living beings possess equal inherent worth and thus command equal moral respect.

Although Paul Taylor believes that his reasoning does show that plants and animals ought to be given legal rights, he refuses to take the last step of ascribing moral rights to all living beings. Some other environmentalists, however, do follow the example of Tom Regan and extend the range of basic moral rights to cover all beings that have inherent value. After all, if the equal inherent worth of human beings grounds human rights, why does not the equal inherent worth of all living beings similarly ground basic moral rights of plants and animals? Surely, the logical conclusion of abandoning the human-centered viewpoint of traditional Kantianism and looking at nature from a life-centered point of view is to adopt an attitude of respect for all of nature and to recognize the moral rights of all living beings.

Plausible as these two lines of reasoning from human rights to environmental rights are, the majority of moral philosophers, even those who believe in animal rights, remain unconvinced. One difficulty is that the case for animal rights rests on the relevant similarity between human and non-human animals, be it the capacity to have interests, as Joel Feinberg argues, or being subjects of a life, as Tom Regan has it. In fact, Regan recognizes that his reasoning applies only to the higher species of animals, those with relatively complex psychological faculties. Now when environmentalists attempt to extend the range of right-holders to the lower species of animals and even to plants, these psychological similarities disappear, and the biological differences become much more pronounced. Although this does not disprove their conclusion that all living beings have moral rights, it does make their argument for it more dubious.

Another difficulty lies in explaining clearly the value theory presupposed by their reasoning. Kenneth Goodpaster rejects Feinberg's conception of an interest presupposing desires, wants, or aims and adopts a much broader conception defined in terms of a teleological or goal-oriented biology.

But since he admits that living organisms do not desire to achieve their biologically determined goals or suffer any frustration when they fail to do so, one wonders where the intrinsic value or disvalue lies. Even if there is some sense in which such teleological processes do involve value, Goodpaster fails to explain why this is the sort of value that grounds moral rights. The inherent value to which Paul Taylor appeals does seem appropriate to command our moral respect. But this may be merely a matter of definition; his only explanation of the nature of inherent value seems to be in terms of whatever it is that commands moral respect and grounds moral rights. The difficulty is to explain what it is about all living beings that gives them inherent value. At this point, Taylor refers us to the theory of Gregory Vlastos that derives the inherent value of human beings from the intrinsic value of freedom and well-being. This, of course, brings us right back to the problem Goodpaster faces: the defense of a theory of intrinsic value applicable to living organisms that have no psychological life at all.

These doubts do not, of course, prove that there are no environmental moral rights. They do, however, suggest that the theoretical presuppositions of the environmentalists who extend the arguments for animal rights to cover all living organisms need further articulation.

Legal Rights

It may have been difficulties such as these that led Paul Taylor to refrain from claiming that all species of living organisms have basic moral rights. Nevertheless, he does maintain that they ought to be given legal rights. Those who do believe in the moral rights of all living beings are usually even more adamant in demanding that these rights be given protection by the addition of environmental rights to our legal system. Even those environmentalists who retain a human-centered moral theory, according to which only human beings can possess any moral rights, often argue that we ought to confer legal rights on natural species and even on natural objects, such as rivers and forests, in order not to violate the moral right of future generations of humans to inherit a hospitable environment. Let us put aside the question of whether future generations have any such right and ask, instead, whether we ought to add environmental rights to U.S. law.

Christopher Stone, a jurist concerned about the moral grounds for environmental law, argues that we could and should give natural objects, such as forests and rivers, legal rights. The necessary conditions for being a legal right-holder are that the thing can institute legal actions at *its* behest, that in granting legal relief the court must take injury to *it* into account, and that the remedy must run to the benefit of *it*. Some might imagine that the very first condition rules out creating any new environmental rights, but this is not so. Infants too young to speak, much less to comprehend the law, can sue in the courts, acting through their proxies—normally their parents or guardians—who speak in their name. It would be quite easy for the courts to appoint guardians for endangered objects in our environment or, alternatively, to recognize environmental organizations as having legal standing to act in their behalf. Granted this possibility, there would be very little difficulty both in taking actual or threatened injury to an object, such as a forest or river, into account when granting relief and in fashioning a remedy that would restore or tend to restore a forest or river to its natural condition of flourishing or nonpollution.

Supposing that it would be possible to confer legal rights on natural objects, why should we do so? Stone gives a number of reasons—none of which presupposes environmental moral rights or the inherent worth of all living organisms—for this reform of U.S. law.

(1) Under our present system of environmental law, when a plaintiff wins her suit, the damages are awarded to the human plaintiff; no money is made available to repair the damages done to the environment itself. If forests or rivers could sue on their own behalf, compensation could be awarded to them and used to remedy the injuries done to them. (2) Existing environmental statutes have limited scope and are therefore inapplicable to many sorts of damage to our environment. Conferring legal rights on natural objects would empower environmental groups to take legal action whenever our environment is threatened, whether or not the injury falls within the scope of current legislation. (3) Lawsuits must now be brought under statutes that distort the real issues. For example, to prevent damage to a forest from acid rain or serious injury to a lake from industrial pollution, the plaintiff must often prove lost "recreational use" of the natural object. The genuinely frightening threats to our environment are very different. The absorption of sunlight upon which the entire life cycle depends may be diminished; the greenhouse effect may warm our oceans so that the polar ice caps will melt, thereby flooding our coastal cities; the portion of the atmosphere that shields us from dangerous radiation may be destroyed. Environmental legal rights would provide a legal basis for bringing the crucial environmental issues before our courts. (4) Giving legal rights to natural objects would help to create a radical new conception of our relationship to nature. Instead of thinking of natural objects exclusively in terms of the property rights of private owners or the public, we would recognize their own rights to flourish and not to suffer injury. This would diminish our concern with manipulation in our own self-interest and render us more broadly benevolent, thus helping to make us better human beings.

It may well be that conferring legal rights on natural objects would enable individuals and agencies concerned about the environment to prevent or at least reduce the damage now inflicted upon it. But should environmentalists adopt this strategy of extending legal rights to nonhuman animals, plants, and even natural objects? Many argue that it would be a grave mistake to rely very heavily on rights. The concept of a right is distributive rather than collective; the paradigm instances of right-holders are individuals. We speak of "the legal right to property" or "the human right to life," but these are merely convenient ways to refer to both the many property rights of many individual owners and the individual rights to life of each and every human being. Jones has legal property rights to her car; Smith has property rights to his house; and so on—for a vast number of distinct rights of different individuals. That these rights are distinct and independent is shown, among other things, by the fact that when Jones sells her car, Smith's property right to his house remains unaffected. This is why Joel Feinberg and Tom Regan assert that although individual animals have moral rights and could have legal rights, it would be impossible for any species of animals to have any right to survive. Even were one to accept group rights of natural species or of collections of living beings like a forest, this would fall short of the holism of any adequate environmentalism. One cannot explain in terms of rights why the extinction of some species or the destruction of some forest is a great loss in and of itself. The fundamental insight of environmentalism is that our world is a vast integrated ecological system in which the well-being and even the very existence of each part depend upon preserving the system as a whole.

Another reason why adopting the strategy of the animal rights movement and simply extending the range of right-holders would not serve the purposes of environmentalists lies in the radical difference between the goals of these two movements. Those who argue that nonhuman animals ought to be given legal rights are morally outraged by the abuse of animals, especially domestic animals. Their goal is to prevent or reduce animal suffering by conferring on animals at least the legal right not to be treated cruelly. Because plants suffer no pain or frustration when they are injured or die, their plight strikes the advocates of animal rights as morally irrelevant. Environmentalists are more concerned with the preservation of each species of wild animal or plant. They recognize that one species preys upon another; the death of the many animals consumed in the food chain does not strike most of them as immoral or even undesirable. In fact, the ecological balance of nature can be preserved only in this way, and it is this balance that environmentalists value and wish to sustain. Hence, their derivative goals are to prevent pollution of the air or water, the extinction of any species, or the destruction of the land upon which all living organisms depend. Perhaps Mark Sagoff, an expert on environmental law, pointed to the bottom line when he entitled one of his journal articles "Animal Liberation and Environmental Ethics: Bad Marriage, Quick Divorce."

So What?

Returning, then, to the animal rights debate, what hinges on its outcome? Why does it matter whether nonhuman animals have any moral rights? The primary concern of the animal rights movement is our abuse of animals. They believe that appealing to the moral rights of animals will provide both a strong moral basis for their demand that human beings cease and desist from our customary cruel and inhumane treatment of animals—especially in factory farming and scientific experimentation—and for modifying our legal system to ensure that animals are protected from those who are unwilling to treat them humanely. But why must the basis for this moral reform be animal rights? Why not simply appeal to our compassion for those animals suffering unnecessary pain and injury?

Rights and Duties

Perhaps if animals have no moral rights, then moral agents have no duties not to abuse them. Some moral philosophers accept the logical correlativity of rights and duties. This is the doctrine that each right implies a corresponding duty and that each duty implies a corresponding right. For example, the creditor's right to be repaid the amount of the loan implies the debtor's duty to repay that amount, and the debtor's duty to repay the loan implies the creditor's right to be repaid the amount loaned. Rights and duties must be logically correlative in this way because they are simply two ways of describing one and the same moral relationship. Seen from the perspective of the creditor, this is a right holding against the debtor; seen from the perspective of the debtor, it is a duty owed to the creditor.

Most moral philosophers, however, reject this doctrine of logical correlativity. Although every right does imply one or more duties, their content does not always correspond precisely with that of the right that imposes them. More to the point, some duties have no correlative right. Thus, anyone with an income more than sufficient to satisfy her own needs has a duty to give to charity, but no particular needy individual or charitable organization has any right to be given any specific amount or anything at all. Each moral agent has discretion as to when and how she will fulfill this duty. Again, every citizen probably has a duty to obey the law of the land, but there is no individual right-holder to whom this duty is owed. Why, then, might there not be moral duties not to abuse animals even though animals have no moral rights?

If nonhuman animals have no moral rights, then moral agents have no moral duties owed to animals. Even those who reject the logical correlativity of rights and duties usually distinguish between duties *to* some second party and duties *regarding* this party. For example, when the owner of a house contracts with a neighborhood youth to mow her lawn every ten days, the youth has a duty to mow that lawn every ten days. But this is not a duty to the lawn; it is a duty regarding the lawn but a duty to the owner with whom the youth has made an agreement that imposes this contractual duty. Why not, then, say that we have duties regarding animals even though nonhuman animals have no rights?

Advocates of animal rights will point out that this misplaces the main ground of these duties. For example, Immanuel Kant, an eighteenth-century philosopher, argued that we have duties not to treat animals cruelly because if we do so, then we will become hardened to suffering and become disposed to treat human beings cruelly. Hence, our duties regarding animals are best explained as duties to human beings. But this ignores the primary reason that we ought not to abuse animals: the pain and injury such mistreatment causes the animals themselves. Any adequate explanation of our duty not to abuse animals must recognize that this is not a duty regarding animals owed to human beings, but a duty owed to animals grounded on their own interests in not being caused to suffer pain or injury.

Still, some argue that if nonhuman animals have no moral rights, then our duties to them will be too easily overridden by human interests. If one interprets our duties to animals as merely duties grounded on their interests, then these duties will often conflict with our duties to human beings, which are grounded on human interests. The reasonable and just method of resolving such conflicts would be to balance animal interests against human interests and to act to further the greater net sum of interests. But this approach will make it too easy, especially in most sorts of scientific experimentation on animals, to judge that the short-term interests of a relatively few nonhuman animals subjected to pain, frustration, and even death are outweighed by the long-term interests of all humanity in the immensely useful, often literally vital, scientific knowledge obtained by using these animals in research. The distinctive strength of any moral right is to resist any such balancing of interests and thereby to render it morally impermissible to use the right-holder merely as a means rather than as an end-in-itself to be respected. Also, if animal rights are equal to human rights, as Tom Regan argues, then our abuse of animals cannot be justified merely by insisting that human interests are greater or more important than the interests of nonhuman animals.

However, Regan admits that moral rights are not absolute; they are prima facie rights capable of being overridden by stronger conflicting rights. Thus one can reply that granting animals moral rights would merely replace the balancing of interests with the balancing of conflicting rights. Might we not then imagine that our human rights to obtain the food we need for a healthy diet and the scientific knowledge we need for a healthy and happy life always or almost always outweigh animal rights? There is no reason to believe that our balancing of human rights against animal rights would be any less prejudicial than our balancing of human interests against animal interests.

The Value of Rights

Joel Feinberg describes Nowheresville, a society in which there are values, virtues, and duties but no rights. He argues that what would be missing in such a society would be claiming, the action of demanding something as one's due. Therefore, he defines a right as a valid claim and explains that to have a right is to be in a position to make a claim, specifically to have standing to demand performance of the corresponding duty. The distinctive value of rights, then, is to enable one to stand up for one's due and to defend the interests protected by those rights. If, then, humans have duties not to abuse animals but animals have no rights, it will be up to human beings whether or not they refrain from abusing animals, but nonhuman animals will not be in a position to demand that human beings cease acting in ways that cause unjustified pain, injury, and death. To be sure, animals lack the linguistic skills and moral understanding to claim their rights themselves; nevertheless human beings speaking as their representatives could claim their rights, just as parents or guardians claim the rights of tiny babies. But some critics point out that although it is usually easy to identify the person who is morally in a position to speak for her baby, how could we know which person or persons have the moral authority to represent each individual animal right-holder? Moreover, would a human representative speaking for some nonhuman animal possess both the love of that animal and the knowledge of what is really in its best interests that parents typically have for their own children?

While Joel Feinberg identifies what is distinctive about rights with the special standing of right-holders in face of the duty-bearers against whom the rights hold, H. L. A. Hart asserts that moral rights regulate the proper distribution of freedom between individuals. Rights thus belong to that special branch of morality concerned to determine both when one person's freedom may be limited by another's and when it is permissible for third parties to intervene coercively. This view suggests that if animals have no moral rights, then it is impermissible to interfere with those who abuse animals and to force them to stop causing unnecessary animal suffering. On the other hand, John Stuart Mill maintains that what is definitive of any duty, whether or not this duty is imposed by some right, is that enforcement is morally appropriate. If this is true, then coercive third-party intervention is permissible to prevent animal abuse in violation of our duties regarding animals, even if animals have no rights.

As usual, we find that moral philosophers disagree about both the practical import of rights and the moral theory presupposed by our assertions and denials of rights. There is, however, considerable agreement that there really is something distinctive and important about moral rights. If only we could identify and define this, then we would be able to know why it matters whether or not animals have rights such as the rights to life, liberty, and not to be tortured.

Notes

1. H. L. A. Hart, "Are There Any Natural Rights?" *Philosophical Review* 64, p. 175.

2. Jeremy Bentham, *An Introduction to the Principles of Morals and Legislation*, eds. J. H. Burns and H. L. A. Hart (London: Methuen, 1970), p. 283.

Suggestions for Further Reading

Callicott, J. Baird. 1989. *In Defense of the Land Ethic*. Albany N.Y.: SUNY Press. He argues that nonhuman species have intrinsic value on pages 129–155.

Elliot, Robert. 1987. "Moral Autonomy, Self-Determination and Animal Rights." *The Monist* 70, pp. 83–97. He argues that some animals have sufficient agency to possess rights.

_____, ed. 1995. *Environmental Ethics*. Oxford: Oxford University Press. A collection of excellent papers on environmental ethics.

Feinberg, Joel. 1980. *Rights, Justice, and the Bounds of Liberty*. Princeton: Princeton University Press. He explains his theory of rights and goes on to argue that animals are possible right-holders on pages 143–184.

Francione, Gary L. 1995. *Animals, Property, and the Law*. Philadelphia Pa.: Temple University Press. Francione argues that in the law animals are considered to be mere property, not persons with the status of right-holders.

_____. 1996. *Rain without Thunder: The Ideology of the Animal Rights Movement*. Philadelphia Pa.: Temple University Press. A strong argument for animal rights rather than animal welfare as the moral basis for political action and legal reform.

Frey, R. G. 1980. *Interests and Rights*. Oxford: Clarendon Press. Frey argues that because nonhuman animals are incapable of having interests, they cannot possess rights.

_____. 1983. *Rights, Killing, and Suffering: Moral Vegetarianism and Applied Ethics*. Oxford: Basil Blackwell. Frey argues that whether vegetarianism is morally required depends on the welfare, not the rights, of nonhuman animals.

Golding, Martin P. 1968. "Towards a Theory of Human Rights." *The Monist* 52, pp. 521–549. A suggestion that although animals cannot have option rights, they might have welfare rights.

Goodpaster, Kenneth E. 1978. "On Being Morally Considerable." *Journal of Philosophy* 75, pp. 308–325. An influential argument that it is simply being alive that makes anything worthy of moral consideration.

Hart, H. L. A. 1955. "Are There Any Natural Rights?" *Philosophical Review* 64, pp. 175–191. Hart suggests that because animals are incapable of moral choice, it is idle to say that they have moral rights.

_____. 1982. *Essays on Bentham*. Oxford: Clarendon Press. The clearest formulation of Hart's choice theory of rights is on pages 162–193.

McCloskey, H. J. 1979. "Moral Rights and Animals." *Inquiry* 22, pp. 23–54. McCloskey argues that because animals lack moral agency, they cannot possess rights.

Morris, Richard Knowles, and Michael W. Fox, eds. 1978. *On the Fifth Day*. Washington D.C.: Acropolis Books Ltd. A useful collection of early essays regarding the humane treatment of animals.

Rachels, James. 1976. "Why Do Animals Have a Right to Liberty?" In *Animal Rights and Human Obligations*, eds. T. Regan and P. Singer. Englewood Cliffs N.J.: Prentice Hall. Defends the thesis that nonhuman animals have a basic moral right to liberty.

_____. 1983. "Do Animals Have a Right to Life?" In *Ethics and Animals*, eds. H. B. Miller and W. H. Williams. Clifton N.J.: Humana Press. An influential argument that animals do have a moral right to life.

Regan, Tom. 1982. *All that Dwell Therein: Animal Rights and Environmental Ethics*. Berkeley: University of California Press. One can watch Regan's theory of animal rights develop in this series of important essays.

_____. 1983. *The Case For Animal Rights*. Berkeley: University of California Press. The best formulation of Regan's theory of animal rights is on pages 266–329.

Regan, Tom, and Peter Singer, eds. 1976. *Animal Rights and Human Obligations*. Englewood Cliffs N.J.: Prentice Hall. An influential collection of essays on animal rights.

Sagoff, Mark. "Animal Liberation and Environmental Ethics: Bad Marriage, Quick Divorce." *Osgoode Hall Law Journal* 22, pp. 297–307. A cogent argument against basing environmental ethics upon rights.

Sierra Club v. Morton. 1972. 405 US 727. The dissenting opinion of Justice Douglas on pages 741–755 is especially relevant.

Silverstein, Helena. 1996. *Unleashing Rights: Law, Meaning, and the Animal Rights Movement*. Ann Arbor: University of Michigan Press. Silverstein argues for expanding the class of right-holders to include animals on pages 27–54.

Singer, Peter. 1975. *Animal Liberation: A New Ethics for our Treatment of Animals*. New York: Avon. An immensely influential attack on the immoral treatment of nonhuman animals.

Stone, Christopher D. 1972. "Should Trees Have Standing?— Toward Legal Rights for Natural Objects." *Southern California Law Review* 45, pp. 450–501. A strong argument to show that natural objects could and ought to have legal rights.

Taylor, Paul W. 1986. *Respect for Nature: A Theory of Environmental Ethics*. Princeton: Princeton University Press. On pages 99–168 and 219–255 Taylor argues that our environment and all of its components are worthy of our moral respect.

Varner, G. E. 1987. "Do Species have Standing?" *Environmental Ethics* 9, pp. 57–72. Varner argues that biological species already have some legal rights and ought to have more rights.

Zimmerman, Michael E., ed. 1993. *Environmental Philosophy: From Animal Rights to Radical Ecology*. Englewood Cliffs N.J.: Prentice Hall. Essays representing five different approaches to environmental ethics.

6

New Medical Rights

The origins of our traditional medical ethics are ancient. Perhaps the most famous of all physicians was Hippocrates, who lived from about 460 to 357 B.C. The oath ascribed to him, but probably Pythagorean, has deeply influenced medical practice since that time. At least from the fourth century A.D., Christian versions of the *Hippocratic Oath* have been administered upon entry into the medical profession in Western Europe and, subsequently, in the United States. This oath consists of a few practical rules of conduct, the central one being, "I will prescribe regimen for the good of my patients according to my ability and my judgment and never do harm to anyone."

Plato, who lived at about the same time as Hippocrates and who mentioned him in his *Dialogues*, provided the theoretical basis for professional ethics in his conception of an art. In fact, Plato used medicine as a paradigm example of an art. There are three essential differences between an art and a mere knack or practical skill.

First, only knowledge derived from reason enables one to practice an art, whereas a knack can be learned from experience and requires only opinion—belief that, unlike true knowledge, can turn out to be false. Second, each art requires knowledge of some specific good, whereas a knack or skill is guided by the practitioner's belief in what seems good. For example, the physician must have knowledge of health, while the cook is merely skillful at creating what tastes good, whether or not the food she serves is really good for one. Third, the purpose of each art is to promote its specific good, to serve the interest of the recipient, whereas the purpose of a knack is to promote the self-interest of the practitioner. It is for this reason that Plato distinguishes between the physician as practicing the art of medicine dedicated to the health of the patient and the physician as practicing the knack of business dedicated to the making of a profit. This

Platonic theory explains both the traditional distinction between the professions and the trades and the reason it has until recently been regarded as unprofessional, and therefore impermissible, conduct for physicians to advertise their services.

For more than a century, medical ethics in the United States was influenced primarily by a book published by the English physician Thomas Percival in 1803. Although entitled simply *Medical Ethics*, its significance is more accurately expressed in its subtitle: *A Code of Institutes and Precepts Adapted to the Professional Conduct of Physicians and Surgeons*. The book consists of a large number of rules of conduct systematically arranged by categories. Like the *Hippocratic Oath*, its spirit is religious but its focus is upon the practice of medicine rather than on any underlying religious or ethical theory. Unlike the *Hippocratic Oath*, its form is more like a code of laws than an oath sworn to the gods or God. Its pronouncements are intended to be precepts both in the sense of the rules of an art and in the sense of divine commands regarding moral conduct.

In 1847, the very year the American Medical Association was formed, it adopted a *Code of Ethics*. Its debt to Thomas Percival is evident in the way that it specifies in some detail the various duties of physicians to their patients, to each other, and to the public, as well as the reciprocal duties of those second parties to physicians and the medical profession. Indeed it often repeats his formulations verbatim. When the AMA switched to its much shorter and simpler *Principles of Medical Ethics* in 1957, it modified the language of this code to make it clear that its ten principles are merely standards to guide the physician not laws to impose strict obligations. This code is not to be followed blindly or imposed in such a manner as to restrict professional autonomy. Neither version of this code of ethics mentions even a single right of patients or those subjected to medical experimentation.

Accordingly, traditional medical ethics was more practical than theoretical. It was not so much applied ethics, ethical theory applied to medical practice, as a rule of conduct generalized from the experience of conscientious physicians and surgeons. Thus medical ethics was created by the medical profession primarily to guide the decisions and regulate the actions of medical professionals. In this respect it was very different from medical law, which imposes an external regulation upon the medical profession. Medical ethics was formulated in the language of duties, or at least principles, specifying how physicians and surgeons ought to conduct themselves. It presupposed a Platonic conception of a profession, insofar as it tacitly assumed both the benevolence and the authority of physicians and surgeons: The purpose of the art of medicine is the health of the patient, and only the person who knows medicine knows what is best for the patient.

During and after the Second World War these two assumptions were challenged radically by revelations of the grossly immoral practices of large numbers of physicians and surgeons in Nazi Germany. These medical scientists advocated a eugenic theory that led in practice to the sterilization of large numbers of persons who suffered from physical or mental illnesses that were at that time thought to be inheritable. Euthanasia was practiced on a large scale to eliminate those who were judged either to have unworthy lives or to be a burden upon society. Under the direction of the Nazi special police, medical professionals carried forward the genocide of the Jewish race and of the Gypsies. Most relevantly, it was the inhumane, and often scientifically useless, medical experiments imposed upon prisoners in the concentration camps that called forth public outrage in England and the United States. Once more the Second World War marks the beginning of a proliferation of rights, this time the alleged moral and actual legal rights of both patients and the subjects of medical research.

The introduction of new medical rights into both U.S. law and the law of many other countries was initiated and sustained by a revolution in medical ethics. Moral philosophers no longer thought of medical decisions and medical institutions from the perspective of physicians and researchers but from the perspective of patients and the subjects of medical experimentation. This led many of them to conclude that the locus of medical authority ought to lie with patients and subjects rather than physicians and medical scientists. As we examine some of the new legal rights and newly alleged moral rights concerning medical practice, let us reflect on whether these changes have been beneficial or harmful.

Consent to Medical Research

In addition to the trials of several Nazi political and military leaders before the Nuremberg Military Tribunals, the most notorious Nazi physicians were indicted for crimes against humanity involving medical experiments without the subjects' consent. At the Dachau concentration camp, human subjects were placed in a low-pressure chamber that subjected many to grave injury and torture. Also at Dachau, some subjects were forced to remain in a tank of ice water for up to three hours, and others were kept outdoors for many hours at temperatures below freezing. In the Ravensbrueck concentration camp, wounds were deliberately inflicted on the experimental subjects, who were then injected with bacteria, such as streptococcus or tetanus, to test the effectiveness of sulfanilamide and other drugs. Sometimes infection was aggravated by forcing wood shavings and ground glass into the wounds. At Buchenwald, experiments were conducted to investigate the effect of poisons secretly administered to the food of the human subjects.

Rights of Consent to Medical Research

The decision of the military court to convict several Nazi physicians of crimes against humanity was based in large measure upon the *Nuremberg Code*: ten moral, ethical, and legal principles limiting permissible experimentation upon human beings. The first principle, and the only one that is spelled out in detail, is, "The voluntary consent of the human subject is absolutely essential." Although the military tribunal did not explain why consent is necessary for morally and legally permissible experimentation upon human subjects, the assumption seems to be that to subject a human being to medical or other experimentation without her voluntary consent is to violate one of her fundamental human rights. Thus Article 7 of the *International Covenant on Civil and Political Rights* reads: "No one shall be subjected to torture or to cruel, inhuman or degrading treatment or punishment. In particular, no one shall be subjected without his free consent to medical or scientific experimentation." Here we find asserted a new medical right, primarily an alleged moral right but also an analogous legal right that has gradually become established in national and international law.

What is the defining content of this human right? Its content is a negative claim-right of each human being, holding against all others, *not* to be subjected to any medical or scientific experimentation unless one has given and not withdrawn one's voluntary consent. The crucial question is what conditions are required for consent to be genuinely voluntary. Probably the most authoritative explanation is given in the *Nuremberg Code*:

> This means that the person involved should have legal capacity to give consent; should be so situated as to be able to exercise free power of choice, without the intervention of any element of force, fraud, deceit, duress, over-reaching, or other form of constraint or coercion; and should have sufficient knowledge and comprehension of the elements of the subject matter involved to enable him to make an understanding and enlightened decision.

Thus the necessary conditions for voluntary consent include (1) the competence of the subject to give consent, (2) the absence of constraint or coercion, and (3) the possession of sufficient information provided in a manner that enables one to understand its relevance to one's choice of whether or not to consent to being subjected to experimentation. As we shall see, each of these conditions is problematic.

When news of the immoral medical experimentation imposed upon those imprisoned in Dachau, Ravensbrueck, and Buchenwald reached the United States, these atrocities were ascribed to the perverted racism of the Nazi ideology and the totalitarian German government under Hitler. There was, of course, no possibility that any such abuses of medical research could happen here. This complacency was rudely shattered over the next few years when information about several medical experiments conducted in the United States became public. At Willowbrook State Hospital in New York a series of studies involved inoculating mentally retarded children with the hepatitis virus. At Jewish Chronic Disease Hospital in Brooklyn live cancer cells were injected into senile patients without their knowledge or consent. And in the notorious Tuskegee Study, funded by the Public Health Service, experiments were conducted in Alabama over a period of thirty years upon hundreds of unsuspecting black men to learn the effects of untreated syphilis on the human body. Thus Congress created a National Commission for the Protection of Human Subjects of Biomedical and Behavioral Research. The recommendations of this commission were adopted, with modifications, in the *Code of Federal Regulations*, thereby introducing the legal right not to be subjected, without one's informed consent, to experimentation or research conducted under the auspices of any institution receiving federal funding. And in *Kaimowitz v. Department of Mental Health for the State of Michigan*, a Michigan circuit court affirmed the legal right, defined very much in the language of the *Nuremberg Code*, not to be subjected to experimentation without one's informed consent. Hence, there is now both a new alleged moral right of informed consent to medical research and a new legal right with very much the same content.

Unresolved Problems

Both the reality of the alleged human right and the desirability of the legal right have remained controversial because of the three conditions required for free informed consent. (1) Under U.S. law, dependent children are not competent to give valid consent to research, and at least very young children lack the psychological capacities required for genuine consent by any plausible moral theory. Do children have any right not to be subjected to medical experimentation without their consent? If they do, then it would appear that medical research for the prevention or cure of those diseases and disabilities normally suffered mostly by children is impermissible. Any such restriction upon medical science would severely limit the ability of physicians to treat their patients effectively in the future and thereby would cause vast amounts of preventable harm. But if children do not possess any such right, then this moral and legal protection against the abuse of these very vulnerable subjects of medical experimentation will be denied to them. In practice, parents or guardians have been granted the power to give consent to experimentation on children, but whether this power is morally justified, and what limits should be put upon it, remains debatable.

There are also problems concerning (2) the absence of constraint or coercion. Millions of U.S. citizens lack access to most forms of medical care because they cannot afford to pay for it out of pocket and are not covered by either public or private medical insurance. Some of these citizens, when they present themselves for treatment at a research hospital, are invited to volunteer to participate in an experiment to determine the effectiveness of some new therapy with unknown side effects. Many consent, even though they fear that they may suffer unanticipated harms. Is their consent genuinely unconstrained? This seems very doubtful, but to conclude that it is impermissible to subject them to therapeutic research will deny them the only medical treatment that is available to them.

Finally, medical researchers sometimes find (3) that fully informing potential subjects would undermine the reliability of their scientific investigation. This is most obviously true when one is conducting a large-scale clinical trial of some experimental therapy and the control group is to receive a placebo rather than an effective therapy. If those who will be assigned to this control group are told in advance that during their participation they will be denied treatment for their illness, they will almost certainly refuse to give their consent. But if they are not given this highly relevant information, then presumably they lack sufficient information for their consent to be fully voluntary. The usual "solution" to this problem is to tell the subjects that they may or may not be assigned to the control group and then to debrief them later by telling them whether or not they have been receiving therapeutic treatment. Many regard this as too little and too late to be any solution at all.

One result of these and other debates concerning the human right to informed consent to medical research has been the *Declaration of Helsinki,* which distinguishes between nontherapeutic and therapeutic biomedical research. In purely scientific research on a human being, it is the duty of the doctor to remain the protector of the life and health of the human subject and never to allow the interest of science or society to take precedence over the well-being of the subject. But in therapeutic research, the health of the patient must be the doctor's first consideration. Therefore, the doctor must remain free to try any new diagnostic or therapeutic measure that in her judgment offers hope of saving life, reestablishing health, or alleviating suffering. Moreover, if the doctor considers it essential not to obtain informed consent, then she is required simply to state the specific reasons for this in the protocol for submission to an independent committee. Does this mean that there is a human right not to be subjected to medical research without one's consent but no comparable human right of the patient not to be treated without her consent?

Informed Consent to Therapy

Although the right not to be operated upon by a surgeon—and, by analogy, the right not to be treated by a physician—without one's consent had its origins in the old common law tort of battery and was explicitly recognized by the Court of Appeals of New York in 1914, the legal right not to be treated without *informed* consent is a relatively new medical right. In 1957, in *Salgo v. Leland Stanford Jr. University Board of Trustees,* a California District Court of Appeal affirmed this right and defined its content in terms of its correlative duty: "A physician violates his duty to his patient and subjects himself to liability if he withholds any facts which are necessary to form the basis of an intelligent consent by the patient to the proposed treatment. Likewise the physician may not minimize the known dangers of a procedure or operation in order to induce his patient's consent."[1] That the court assumed that consent is legally valid only if there is no constraint or coercion is made clear by the second sentence. Thus the patient's right not to be given medical treatment without her free informed consent entered U.S. law.

At the same time, the court introduced an exception to or limitation on this right. It asserted that the physician must place the welfare of her patient above all else. Were the physician required to explain to every patient every risk, however remote, she might alarm a patient already overly worried, actually increase the risks because of the physiological results of this fear, and even cause the patient to refuse consent to some therapy essential to preserve his or her life or restore his or her health. Therefore, the physician has the therapeutic privilege or liberty to use her discretion regarding whether or not to disclose some risk to her patient, "consistent, of course, with the full disclosure of facts necessary to an informed consent."[2]

But how can the liberty not to disclose risk be consistent with full disclosure? What standard should the law use to specify the facts that are necessary to form the basis of an intelligent consent by the patient? (1) At first the courts adopted the professional standard. The physician's duty was to provide that amount of information usually provided by physicians in their community. The rationale for this standard was that it is the physician who knows best both what information is relevant to the choice of a therapy and what disclosures might jeopardize treatment by having an adverse effect upon the patient. (2) The courts have subsequently rejected the professional standard as giving too much discretion to the physician and too little attention to the patient's need for information. Currently the physician's duty to disclose is defined in terms of the objective standard. The physician must provide whatever information a prudent person in the patient's position would want before deciding whether to consent to the proposed medical treatment. This is an objective standard because it is defined in terms of the impersonal ideal of prudential rationality. (3) Some moral reformers argue that respect for the patient's autonomy requires the adoption of the subjective standard. This standard would require the physician to disclose all the information that this particular patient—with all her wishes and fears, some of which may be unreasonable—would want before deciding whether to consent to the proposed therapy. The law has been reluctant to adopt this more demanding standard of full information both because it would be much more difficult to provide the kind of evidence needed to decide cases of medical malpractice before the courts and because it would limit the therapeutic privilege in a manner that might be seriously harmful to the patient. Even those who admit that the objective standard is more appropriate for the law often insist that the subjective standard is a moral ideal that physicians ought to strive to achieve as far as practicable.

The law does, however, give the patient the power to waive her right to informed consent. If the patient requests not to be informed wholly or in part regarding diagnosis, alternative therapies, or the risks attendant to the recommended therapy, then the physician's legal duty to provide *full* information is canceled. Thus the law gives the patient the opportunity to make a free informed choice to consent to medical treatment, but it also permits the patient to consent more or less blindly to treatment, if she trusts her physician and prefers that the physician shoulder the burdens of choosing between several alternative therapies. Although some believe that this limitation on the legal right to informed consent endangers the health of patients by permitting them to choose irresponsibly, others defend it as enabling the patient to exercise her autonomous choice at a higher level by choosing the kind of patient-physician relationship she thinks best for herself.

Legal Grounds

What are the legal grounds of this right to informed consent? Originally the courts tended to find the right to informed consent to medical treatment in the common law of assault and battery. Although the angry man who beats up his victim commits a battery, the boxer who batters his opponent does not, because his opponent has consented to participate in a boxing match. Indeed, any unwelcome touching of one's person normally constitutes the tort of battery, but consent is a defense against this charge. By analogy, just as a criminal who knifes one commits a battery, so does a surgeon who cuts into one's body without one's consent.

As Justice Cardozo said in the landmark case of *Schloendorff v. Society of New York Hospital:* "In the case at hand, the wrong complained of is not merely negligence. It is a trespass. Every human being of adult years and sound mind has a right to determine what shall be done with his own body; and a surgeon who performs an operation without his patient's consent commits an assault, for which he is liable in damages."[3] The right not to be subjected to medical treatment without one's consent gradually became the right to informed consent. Only if one understands what one is agreeing to is one's consent genuine, and this understanding requires that one know both the nature of the proposed therapy and the risks associated with it. In this reasoning the ultimate legal ground is the fundamental common law right of self-determination.

More recently the courts have tended to ground the right to informed consent upon the law of negligence. Although the common law does not recognize any general duty to rescue others from harm, it does hold that those with certain special relations to a person have a duty of care toward that person. For example, a parent has a special obligation to protect his or her child from harm, and to fail to do so is to be guilty of child neglect. Similarly, when a physician accepts someone as her patient, she acquires a special duty of care, a legal obligation to provide competent medical treatment in return for payment received. The required standard of professional conduct is set by good medical practice, and this is determined by the usual practices of physicians who are knowledgeable, skillful, and conscientious. Increasingly, the courts have decided that one who neglects to obtain the informed consent of her patient before treatment engages in medical malpractice and is liable for damages. Thus the ultimate ground of the patient's right to informed consent are the understandings implicit in the contractual relation of physician and patient.

Moral Justification

Many, although not all, moral philosophers argue that the moral justification for having a legal right to informed consent parallels its legal grounds. There ought to be this legal right not to be treated medically without one's informed consent in order both to protect the patient from harm and to respect her autonomy.

Some who grant that society ought to protect its citizens from avoidable harm doubt that a legal right to informed consent will provide such protection. When a patient has come to a physician with a medical problem, presumably it is the physician who knows—by virtue of her knowledge of medical science and her experience in treating similar cases—which of the available therapies is most likely to be effective and to have the least harmful side effects. This presumption may not, however, be correct. For one thing, the concepts of disease, disability, and health are not purely impersonal objective concepts. A mild allergy that causes slight post-nasal drip might constitute an illness for a professional singer, whereas for most persons it would not detract significantly from good health. After all, perfect health is an ideal that is never fully realized but is achieved only to a greater or lesser degree in actuality. Similarly, a disproportionately large nose might threaten the psychological health of an overly sensitive person and therefore call for plastic surgery for one patient but be no reason at all for another patient to consent to any such therapy.

For another thing, those who doubt that a right to informed consent would protect the patient from harm argue that the decision of whether to consent to some proposed therapy is not a purely medical decision. Which treatment is best, indeed whether any treatment is really needed, depends upon one's life-plan and the relative values one places upon the many and varied things that can make one's life go better or worse. Even the slightest damage to a knee or ankle might constitute a major medical problem to someone hoping to run the 200 meter dash or the 400 meter hurdles in the next Olympics, but for someone who lives a largely sedentary life it would not be a reason to undergo an operation. Whether it would be prudent for one to undergo chemotherapy—with its painful and even dangerous side effects—in the hope of extending one's life a year or two would depend both upon the relative value one places on longevity versus quality of life and upon whether one is deeply invested in a major project that requires another year or so for completion.

The second crucial moral consideration is respect for the patient's autonomy. Human beings, at least those with normal psychological capacities, have a strong interest in self-determination: selecting their own values, setting their own goals in life, and acting to achieve the kind of life that they think best for themselves. Because the value of reaching any goal depends upon its significance for one's life as a whole and because one suffers frustration when prevented from pursuing one's chosen goals, autonomous choice and action have tremendous instrumental value for most persons. Also a sense of having made something of one's life has great intrinsic value for most of us. Therefore, it matters a great deal that others respect one's autonomy and let one make one's own choices, even if those choices are mistaken; and because choices of life or death, health or disability have such an important place in one's life as a whole, it is especially important that one have the right to informed consent to medical treatment.

Withholding Information

The patient's right to informed consent imposes a correlative duty upon the physician to explain to the patient, in a manner that the patient can understand, all the facts relevant to her choice of whether to consent to the proposed therapy. This legal and moral requirement runs counter to a long and firmly established tradition. The original *Code of Ethics* of the American Medical Association reads in part:

> A physician should not be forward to make gloomy prognostications, . . . but he should not fail, on proper occasions, to give to the friends of the patient timely notice of danger, when it really occurs; and even to the patient himself, if absolutely necessary. . . . The life of a sick person can be shortened not only by the acts, but also by the words or the manner of the physician. It is, therefore, a sacred duty to guard himself carefully in this respect, and to avoid all things which have a tendency to discourage the patient and to depress his spirits.

Although this duty to withhold depressing information from the patient is omitted from the current AMA *Principles of Medical Ethics,* it contains no suggestion at all that the physician ought to inform the patient concerning diagnosis, prognosis, or the alternative therapies available.

Physicians often refrain from providing full and frank information to their patients, and moral philosophers often argue against the right to informed consent for at least three reasons. (1) It is impossible in practice to meet the legal standard of providing to the patient all the material facts in a manner she can understand, because the patient lacks knowledge of medical science as well as the experience of similar cases that are required to interpret so much, often technical, information. (2) Both the awareness that there are available therapies other than the one proposed by the physician and the knowledge of the risks, often remote, of the recommended treatment will damage the patient's trust in her physician and her confidence in the proposed therapy, thereby undermining those psychological factors on which cure depends to a considerable degree. (3) When the prognosis is dismal, or the risks of the proposed therapy are serious, this kind of information may produce anxiety and depression with serious attendant physiological changes. These effects can worsen the patient's medical condition, cause the patient to refuse consent to necessary medical treatment, and even tempt her to commit suicide. Informed consent cannot be required by the physician's duty of care to the patient when it often prevents the physician from giving the best, sometimes even minimally good, medical treatment.

These and similar arguments lead many to conclude that the new legal right of the patient not to be treated without informed consent ought to be repealed or, if this is impossible, that the therapeutic privilege ought to be wide enough to permit physicians to withhold information from their patients whenever they deem this desirable. The same arguments challenge the allegation that the patient has a more fundamental and perhaps more demanding moral right to fully informed consent. As one would expect, however, the patient's rights movement defends both the existing legal and the alleged moral rights to informed consent on the grounds that these rights prevent harm to and respect the autonomy of the patient. But what if full information often harms the patient? And why should the physician respect the autonomy of the patient when doing so will often prevent her from fulfilling her primary duty to provide the best medical care for her patient?

The Right to Die

The right to informed consent implies the right to refuse medical treatment. This is because consent is legally valid and morally acceptable only if it is voluntary and free. But if one is forced or legally required to "consent" to some proposed therapy so that one is not free to refuse it, then one has not really consented at all. But what are the limits of one's right to refuse to consent? May one refuse even medical treatment necessary to prolong one's very life? To do so would be to render the necessary therapy legally and morally impermissible, and this presumably would result in one's death. Does one, to anticipate language only later accepted in the law, have the right to die?

Opinions of the Courts

On this issue, the leading case is *In the Matter of Karen Quinlan*. On the night of April 15, 1975, for reasons unknown, Karen Quinlan ceased breathing for at least two fifteen-minute periods. As a consequence she was rendered irreversibly comatose and reduced to a persistent vegetative state. Nevertheless, the attending physician could not certify her death and, because she did not satisfy the legal criterion for brain death, could not disconnect her from the artificial respirator that seemed to be sustaining her biological life. Joseph Quinlan, her father, petitioned the court to be appointed Karen's guardian with the power to authorize the discontinuance of all extraordinary medical procedures.

The Supreme Court of New Jersey acknowledged that Karen Quinlan's right to life was at issue but decided that, given her condition, her constitutional right to privacy was broad enough to encompass her right to refuse even life-sustaining medical treatment. It reasoned that the individual's right to privacy grows and the state's interest in preserving life weakens "as the degree of bodily invasion increases and the prognosis dims."[4] Because Karen was not competent to exercise it herself, the only practical way to protect her right to refuse medical treatment was to authorize her family to exercise it on her behalf. Accordingly, the court granted Joseph Quinlan's petition and—in effect, although not in so many words—recognized Karen Quinlan's legal right to die. Still, the court defined this right narrowly. It is the legal right to refuse only extraordinary therapy when the prognosis for the patient is extremely poor. Whether this would permit the termination of artificial nutrition and hydration remained in doubt.

In a subsequent case, *In re Conroy*, the same court recognized a much broader right to die. It decided, on the ground not of the constitutional right to privacy but of the common law right to self-determination, that a nasogastric feeding tube could be removed from an eighty-four-year-old, incompetent nursing home resident suffering irreversible mental and physical ailments. Of special importance is its rejection of several distinctions traditionally used to distinguish between impermissible and permissible cases of refusing medical treatment: the distinction between actively hastening death by terminating treatment versus passively allowing a person to die of a disease; between withholding treatment initially versus withdrawing treatment afterwards; between ordinary versus extraordinary treatment; and between treatment by artificial feeding versus other forms of life-sustaining medical procedures. Hence, the patient's legal right to die could no longer be limited on the basis of any of these distinctions.

The most definitive right-to-die case to date, and the first to reach the United States Supreme Court, is *Cruzan v. Director, Missouri Department of Health*. On the night of January 11, 1983, Nancy Cruzan lost control of her car and was later discovered lying face down in a ditch without any detectable respiratory or cardiac function. Although paramedics were able to resuscitate her, the permanent brain damage she had suffered left her irreversibly comatose and in a permanent vegetative state. Her parents petitioned a Missouri court for authority to terminate all artificial nutrition and hydration procedures. The trial court granted their petition, but the Supreme Court of Missouri reversed on the ground that there was no clear and convincing, inherently reliable evidence of Nancy's desire to die under the given circumstances.

The United States Supreme Court granted certiorari to decide whether Nancy Cruzan had a constitutional right that would require the hospital to withdraw life-sustaining treatment from her. Chief Justice Rehnquist, speaking for the court, said: "In this Court, the question is simply and starkly whether the United States Constitution prohibits Missouri from choosing the rule of decision that it did. This is the first case in which we have been squarely presented with the issue whether the United States Constitution grants what is in common parlance referred to as a 'right to die.'"[5] Justice Rehnquist traced the derivation of the patient's right to refuse life-prolonging treatment from the common law right to bodily integrity and, after *Quinlan*, from the constitutional right to privacy. He concluded: "The Fourteenth Amendment provides that no State shall 'deprive any person of life, liberty, or property, without due process of law.' The principle that a competent person has a constitutionally protected liberty interest in refusing unwanted medical treatment may be inferred from our previous decisions."[6]

Thus, Justice Rehnquist recognized the patient's constitutional as well as common law right to die. Of the five opinions reported in this controversial case, only that of Justice Scalia rejected this part of the reasoning of the Court. Hence, the right to die has become entrenched in U.S. law.

Nevertheless, the United States Supreme Court sustained Missouri's refusal to grant the petition of Cruzan's parents for the authority to terminate all artificial nutrition and hydration procedures. The granting of the constitutional right to die is not decisive in this case because no right is absolute. The Court asserted that the Due Process Clause protects an interest in life as well as an interest in refusing life-sustaining medical treatment. Therefore, Nancy Cruzan's liberty interest in choosing to die must be weighed against the state interest in preserving life. Rehnquist reasoned that because the choice between life and death is a deeply personal decision of obvious and overwhelming finality, Missouri may legitimately seek to safeguard the personal element of this choice through the imposition of heightened evidentiary requirements.

Dissenting Opinions

It is from this part of his reasoning, and not his derivation of a constitutional right to die, that four of the nine justices dissented. They argued that a stronger right to die is entirely consistent with the right to life. Justice Brennan, with whom Justices Marshall and Blackmun joined, objected to the way in which the Court had weighed the state interest in preserving life against the patient's interest in refusing life-prolonging treatment: "But the State has no legitimate general interest in someone's life, completely abstracted from the interest of the person living that life, that could outweigh the person's choice to avoid medical treatment."[7] Two theses are implicit here: that the individual's right to life is the right to having a life, not merely to remaining alive, and that this right is grounded on the value of that life for the right-holder not the value of that life for the state.

These theses are made explicit in the opinion of Justice Stevens:

> But for patients like Nancy Cruzan, who have no consciousness and no chance of recovery, there is a serious question as to whether the mere persistence of their bodies is "life" as that word is commonly understood, or as it is used in both the Constitution and the Declaration of Independence. . . . Life, particularly human life, is not commonly thought of as a merely physiological condition or function. Its sanctity is often thought to derive from the impossibility of any such reduction. When people speak of life, they often mean to describe the experiences that comprise a person's history, as when it is said that somebody "led a good life."[8]

It is worthy of note that Justice Stevens applied his interpretation of "life" both to the constitutional right to life recognized in the Due Process Clause and to the alleged moral right to life asserted in the *Declaration of Independence*.

Because the justices of the Supreme Court disagreed so fundamentally, *Cruzan* leaves at least two legal issues to be decided as right-to-die cases come before the courts in the future. (1) How should courts weigh the patient's liberty interest in choosing to die against the state's interest in protecting the lives of those subject to its jurisdiction? Justice Brennan probably went too far when he asserted that the state has no general interest in protecting a patient's life other than the value of that life for that individual. Many argue that the inviolability of each and every person's life is essential for the security of person necessary to maintain public order. For the state to permit an indigent homeless person to be murdered, for example, is to endanger the security of a wider public and is thus to engender in the general population both fear and the resulting preemptive violence. (2) How should the courts interpret "life" when they must decide cases involving the constitutional right to life? To agree with Justice Stevens that this fundamental legal right is not applicable to human beings with a merely biological life would threaten to leave unprotected both the irreversibly comatose and severely brain-damaged infants. To say that this right is not applicable to those with a merely biological life would also leave the severely brain-damaged and the elderly, whose dementia has caused them to lose all contact with their past experiences, without its legal protection. Many judges and most citizens will regard this as too great a danger to introduce into our law.

In his legal reasoning, Justice Stevens appealed to the sanctity of human life. This raises the underlying moral issue: Why is human life sacred or inviolable? The word "sanctity" reminds us that this conviction was originally derived from our Judeo-Christian tradition. Each human life is sacred either because it belongs to God who created us or because human beings are made in the image of God. Thus to destroy or even to fail to preserve the life of anyone is to destroy or to fail to preserve either the property of God or a spark of the divine. However, the constitutional separation of church and state precludes this religious justification for the legal right to life, and these theological premises are no longer common ground in the moral reasoning accepted in our pluralistic society.

Moral philosophers today tend to appeal either to a Kantian theory that demands respect for the rational autonomy of every moral agent or, more often, to the inherent value of human life. But the former seems inapplicable to any individual whose rationality is not sufficient to enable her to make genuinely autonomous choices; and the latter poses anew the question of why, if at all, the lives of the irreversibly comatose, severely defective neonates, the very senile, and especially the terminally ill who suffer acute physical pain or psychological agony have any significant inherent value. Until some of these recalcitrant moral problems are solved, we will not know how best to interpret the human right to life and to weigh it properly against the alleged right to die.

The Right to Assisted Suicide?

Of the divided opinions of the members of the United States Supreme Court in *Cruzan*, only that of Justice Scalia refused to admit any constitutional right to die. He argued both that the Constitution says nothing about the matter and that to invent any such right would render suicide legally permissible. This suggests a highly controversial question. Does the constitutional right to die imply or include a legal right to assisted suicide?

Compassion in Dying

The Ninth Circuit United States Court of Appeals has decided in the case of *Compassion in Dying v. State of Washington* that it does. Three mentally competent terminally ill patients challenged the constitutionality of a Washington statute providing, "A person is guilty of promoting a suicide attempt when he knowingly causes or aids another person to attempt suicide." Because attempting suicide is a crime in that state, as it is in many other states, this statute makes any physician who assists a patient who wishes to commit suicide a criminal. The plaintiffs alleged that the words "or aids" violate the Due Process Clause.

Speaking for the Court, Judge Reinhardt agreed. His judicial reasoning consisted of two stages. First, he argued that there is a constitutional right to die. He reviewed a long line of previous due process decisions of the Supreme Court and said:

> A common thread running through these cases is that they involve decisions that are highly personal and intimate, as well as of great importance to the individual. Certainly, few decisions are more personal, intimate or important than the decision to end one's life, especially when the reason for doing so is to avoid excessive and protracted pain. Accordingly, we believe the cases from *Pierce* through *Roe* provide strong general support for our conclusion that a liberty interest in controlling the time and manner of one's death is protected by the Due Process Clause of the Fourteenth Amendment.[9]

He also argued that this conclusion is supported much more strongly and specifically by the decision in the case of *Cruzan v. Director, Missouri Department of Health:* "In *Cruzan* the Court considered whether or not there is a constitutionally-protected, due process liberty interest in terminating unwanted medical treatment. The Court said that an affirmative answer followed almost inevitably from its prior decisions holding that patients have a liberty interest in refusing to submit to specific medical procedures."[10] But whether this liberty interest of a patient who wishes to die outweighs the relevant interests of the state of Washington remains to be decided.

In the second stage of his reasoning, Judge Reinhardt argued that in the case before the court the liberty interest of the patient does outweigh the interests of the state. Of the six state interests he considered, the protection of life and the prevention of suicide are the most relevant for our purposes:

As the laws in state after state demonstrate, even though the protection of life is one of the state's most important functions, the state's interest is dramatically diminished if the person it seeks to protect is terminally ill or permanently comatose and has expressed a wish that he be permitted to die without further medical treatment (or if a duly appointed representative has done so on his behalf).

Reinhardt went on:

While the state has a legitimate interest in preventing suicides in general, that interest, like the state's interest in preserving life, is substantially diminished in the case of terminally ill, competent adults who wish to die. One of the heartaches of suicide is the senseless loss of a life ended prematurely. In the case of a terminally ill adult who ends his life in the final stages of an incurable and painful degenerative disease, in order to avoid debilitating pain and a humiliating death, the decision to commit suicide is not senseless, and death does not come too early.[11]

And finally Reinhardt argued: "We hold that a liberty interest exists in the choice of how and when one dies, and that the provision of the Washington statute banning assisted suicide, as applied to competent, terminally ill adults who wish to hasten their deaths by obtaining medication prescribed by their doctors, violates the Due Process Clause."[12]

Thus, the circuit court recognized a constitutional right to die, including a right to physician-assisted suicide. Whether this precedent will be, or ought to be, followed by other courts in future cases remains very much in doubt.

A crucial passage in the opinion of the court reads as follows: "We do not ask simply whether there is a liberty interest in receiving "aid in killing oneself" because such a narrow interest could not exist in the absence of a broader and more important interest—the right to die. In short, it is the end and not the means that defines the liberty interest."[13] The interpretation of this language is doubly problematic. For one thing, it conflates the interest of the patient in dying with the legal right intended to protect the interest; for another, it fails to define the meaning of "the right to die." Is this the right to be allowed to die (to be left alone by the physician, not kept alive against one's will) or the right to be enabled to die (including the right to be provided with the means to, or the right to be assisted in, dying)? Although the former interpretation seems more appropriate for the reasoning of the Supreme Court in *Cruzan*, Reinhardt's reasoning seems to require the latter.

Circuit Judge Beezer, dissenting, appealed to this ambiguity in his opinion denying that the Due Process Clause implies any constitutional right to physician-assisted suicide:

Plaintiffs ask us to blur the line between withdrawal of life-sustaining treatment and physician-assisted suicide. At the same time, some proponents of physician-assisted suicide would maintain a conceptual distinction between physician-assisted suicide and euthanasia. . . . The proper place to draw the line is between withdrawing life-sustaining treatment (which is based on the right to be free from unwanted intrusion) and physician-assisted suicide and euthanasia (which implicate the assistance of others in controlling the timing and manner of death). The former is constitutionally protected (under *Cruzan*), the latter are not.[14]

Presumably this is because *Cruzan* recognized the "right to die" only in the sense of the right to refuse unwanted medical treatment in the special case of life-sustaining procedures, a right implied by the right *not* to be subjected to medical treatment without one's consent that is in turn derived from the common-law right to determine when others may intrude into one's body and the constitutional right that others not intrude into one's privacy.

Glucksberg

In *Washington v. Glucksberg*, the United States Supreme Court reversed the decision of the Ninth Circuit Court of Appeals. Chief Justice Rehnquist delivered the opinion of the Court. He defined the question presented in this case as whether the statute of the state of Washington prohibiting any person from causing or aiding another to commit suicide offends against the Fourteenth Amendment to the United States Constitution. More specifically, it is whether the liberty protected by the Due Process Clause includes a right to commit suicide, including a right to assistance in so doing.

Rehnquist noted that the liberty protected by the Due Process Clause includes more than the absence of physical restraint; it protects individual liberty against any arbitrary governmental action and provides heightened protection against governmental interference with certain fundamental rights and liberty interests. In a long line of cases, the Supreme Court has held that these fundamental freedoms include the rights to marry, to have children, to direct the education and upbringing of one's children, to have marital privacy, to use contraception, to have bodily integrity, to have an abortion, and even to refuse unwanted lifesaving medical treatment.

The question is whether this last right implies any right to physician-assisted suicide. What method ought the Supreme Court use to decide this question?

Our established method of substantive-due-process analysis has two primary features: First, we have regularly observed that the Due Process Clause specially protects those fundamental rights and liberties which are, objectively, "deeply rooted in this Nation's history and traditions". . . Second, we have required in substantive-due-process cases a "careful description" of the asserted fundamental liberty interest.[15]

The reason to insist upon the tests of this rather conservative method is to rein in the subjective evaluations present in judicial review and to avoid irresponsible judgments in the uncharted areas of liberty.

Justice Rehnquist argued that the case for physician-assisted suicide failed both tests. He began by examining our nation's history, legal traditions, and practices and concluded that although attitudes toward suicide itself have changed over the years, "our laws have consistently condemned and continue to prohibit suicide."[16] Moreover, the Ninth Circuit Court of Appeals had not formulated carefully the liberty interest at stake. In various places it had described it as "a liberty interest in determining the time and manner of one's death," "the right to die," "a liberty to choose how to die," "a right to control of one's final days," "the right to choose a humane, dignified death," and "the liberty to shape death."

Hence, Harold Glucksberg, Abigail Halperin, and Thomas A. Preston, the three physicians who had originally petitioned to be permitted to assist their terminally ill and suffering patients to commit suicide, had failed to prove that Washington's prohibition against assisted suicide violated any fundamental constitutional right.

Still, the prohibition against assisted suicide might offend against the Due Process Clause if it were an arbitrary prohibition unrelated to legitimate governmental interests. However, this is clearly not the case. The state of Washington has legitimate interests in preserving human life, alleviating the serious public-health problem of suicide, protecting the integrity and ethics of the medical profession, protecting vulnerable groups, and avoiding starting down the path to voluntary and perhaps involuntary euthanasia. Accordingly, the Court overruled the decision of the Ninth Circuit Court of Appeals in *Compassion in Dying v. State of Washington.*

Although the justices of the Supreme Court were unanimous in ruling that there is no constitutional right to physician-assisted suicide, their decision in *Glucksberg* does not require the continuation of state statutes prohibiting physicians from assisting suffering patients to commit suicide: "Throughout the Nation, Americans are engaged in an earnest and profound debate about the morality, legality, and practicality of physician-assisted suicide. Our holding permits this debate to continue, as it should in a democratic society."[17] The concurring opinions suggest that among the relevant considerations are whether medicine is or will soon be able to prevent or substantially reduce the suffering of all patients, whether permitting physicians to assist suffering patients to commit suicide would undermine the moral integrity of the medical profession, and whether experiments in permitting physician-assisted suicide—such as those in the Netherlands—lead to abuses such as involuntary euthanasia.

The Moral Question

Whether state legislatures prohibit or permit assisted suicide, and however the courts decide cases that challenge the constitutionality of such statutes, the moral question remains: *Ought* there to be a legal right to physician-assisted suicide? Increasing numbers of moral philosophers and social reformers are arguing that some such legal right is needed to respect and protect the patient's moral right to physician-assisted suicide. However this alleged moral right is defined, it seems to presuppose both the patient's right to commit suicide and a right to assistance by her physician in doing so. Are there really any such rights?

Many moral philosophers are convinced that there can be no moral right to commit suicide because suicide is always or is generally morally wrong. Historically this conviction originated in our Judeo-Christian tradition. Saint Augustine and other theologians have asserted that suicide violates the sixth commandment: Thou shalt not kill. But even granted that the commands of God constitute the moral law, the interpretation of this law remains in doubt. Biblical scholars now believe that the Hebrew word traditionally translated "kill" really means "wrongfully kill." Thus one must establish the wrongfulness of suicide before one can conclude that it violates the sixth commandment; one must not deduce its wrongfulness from that divine command. Moreover, most theologians have recognized that there are exceptions implicit in the moral prohibition of killing. For example, it is morally permissible for one to kill an attacker if this is necessary to save one's life, for a soldier to kill in a just war, and for the state to execute condemned murderers. Given the ability of modern medicine to keep patient's alive biologically in a merely vegetative state or in a condition of acute suffering, it seems to many that at least suicide and perhaps euthanasia are also exceptions to the moral law prohibiting killing.

Other traditional religious arguments against suicide depend upon an appeal to moral analogies. Just as a statue belongs to the sculptor who made it, so we are the property of God our Creator. But to admit that God owns human beings seems to imply the repugnant conclusion that slavery may not be always morally wrong. Again, human beings are assumed to be servants of God and instruments of divine providence. No doubt it is normally wrong for a servant to fail or refuse to serve her master. But what if a master is so cruel as to inflict extreme suffering upon the servant? Just as a public servant, such as a firefighter or police officer, is not morally required to enter a burning building or pursue an armed criminal into the dark, so there are surely limits to one's duty to persevere in the service of God.

There are also traditional nonreligious arguments used to prove that suicide is morally wrong. Kant held that the fundamental moral obligation is always to treat humanity, whether in one's own person or that of another, always as an end-in-itself and never as a means only. But to commit suicide is to use one's person merely as a means to escape from suffering or to end an empty life. Hence, everyone has a duty to refrain from suicide. Many moral philosophers now reject this reasoning as inconsistent with the fundamental insight of Kantianism. What commands moral respect in each and every human being, including oneself, is moral agency, the capacity to act on moral reasons. But irreversibly comatose patients no longer possess moral agency, and a terminally ill patient who commits suicide in order to prevent the dehumanizing effects of intense pain or deteriorating faculties is respecting, not failing to respect, her personality.

Then there are the utilitarian arguments that condemn suicide because it prevents goods and produces evils. To kill anyone, even oneself, is to destroy the potential of any life for future goods it could enjoy or create. Even worse, in most cases suicide inflicts avoidable harm on others. At the very least, it causes grief in friends and family. Typically it leaves those who are dependent upon one without the income one could have earned or the services one could have performed. But these considerations seem inapplicable to patients whose lives now have only the potential of suffering or unconsciousness, rather than intrinsic value. Such patients are more of a burden on family and society than they are contributors to the welfare of others.

In short, the traditional arguments intended to prove that suicide is always morally wrong are now unconvincing to increasing numbers of conscientious persons. When they reflect upon the plight of many patients, especially terminally ill patients suffering unrelieved physical pain or mental agony, they are led to conclude that suicide is not *per se* morally wrong. This is not, however, sufficient to establish any moral right to commit suicide. Any such right worth taking seriously must be at least a protected liberty: a moral liberty to kill oneself together with a moral claim against others not to prevent one from so doing.

The Right to Commit Suicide

The defining core of the alleged moral right to commit suicide is the moral liberty of killing oneself. What could be the ground of this liberty? Advocates of physician-assisted suicide differ in their answers to this question. Some hold that the liberty to commit suicide is an innocent liberty grounded simply on the absence of any moral duty not to do so. On this view, the duty not to kill is limited to the murder or the killing of another human being. Killing oneself is a very different species of action because it is not motivated by malice or hostility and does not threaten the general peace or personal security of others. On this view, the moral right to commit suicide is a general prima facie right possessed by all human beings but often overridden by conflicting obligations, such as one's duty not to inflict unnecessary grief upon one's spouse or not to abandon one's dependent children. The problem, of course, is to explain why killing oneself can be a morally innocent action, whereas killing anyone else is one of the most serious moral wrongs.

Therefore, others admit that there is a general duty not to kill any human being but insist that this duty is undermined by excessive sacrifice in certain unfortunate circumstances. The demands of duty are limited. Although a lifeguard has a duty to save swimmers in danger of drowning, she has no obligation to plunge into a whirlpool or riptide when to do so would be a futile loss of her own life. Similarly, one has no duty to refrain from killing oneself when one's own life has lost its value and when to continue living would only impose great suffering. On this view, the right to commit suicide is a special right, a moral right possessed by some persons but not by all.

Whichever view one adopts, the moral right to commit suicide is strong enough to deserve legal protection only if this core moral liberty to kill oneself is morally protected by a claim against others, such that they not prevent one from exercising it. What could be the ground of this moral claim and the correlative duty it imposes on others? Two answers are widely accepted by the advocates of physician-assisted suicide. The moral claim against interference is grounded both by respect for the autonomy of the psychologically competent patient and by the harms (including the continued suffering of the patient, the hardships imposed on her family, and the waste of scarce resources of society) that would result from preventing the patient from ending her life.

The Right to Assistance

Although these arguments for the existence of the moral right to commit suicide are controversial enough, it is the alleged moral right to assistance by one's physician that is most often and vehemently denied by judges and conscientious physicians. Although this right to assistance could be taken to be merely a liberty-right of the physician to assist a patient who wishes to commit suicide, most advocates of physician-assisted suicide insist upon a stronger right, a claim-right. The defining core of this asserted right is the moral claim of a patient whose life has become intolerable against his physician that she either assist him to kill himself or transfer his case to another physician who is willing to do so. What could be the ground of this alleged moral right? Many argue that it is simply one aspect of the physician's professional duty of care to her patient, because medical care includes relief from suffering as well as treatment intended to cure. In addition to this argument others appeal to either the general moral obligation to rescue anyone in distress or even the duty of benevolence. Although these moral reasons would not be applicable to all human beings, and thus could not ground any universal moral claim of all patients against their physicians, they do make a plausible case for the right of a patient to commit suicide with the assistance of his physician, if the patient is inevitably dying and undergoing great suffering.

This case is plausible but far from conclusive. To assume the complete autonomy of the patient in the choice to commit assisted suicide seems to wrongly restrict the autonomy of the physician who conscientiously objects to suicide and to impose upon her a demand that she become an accomplice in what she sincerely believes is moral wrongdoing. Nor is the physician's objection obviated by the alternative of transferring care of the patient to another physician, for this also renders her an accomplice by virtue of her cooperation in what she takes to be a wrongful suicide. Besides, there is a serious practical question as to whether any patient, by the time he has become terminally ill and is suffering great physical pain or mental agony, retains the capacity to make any genuinely autonomous choice.

The appeal to the principle of benevolence, or to the duty to rescue a patient in distress, seems to many equally inadequate to ground any moral claim to assistance by the physician. The combination of modern medical science and compassionate treatment can now relieve almost all acute physical pain or psychological anguish. Moreover, the option of assisting a patient to end his life reduces the moral demand on the physician to expend the time, effort, and care necessary to control the suffering of the patient.

The most obvious objection to admitting any duty of the physician to cooperate with a patient who chooses to commit suicide is that it would undermine the patient's trust in his physician. The danger is that the physician's personal values and acceptance of assisted suicide will unconsciously shape how aggressively she treats the patient or how dismally she presents the prognosis. Given the ability of physicians to influence the choices of their patients, how can any patient know whether his physician is subtly enticing or coercing him to choose death? Although one aspect of the physician's professional duty of care is to relieve suffering, this duty should be subordinated to the primary duties both to cure, if possible, and to preserve life. We can see that although a case can be made for the moral right to physician-assisted suicide, there are strong moral reasons to deny that any such right exists.

Legal Protection?

Let us, however, assume for the sake of the argument that some such strong moral right to physician-assisted suicide really exists. It does not necessarily follow that this moral right ought to be protected by some similar legal right. This patient's right may well be overridden both by the state's obligation to protect the more fundamental human right to life and by the public interest in preserving the integrity of the medical profession. Many jurists and conscientious citizens also use an opening wedge or slippery slope argument to oppose the legalization of physician-assisted suicide. Although it may be true that in some rare cases it is morally permissible for a physician to cooperate with a patient who wishes to end his life, in most cases to introduce a right to physician-assisted suicide into the law would lead to morally repugnant consequences. Once a society abandons the principle of the inviolability of every human life, it will inevitably permit the killing of genetically defective infants, elderly persons inflicted with degenerative diseases, and eventually persons judged to be a burden on society. It is much safer to maintain the legal prohibition against physician-assisted suicide, leaving it to the discretion of each individual physician whether or not to disobey the law in cases where she conscientiously believes that the patient has a moral right to die.

Advocates of physician-assisted suicide reply that it is not a satisfactory solution to place upon the physician the burden of responding morally to the plight of incurably ill patients suffering unrelieved physical pain or mental agony and at the same time to expose these physicians to the risk of legal sanctions for their conscientious action. This solution is clearly unfair to medical practitioners. It will also result in the unjust treatment of many patients who have a moral right to physician-assisted suicide. While some will have their right respected by their physicians, others will be denied their moral right to assistance by their physician, either because her moral values differ from theirs or because she is unwilling to endanger her practice by running the risk of being indicted for murder. Finally, as long as assisting a patient to end his life is illegal, the attending physician will be unwilling to consult with other physicians when in doubt about some case and will be unable to ask the advice of the ethics committee of her hospital. It would be far better to introduce a right to physician-assisted suicide into the law and to regulate its exercise in ways that would reduce the probability of its abuse. As long as the existing practice of many physicians to cooperate with some patients who wish to die remains outside the law, the danger of abuse remains and has, in fact, increased.

The debate over the right to die has not yet been resolved in our society. Although the right to die appears to be firmly established in constitutional law, its boundaries are not yet clearly drawn. Most recently the United States Supreme Court has denied that it is broad enough to imply any legal right to physician-assisted suicide. But state legislators, social reformers, conscientious citizens, and moral philosophers continue to disagree on the underlying moral issues. While some believe that there is not any moral right to die at all, others argue strenuously that this right does exist and that it implies a right to physician-assisted suicide. Does our law contain one right too many or one right too few? And which, if any, of the alleged moral rights to die and to physician-assisted suicide, are real?

The Rights to Medical Care

The *Universal Declaration of Human Rights* of 1948 asserts the right to an adequate standard of living. Article 25 reads in part: "Everyone has the right to a standard of living adequate for the health and well-being of himself and of his family, including food, clothing, housing and medical care and necessary social services." This fundamental moral right is clearly broad enough to contain the right of each individual human being to medical care adequate for his or her health and well-being. This is usually interpreted as a claim-right holding primarily against one's state, but secondarily against all other individuals and private associations, to be provided with those goods and services included in both preventive and therapeutic medicine.

Is there any reason to believe that this alleged moral right to adequate medical care really exists? Many moral philosophers argue that it is grounded on a fundamental human need. They do not pretend that one has a moral right to everything one needs. I need a computer upon which to draft and revise the journal articles and books I write in fulfilling my duty as a member of the Washington University faculty; but this need does not ground any moral right, much less a human right, to be provided with a computer. There are, however, certain fundamental needs that everyone has simply by virtue of human nature. These possess the universality and importance required to ground human rights. Because every human being is vulnerable to illness and disability, everyone has a basic human need for medical care. Therefore, everyone has a human right to medical care.

Alternative Definitions

But to how much medical care of what kind does one have a fundamental moral right? The *Universal Declaration* asserts a human right to medical care adequate for health and well-being. The problem is that both health and well-being admit of degrees. The former can vary from very poor health to almost perfect health, and the latter can range from a life that is not quite intolerable to one that is almost entirely satisfactory and greatly rewarding. What degree of health and well-being is required for living adequately? Because no convincing or even plausible answer has been given to this question, the content of this alleged human right to adequate medical care remains indeterminate and undefined. This lack of definition renders it useless in determining what moral duties, if any, it imposes on society or others. Therefore, even if this human right does exist, it seems to be of no practical importance to anyone.

In the *International Covenant on Economic, Social and Cultural Rights* of 1966 the United Nations attempted to solve this problem of indeterminacy by adopting a second definition. It first asserted "the right of everyone to the enjoyment of the highest attainable standard of physical and mental health." It then described in specific terms some of the duties this human right imposes upon the states who have agreed to the *Covenant*. Among these are the duties to take the steps necessary for "the prevention, treatment and control of epidemic, endemic, occupational and other diseases" and "the creation of conditions which would assure to all medical service and medical attention in the event of sickness." Here the human right to medical care has been redefined as the fundamental moral right of each human being to medical care sufficient for the highest attainable standard of physical and mental health.

At best, the *International Covenant* is only a partial solution to the problem of specifying the content of the human right to medical care. Because it describes only some of the duties imposed upon the states parties by this human right and gives no hint of how these duties are implied by its definition of that right, there is no way of knowing what other moral obligations, if any, fall upon those states that have ratified this document.

Presumably the content of any right is determined by its ground. What, then, could be the ground of this alleged human right? Most likely it is some conception of human flourishing that includes or presupposes the best possible health of the individual. No doubt this ideal, if it can be spelled out and some rationale can be given for it, would be worthy of pursuit by public policy, but is it more than an eminently desirable social goal? Does it really justify any moral claim of each individual against her state that it actually achieve this ideal in her case?

The most serious objection to this conception of the human right to medical treatment is that it poses the problem of scarce resources in its most acute form. The amount of goods and services that can be created in any society is limited, and not all of those goods are available for distribution by its government. To achieve the highest attainable standard of physical and mental health for each and every individual, especially given the potentialities of modern medical science and the cost of many modern medical technologies, would certainly require the expenditure of vast resources. Many societies would lack these medical resources. How, then, can there be any universal human right that would imply a correlative duty that could not possibly be universally fulfilled? Even in relatively affluent societies such as ours, this duty would probably require neglecting other equally stringent state obligations, such as providing for public education, police and fire protection, and national defense. How can there be any fundamental human right that would impose a duty that would in turn require the neglect of other equally or more urgent moral obligations? Surely, any genuine moral right to medical care will allow for a level of cost containment consistent with a reasonable quality of medical care.

Accordingly, some moral philosophers propose a third conception and assert only a fundamental moral right of every individual to a minimum level of medical care. To be sure, some qualify this as a "decent" minimum of medical care, but this reintroduces the problem of indeterminacy because it is no easier to specify the amount and kinds of medical care required by moral decency than those required by adequacy for health and well-being. It seems much wiser to define minimum care as only that necessary to sustain human life, for this criterion is much easier to apply in practice and makes by far the least demands upon the scarce resources of society.

Another advantage of this conception of the human right to medical care is that there is a distinctive and plausible argument for its existence; it might well be grounded on the inalienable right to life of each individual. This conception does, of course, presuppose that the human right to life is stronger than the merely negative right not to be killed; the right to life also includes the right to have one's life preserved or sustained. But both theologians who believe that one has a right to life because one has been created by or given one's life by God and moral philosophers who explain this right by the inherent value of each human life often define the right to life in positive as well as negative terms.

Nevertheless, to assert the fundamental moral claim of each individual against her society to be provided with a minimum level of medical care, care sufficient to sustain her life, seems to demand both too much and too little. Unfortunately, some diseases are incurable and some injuries irremediable, even by the very best modern medicine; the individual can have no moral claim against her society that it provide medical care sufficient to do the impossible. Some medical problems can be dealt with by modern medicine only by the use of resources, such as transplantable human hearts, not available in sufficient numbers to save the lives of every individual who will die without this sort of medical care. Other life-preserving medical technologies are so expensive that to recognize a right of everyone to these kinds of medical care would require that society neglect other more urgent moral obligations. Hence, in many cases this definition of the human right to medical care seems to demand too much. At the same time, to assert a human right to a merely minimum level of medical care seems to demand too little, at least of any affluent society. Surely every state ought in most cases to do more than barely sustain the lives of its citizens; it ought to ensure some degree of health and welfare for them.

Because there seems to be no satisfactory way to define the level of medical care to which everyone has a right, many moral philosophers advance a fourth conception of this human right. Every human being has a fundamental moral right to equal access to medical care proportional to need. If real, this right would rule out discrimination against any patient because of religion, race, or sex and would also require that access to medical care depend on need alone, not on one's political power, geographical location, or ability to pay. Those who assert this human right are responding to the perceived injustice that our medical institutions wrongly deny access to medical care to certain disadvantaged persons, such as African-Americans or Hispanics, those who live in depressed urban cores or isolated rural areas, and the poor.

Advocates of equal access argue that this human right is grounded on a fundamental principle of justice—"treat similar cases similarly"—together with the moral judgment that need is the morally relevant similarity for the distribution of medical care. The presupposed principle of justice is relatively uncontroversial. Surely it would be unfair for me to give one student a higher grade than another for term papers that are equally well researched, logically argued, and original in conception. It would also be unfair were I to give two students the same grade even though one has submitted a much better paper than the other. Thus a more explicit formulation of the presupposed principle of justice is, "treat similar cases similarly and different cases differently."

This leaves open the question of which similarities and differences are morally relevant. I could not defend my act of giving John a higher grade than Jane on their term papers by pointing out that John is male and Jane female, because sexual differences are irrelevant to grading philosophical papers. Why, then, is need the relevant similarity for the distribution of medical care? The defining purpose of medicine is to prevent or remedy disease or disability; it would be pointless and a misuse of medicine to give medical care to persons who have no need for it. Hence, justice demands that patients with equal medical need be given equal medical care and that when two patients have unequal need, the one with the greater need should receive a proportionally greater amount of medical care.

This attempt to ground a human right to equal access to medical care on justice is open to serious challenge. Let us assume that it has been put into practice and that the medical institutions of our society ensure that each individual has access to medical care equal to that of every other individual who has an equal need for it. To accomplish this practice, wealthy persons must be prevented from purchasing any medical care not provided to everyone else in the society. But this seems unjust. Presumably they have a fundamental human right to property that includes their right to use their earned income, savings, or acquired assets as they choose. Egalitarian medical institutions are also morally objectionable because they would require that some curable illnesses and disabilities must remain untreated merely because these social institutions cannot guarantee a cure for all.

An even more fundamental objection is that need is not the only similarity or difference morally relevant for the distribution of medical care. Personal responsibility is at least as relevant to the justice of medical institutions. Does a heavy smoker with lung cancer or an alcoholic who needs a kidney transplant have a right to medical treatment equal to that of a patient in equal need through no fault of her own? Surely not. This is not to say that society ought to deny medical treatment to its less responsible citizens. But it is the moral duty of benevolence—or perhaps the moral right to rescue when in distress—not any moral claim-right to equal access grounded on justice that is relevant here. Other things being equal, it is unfair to treat those who are responsible for their medical need the same as those who need medical care through no fault of their own.

Some moral philosophers go even further. Access to medical care is an individual not a social responsibility. Each individual—or in the case of dependent children or elderly persons, each family—is fully responsible for his or her medical care. In our society, as in many others, medical care is provided by physicians, surgeons, nurses, hospital orderlies, and other medical practitioners who sell their services much as teachers, lawyers, plumbers, and hairdressers do. It would be entirely unrealistic to expect them to provide their services without recompense and unjust to require them to sacrifice their own standard of living for the sake of those unwilling or unable to pay for their services. As the *Universal Declaration of Human Rights* itself recognizes, it is up to each breadwinner to earn an income sufficient to provide for oneself and for one's family an adequate standard of living, including adequate medical care. If there is any relevant human right, it is a right to an equal opportunity to earn a living not a right to equal access to medical care proportional to need alone.

The Right to Emergency Treatment

Although U.S. law does not contain a right analogous to any of the alleged human rights to medical care that we have considered, three new legal rights have been introduced to increase access to medical treatment—the rights to emergency treatment, to financial assistance under Medicare, and to financial assistance under Medicaid. There is a general common law right of anyone experiencing a medical emergency to receive appropriate treatment by any hospital with emergency facilities or, if it is unable to provide such treatment, to be referred to another hospital with the necessary facilities. This right is, however, contingent upon the person needing emergency treatment presenting herself or being presented, often by ambulance or police, to the emergency room of some hospital; hospitals have no legal duty to seek out persons experiencing a medical emergency. A medical emergency is defined roughly as any injury or acute medical condition likely to cause death, disability, or serious illness if not treated at once. The hospital has a legal duty to attend to the patient within a reasonable time and continue treatment until the patient can be transferred or discharged without harm.

The leading case regarding this right to emergency treatment is *Wilmington General Hospital v. Manlove,* which was decided in 1961. In its opinion the court appealed to the common-law principle that if one voluntarily undertakes to render services, service cannot be refused or negligently terminated to the detriment of one who has reasonably relied on the representation that service would be provided. Hence, persons should be able to rely on the established custom that hospitals that have emergency facilities treat those who present themselves or are presented for treatment.

Rights to Financial Assistance

The other two new medical rights—conferred by the Medicare Program and the Medicaid Program, respectively—differ from the legal right to emergency care in three important ways. They are statutory rights conferred by legislation rather than common-law rights arising from judicial precedents. They are special rights, rights for which only some limited category or categories of citizens are eligible, rather than general legal rights possessed by everyone subject to U.S. law. And they are rights to financial assistance in meeting the cost of medical care not rights to medical care itself.

The Medicare Program, created by Title 18 (Health Insurance for the Aged) of the Social Security Amendments of 1965, is financed out of Social Security payroll taxes. It confers upon persons over sixty-five who have paid the Social Security payroll tax for a sufficient number of years, and upon their elderly dependents, a legal right to financial assistance in paying for hospital services and, if they have enrolled in Part B, to physician and related services. Elderly disabled persons are also eligible under special conditions, and elderly persons who are not automatically covered under Social Security can become eligible by paying a monthly premium. Part A provides financial assistance for almost all inpatient hospital care, including diagnostic and related services; but there are limits on the amount, scope, and duration of payment, as well as some cost sharing requirements. Part B covers a wide range of physician and other medical services. Those who are eligible for Part A may, but are not required to, enroll in Part B by paying a substantial monthly premium. In Part B there are also limitations on payments for covered services, and significant co-payments are required. In spite of all these limitations and restrictions, Medicare payments amount to many billions of dollars each year and enable millions of elderly patients to receive medical care they could not afford without this financial assistance.

The right to financial assistance under Medicaid was created by Title 9 (Grants to States for Medical Assistance Programs) of the Social Security Amendments of 1965. Only those persons whose financial resources place them below the official poverty line and who are deemed worthy of assistance possess this new medical right holding against the state in which they reside to receive financial assistance to pay for covered medical treatments. Because the Medicaid Program is governed by both federal and state legislation and jointly funded, the right to financial assistance it confers differs significantly from state to state. Still, one can describe a few common features. Those who are eligible for Medicaid have traditionally consisted primarily of the aged, blind, disabled, and of poor dependent children. Federal legislation specifies a broad range of basic medical services that must be covered under any state Medicaid program, but each state is permitted to cover additional treatments if it so chooses. Moreover, each state has wide discretion as to the amount of financial assistance it will provide for any covered medical service. It can, and most states do, also limit the duration of medical treatment and insist that the patient share in the cost of the medical service.

The Moral Debate

Many ethicists and conscientious citizens believe that these new legal medical rights are three steps in the right direction, but still morally inadequate. Because only a few categories of poor persons are eligible for Medicaid, the legal right to financial assistance under the Medicaid Program leaves millions of individuals below the poverty level without access to even basic medical care. There are additional millions of citizens above the poverty line but below the age of sixty-five who are denied needed medical care because they cannot afford to purchase private medical insurance. Therefore, even taken together, these new medical rights fail to satisfy any of the alleged human rights to medical care. Not everyone, of course, admits that there is a fundamental moral right, however its content may be defined, of every individual to be provided with medical care. Nevertheless, many people are convinced that justice demands that our government do more to equalize access to needed medical treatments. Perhaps complete equality of access is not morally required, but any society in which the affluent can and do obtain luxurious and often unnecessary medical care, while millions of others are denied access to even the most basic and urgently needed medical treatment, is inequitable and unjust.

On the other side of the debate over recent changes in medical law are some moral philosophers who argue that these three new medical rights are harmful and unjust. These steps toward socialized medicine are both very harmful governmental handicaps to the efficient functioning of our traditional free enterprise system of health care and disastrously strong disincentives to the private charity of hospitals, physicians, charitable organizations, and private citizens. The billions of dollars spent on Medicare and Medicaid have exacerbated the increasingly urgent problem of the cost containment of medical care; at the same time rigid governmental regulations have added bureaucratic burdens to our medical institutions and have interfered with the best medical judgment of physicians. And the vast impersonal governmental agencies that administer Medicare and Medicaid lack both the flexibility necessary to deal with the highly variable cases of diverse individuals and the sensitivity required to treat with genuine charity those who cannot afford to pay the full cost of medical treatment.

Moreover, these philosophers argue that far from making our law more just, these three new medical rights are fundamentally unjust. They do not serve to protect or even to move us closer to fulfilling any human right to medical care because there is no such right. Human rights, the rights traditionally called natural rights, are negative rights *not* to be harmed in one's person or hindered in one's liberty; they are not positive rights to be provided with economic goods or social services. Indeed, the taxes imposed to fund Medicare and Medicaid violate both the property- and liberty-rights of those upon whom they are imposed by law. They violate the owner's right to dispose of her property as she wishes and the liberty of those who must engage in what amounts to forced labor to earn the income required to pay taxes enforced with legal sanctions. Thus the political struggle and moral controversy between those who wish to expand our legal rights to medical treatment and those who wish to restrict or repeal them continue unabated.

Conclusion

There has been, as we have now seen, a revolution in medical ethics and a similar but less radical development in medical law. New moral medical rights have been claimed and new legal medical rights have been created, either by judicial decision or by legislation. Why does it matter whether these alleged new moral rights really exist? Why does it matter that U.S. law now includes the rights to consent to medical research, to informed consent to therapy, to die, to emergency medical care, and of some persons to financial assistance in paying for medical care? Why do many believe that both the traditional professional duties, moral and legal, of physicians and the charitable provision of medical care to those who cannot afford to pay for it are insufficient?

The central issue is the proper locus of authority. Traditionally the physician, by virtue of her knowledge of medicine and dedication to the well-being of her patient, had authority over medical decisions. It was believed to be up to her to decide what treatments are best and up to the patient to obey her orders. And it was up to medical providers, charitable organizations, and kindly individuals to decide whether those who cannot purchase medical care shall obtain it.

The new medical rights have shifted authority over their defining contents to the subjects of medical research and the patients of medical treatment. Thus only those who choose to participate in a medical experiment may be subjected to it, and they are free to discontinue participation at any time. Although the physician should inform the patient of alternative therapies and recommend the one that in her judgment would be most beneficial, the patient is free to accept or reject her recommendation. Medical duties, it is argued, are insufficient because whether the physician fulfills her moral duties is a matter between the physician and her god, or her conscience, and whether she fulfills her legal duties is a matter between the physician and the courts. Medical rights are needed to transform the subject of research and the patient of treatment from a passive dependent of the medical provider to an active right-holder exercising freedom and control over the domains of these new medical rights.

But is this a desirable or an undesirable change in our medical ethics and law? The advocates of medical rights argue that these new medical rights, and several others, are morally required both by respect for the autonomy of the patient or the subject of research and by the need to protect her from harm. Each normal human being, and to a lesser extent persons with more limited psychological abilities, possess practical reason: the capacity to choose and act on the basis of reasons, moral as well as prudential. It is this capacity that commands our moral respect and imposes upon us the obligation to respect the autonomy of each individual by allowing her to choose for herself how to live her own life. Because medical treatment and biomedical experimentation affect for better or worse primarily the patient or the subject, respect for autonomy requires that she have the authority conferred by these new medical rights.

These new medical rights are also morally required to protect the patient or the subject of research from harm. Each individual person is a better judge than others of what will benefit or harm her, because she is more familiar with her special circumstances, more sensitive to her personal values, and more strongly motivated to pursue her well-being and avoid injury to herself. This is not to say that the patient or the subject is infallible and always makes the right decision; it is merely to recognize that reasonable persons will be more concerned to avoid risks than will be their physicians or those whose careers require them to conduct medical research with as yet unknown dangers.

Many physicians and some moral philosophers remain unconvinced by these arguments for locating authority in the hands of patients and the subjects of medical research. No doubt, one ought to respect the autonomy of every human being, but this requires that one defer to a person's choice only when it is a genuinely rational choice. Even disregarding persons with limited rationality, psychologically normal patients and subjects are often incapable of exercising full autonomy. As the advocates of medical rights themselves insist, voluntary consent or refusal must be fully informed. But patients and subjects lack both the knowledge of medical science and the familiarity with similar cases that is required for any accurate and reliable assessment of either the relative advantages of alternative therapies or the risks of a medical experiment. Moreover, when one is ill, as every patient and subject of clinical research is, one becomes insecure, dependent, and psychologically less able to confront difficult choices calmly, clearly, and rationally. What respect for autonomy really requires in most medical contexts is that the physician restore the patient to full autonomy and not submit to unwise decisions in the name of a spurious autonomy.

These critics also maintain that the argument for medical rights as protections for the well-being of the patient or the subject of research is even weaker. When one is ill or suffering from some disability, what one needs first and foremost for one's well-being is being well; what one needs is to be cured or at least to receive the most effective medical treatment. Therefore, medical authority ought to be in the hands of the physician, whose medical knowledge and dedication to the preservation of the health and very life of the patient are by far the most reliable protections of his well-being. One should, of course, choose a conscientious physician who will fulfill her professional duties. But whatever may be true of other areas of human life, in the medical context it is the good of the patient, not his rights, that should come first. After all, why should anyone, least of all the patient, value medical rights when they so often endanger rather than protect the patient's well-being? Here, as in previous chapters, we see that the recent proliferation of alleged moral and actual legal rights remains controversial.

Notes

1. *Salgo v. Leland Stanford Jr. University Board of Trustees*, 317 P2d 170, 181 (1957).
2. *Salgo*, 181.
3. *Schloendorff v. Society of New York Hospital*, 105 NE 92, 93 (1914).
4. *Matter of Quinlan*, 355 A2d 647, 664 (1976).
5. *Cruzan v. Director, Missouri Department of Health*, 497 US 261, 277 (1990).
6. *Cruzan*, 278.
7. *Cruzan*, 313.
8. *Cruzan*, 345.
9. *Compassion in Dying v. State of Washington*, 79 F3d 790, 813 (1996).
10. *Compassion in Dying*, 820.
11. *Compassion in Dying*, 820–821.
12. *Compassion in Dying*, 838.
13. *Compassion in Dying*, 801.
14. *Compassion in Dying*, 840.

15. *Washington v. Glucksberg*, 138 LEd2d 772, 787-788 (1997).
16. *Glucksberg*, 787.
17. *Glucksberg*, 797.

Suggestions for Further Reading

Annas, George J. 1992. *The Rights of Patients*. Totowa, N.J.: Humana Press. A very clear account and defense of the rights of patients.

Annas, George J., Sylvia A. Law, Rand E. Rosenblatt, and Kenneth R. Wing. 1990. *American Health Law*. Boston: Little, Brown and Company. A respected legal textbook on health law including medical rights.

Battin, Margaret Pabst. 1995. *Ethical Issues in Suicide*. Englewood Cliffs N.J.: Prentice Hall. A clear discussion of the morality of suicide with a chapter on physician-assisted suicide.

_____. 1994. *The Least Worst Death: Essays in Bioethics on the End of Life*. New York: Oxford University Press. A sustained defense of euthanasia and suicide with a chapter on the human right to suicide.

Bok, Sissela. 1978. *Lying: Moral Choice in Public and Private Life*. There is an illuminating contrast between the perspective of physician's duties and that of patient's rights on pages 232–255.

Compassion in Dying v. State of Washington. 1996. 79 F3d 790. A decision in which a United States Court of Appeals affirmed a constitutional right to assisted suicide.

Cruzan v. Director, Missouri Department of Health. 1990. 497 US 261. A case in which the United States Supreme Court recognized what is commonly called "the right to die."

Donnelly, John, ed. 1990. *Suicide: Right or Wrong?* Buffalo N.Y.: Prometheus Books. Essays old and new on the morality of suicide.

Downing, A. B., ed. 1969. *Euthanasia and the Right of Death*. London: Peter Owen. A collection of early influential essays on the ethics of euthanasia.

Dworkin, Ronald. 1997. "Assisted Suicide: What the Court Really Said." *New York Review of Books* 44, no. 14. (September 25, 1997), pp. 40, 42–44. An interpretation of the significance of the decision of the Supreme Court in *Washington v. Glucksberg*.

Engelhardt, H. Tristram. 1986. *The Foundations of Bioethics*. New York: Oxford University Press. An approach to bioethics in terms of rights.

Hamel, Ronald P., and Edwin R. DuBose, eds. 1996. *Must We Suffer Our Way to Death?: Cultural and Theological Perspectives on Death by Choice*. Dallas: Southern Methodist University Press. A collection of essays on assisted death.

Matter of Quinlan. 1976. 355 A2d 647. The leading case concerning the right to die.

Pellegrino, Edmund D., and David C. Thomasma. 1988. *For the Patient's Good*. New York: Oxford University Press. They argue that a benevolent concern for the patient's good rather than for the patient's rights is basic to ethical medical practice.

Percival, Thomas. 1849. *Medical Ethics*, 3d ed. Oxford: John Henry Parker. An immensely influential code of medical ethics.

Reich, Warren T., ed. 1978. *Encyclopedia of Bioethics*. New York: The Free Press. The appendix contains the most convenient source for the most important codes and statements concerning medical ethics.

_____. 1995. *Encyclopedia of Bioethics*, rev. ed. New York: Macmillan. The expanded appendix includes a wide range of codes, oaths, and directives on medical ethics.

Salgo v. Leland Stanford Jr. University Board of Trustees. 1957. 317 P2d 170. The case that first recognized the legal right to informed consent to medical treatment.

Schloendorff v. Society of New York Hospital. 1914. 105 NE 92. The leading case establishing the patient's right not to be treated without consent.

Wallace, Samuel E., and Albin Eser, eds. 1981. *Suicide and Euthanasia: The Rights of Personhood*. Knoxville: University of Tennessee Press. An illuminating collection of essays on suicide and euthanasia.

Washington v. Glucksberg. 1997. 138 LEd2d 772. The Supreme Court decision holding that there is no constitutional right to physician-assisted suicide.

7

An Appraisal

Over the last few decades there has been a widespread and controversial proliferation of rights in our society and, to a lesser degree, in other societies around the world. The previous chapters have described some examples of new legal rights and newly alleged moral rights in the areas of human rights, civil rights, women's rights, animal rights, and medical rights. They have also reported some of the more important arguments for and against each of these actual legal rights and alleged moral rights. But this piecemeal discussion has not offered any comprehensive understanding of this complex social development. In order that the manifold details shall not obscure the overall pattern, this chapter will go beyond the fragmentary treatment of sample rights and particular arguments presented so far to provide a more general perspective on the proliferation of rights as a whole.

Moreover the previous chapters have, for the most part, maintained an objective and neutral stance. However, I am not neutral, and I should not conclude this discussion without explaining where I stand, if only to invite the reader to draw her own evaluative conclusions. In short, it is time for a general appraisal.

What follows will be an appraisal in the sense of an evaluation of the merits and defects of something, in this case of the proliferation of rights. Because this proliferation has been a complex social development in which three strands have been interwoven, I will give a threefold appraisal. I will evaluate the merits and defects of the proliferation of actual legal rights, the proliferation of alleged moral rights, and the proliferation of the language of rights in political discourse.

Legal Rights

One strand in the recent proliferation of rights has involved the introduction of new rights into international law and the legal systems of many nation states—along with continuing attempts of social reformers to create additional legal rights. Has this proliferation of legal rights improved our international and domestic law?

Possible Defects

Many jurists and moral philosophers argue that on the whole it has been highly undesirable. Each new legal right provides an opportunity, and even an invitation, for those who believe, often on the basis of little or no solid evidence, that someone has not respected this right in their case to initiate legal proceedings to remedy the wrong they imagine they have suffered. Therefore, the increased number of legal rights has multiplied the number of legal disputes and interpersonal conflicts in our society. One consequence has been that we have become a more litigious people, a people more given to and fond of litigation. In this way, the proliferation of rights in our adversarial legal system has infected our personal interactions by making them more confrontational. Witness the manner in which the proliferation of medical malpractice suits in our society seems to have made patients distrustful of their physicians and forced physicians to practice defensive medicine, whereby they are more concerned to protect themselves against litigation than to do what is best for their patients.

An obvious response to this argument is that these disputes have not been created by the introduction of new legal rights. Patients who have suffered from medical malpractice have always resented their mistreatment; it is simply that in the past they have merely withheld payment from their physicians and often changed doctors.

Still, even if the introduction of new legal rights does not create new disputes *ex nihilo*, it may very well intensify interpersonal conflicts in our society. Thus the patient's awareness of her right to informed consent to therapy has caused her not only to resent having been harmed by medical treatment that she believes was not fully explained to her but also to become indignant at what she now takes to have been a violation of her rights. At the same time, her physician can no longer see himself as a trusted and benevolent medical practitioner cooperating with his patient; he must recognize that she is a potential adversary in a legal suit that may cost him vast sums of money and even the loss of his medical practice.

Once it is recognized that the introduction of new legal rights typically reflects rather than creates new or hitherto unrecognized interpersonal conflicts, the danger remains that these new rights may intensify these conflicts in a harmful manner. This very real danger must be balanced against the possibility that a new legal right could reduce conflict by discouraging the offensive conduct that engenders antagonism. To my mind, this suggests that it is not the proliferation of rights per se that should worry us. Nevertheless, because a primary purpose of any legal system is the peaceful resolution of disputes, one should add a right to some legal system princi-pally when there is reason to believe that it will reduce rather than increase the conflict that seems to call for its creation.

Another criticism of the proliferation of legal rights is that these new rights have overburdened our legal system. Because each new right provides the basis for a new set of lawsuits, the sheer number of rights now clogs our courts so that there are intolerable delays before an aggrieved plaintiff can obtain even a first hearing in court; and the new rights often conflict, or at least seem to conflict, with established rights, so that appeals to higher courts have become more common and more prolonged. The introduction of new rights has also spread the enforcement of rights too thinly; in their efforts to enforce newfangled and less important rights, the police and other agencies of the law have had to divert their energies away from the enforcement of older and more vital rights of our citizens.

There is, I believe, no doubt that our legal system is presently overbur-dened, so that justice is frequently delayed and sometimes denied alto-gether. Whether this is because U.S. law now recognizes and attempts to en-force too many rights or because taxpayers are unwilling to provide legal resources sufficient to secure the rights they have demanded is not clear. In any event, it is a mistake to try to solve every social problem or to prevent every kind of immoral act by passing another law. Legal resources will al-ways be scarce relative to the demand for them, and there are many areas of human conduct where legal intervention will not be effective and may even be harmful. It is better, as these critics of the proliferation of rights ar-gue, to limit legal rights to a manageable number of very important rights.

The question remains, of course, as to which legal rights are most impor-tant. This will depend in part upon utilitarian considerations, such as the degree to which a new right would be both practicable and beneficial. But there are also moral reasons for or against any proposed reform of the legal system: whether it would make the law more or less just and whether it would protect or violate some moral right. No wholesale assessment of new legal rights is reasonable; rather, we should assess each legal right, old or new, on its own merits. In the end, it may not be the number of legal rights that is most important but how wisely they are selected and how ju-diciously the content of each is defined.

Probable Merits

Although the creation of new legal rights is no panacea and the unrestrained proliferation of rights is harmful, some of the rights recently added to U.S. law have promoted the public welfare by solving, or at least contributing to the solution of, urgent social problems. For example, the rights to financial assistance under the Medicare and Medicaid Programs were introduced to enable those who could not afford desperately needed medical care under our traditional free market system to obtain necessary medical treatment. The relief from much hardship and suffering of those previously denied medical care is obvious. But these new rights have also reduced both the economic loss resulting from the inability of the ill and disabled to be productive workers and the increased costs of medical care that would have been unnecessary had the elderly and poor been able to afford preventive medicine and early treatment. To the extent that this and other new legal rights have promoted the public welfare by solving urgent social problems, there is merit in the recent proliferation of rights.

Although public welfare is constituted by the sum total of the well-being enjoyed by the members of a society, legal rights are distributed among those members as individuals. Thus I have my right to vote, my neighbor has her right to vote, and every other citizen is the possessor of his or her right to vote. Similarly, my right to be paid by Washington University is distinct from the similar right of each and every other member of its faculty. This is fortunate because it means that when one of my colleagues resigns or retires, thereby terminating her right to her monthly salary, my own right to my monthly paycheck remains intact. Accordingly, many jurists argue that the distinctive value of legal rights is not the promotion of public welfare but the protection of individuals. If this is so, then the special value of many new legal rights will consist in their protection of the interests or the liberty of the individual members of our society.

It certainly seems true that the new legal right to emergency medical care has protected the interests of large numbers of people. This right has enabled many persons to obtain the medical treatment they have needed when their health, and even their very lives, were threatened and thereby has protected countless individuals from the harms of protracted disease, permanent disability, or death.

Other legal rights seem to protect individual liberty more than individual interests. For example, the new legal right to abortion protects the liberty of the individual woman to choose whether to terminate her pregnancy or to continue to carry her unborn child. Although the exercise of this liberty may often protect a pregnant woman from having an unwanted child, or protect her fetus from being born with serious genetic defects, on other occasions the exercise of this liberty may fail to protect a healthy and potentially happy unborn child from the ultimate harm of death. This failure helps to explain why this new legal right remains so controversial. Still, because legal rights tend to protect individual interests and the liberty of individuals, there is always some merit in introducing a new legal right when it is capable of doing so effectively.

Another alleged merit of some legal rights is that they secure more fundamental moral rights. Moral reformers often advocate the addition of some right to the legal system on the ground that this is necessary in order to enforce an analogous moral right. This kind of argument presupposes that the alleged moral right is real, that it really needs protection because it is threatened, and that the advocated legal right will effectively secure it. If all this is true of the majority of the new legal rights, there is a strong moral justification for the recent proliferation of legal rights.

The civil right to interracial marriage introduced by the Supreme Court in *Loving v. Virginia* can almost certainly be justified in this manner. There does seem to be a human liberty-right to marry or not marry a willing partner of the opposite sex, whether or not there is any moral right of same-sex marriage. This fundamental moral right was violated by statutes in many states prohibiting the marriage of persons of different races. And this new constitutional right has reasonably and effectively secured this human right by rendering these prohibitions null and void. Although it has not eliminated all personal prejudice and informal social sanctions against interracial marriages, it has reduced these to a considerable extent by helping to change public opinion in the United States.

There is little doubt that the woman's constitutional right to abortion recognized by the Supreme Court in *Roe v. Wade* has been effectively protected in our legal system. What remains in doubt is whether this new legal right secures any fundamental moral right. Many pro-choice advocates allege that the legal right to abortion protects the moral right of a pregnant woman either to choose whether or not to remain pregnant or, more broadly, to choose what happens in and to her body. Many other moral philosophers argue that it protects one aspect of her right to privacy: her right to make and act on choices that fundamentally affect her life for better or worse. On the other hand, conservatives argue that there can be no moral right to choose to murder an unborn child. What is lacking in contemporary moral theory is any persuasive explanation of the grounds for any of these alleged moral rights. Although I am tempted to believe that there is a human right to privacy, I have not been able to justify this belief even to myself, nor to define this right with enough precision to determine whether it embraces the right of a pregnant woman to abort her unborn child whenever she chooses to do so.

At this point, my appraisal of the recent proliferation of *legal* rights must await my appraisal of the proliferation of alleged *moral* rights. What I can conclude here and now is that it is a mistake to praise or condemn the proliferation of legal rights wholesale; one should assess the merits and defects of each new legal right individually.

Alleged Moral Rights

A second strand in the recent proliferation of rights has been the assertion of many previously denied or even unimagined moral rights. Whereas the introduction of the appropriate changes into a legal system creates a new legal right, moral rights cannot be created either by being claimed or by the widespread acceptance of any such claim. Because the existence of moral rights is independent both of our moral convictions and of the moral code of any society, it is hard to know whether any alleged moral right is genuine. Whether some moral right really exists depends upon whether it has adequate grounds, whether there are moral reasons sufficient to justify its assertion. Because moral philosophers and conscientious lay persons disagree about what kinds of reasons are required to ground moral rights, the existence of any alleged moral right remains in doubt. Indeed, our inability to prove convincingly that some alleged right is illusory is one of the main sources of the proliferation of rights. Even if some such right does exist, it may not have exactly the content presupposed by its advocates, so that it may not justify the moral conclusions drawn from it. Hence, the proliferation of alleged moral rights is even more controversial than the proliferation of legal rights.

Moral Insight

Many philosophers regard the recent proliferation of alleged moral rights as healthy because it reflects and communicates increased moral insight. Those who assert some new moral right usually do so with the intention of righting some previously unrecognized moral wrong. For example, the right to equal pay for equal work was affirmed by the women's rights movement in protest against the common but unjust practice of paying female workers less than male employees doing the same work. That this is unfair had not been recognized because most employers and many employees believed that women, who could and should rely upon the male breadwinners in their families for financial support, had much less need for income than male workers. Accordingly, the proliferation of moral rights has greatly enlightened our consciences by calling to our attention the immorality of individual actions and social institutions we had accepted without question.

Although the proliferation of alleged moral rights has often challenged our moral prejudices, it is also possible to disguise one's prejudice by appealing to some alleged right. Some, but not all, moral philosophers believe that those who oppose abortion as a violation of the right to life of the human fetus are using the language of rights to express their religious dogmas and protect themselves from the need to reexamine their moral assumptions. Others contend that the alleged right of essential workers to strike is simply a cloak for the selfish and irresponsible demands of teachers or firefighters. Whatever one may believe about these two moral rights, one must recognize that the assertion of a new moral right will sometimes express immoral prejudice rather than moral insight. Still, even then it can sometimes lead to heightened moral sensitivity by stimulating those who are less prejudiced to rethink their own moral convictions. It seems to me that for the most part the recent proliferation of alleged moral rights in our society has been valuable because it has enriched our individual consciences and created a public opinion that is more sensitive to important moral concerns.

Moral Reform

Another important value of the recent proliferation of alleged moral rights is that it has provided a rational basis for many moral improvements in our society. To assert a previously unrecognized moral right is very often not merely to demand some change in personal conduct or some social institution but, if this alleged right is real, to justify this demand. Moreover, because moral rights are typically strong reasons for moral claims that often, but not always, outweigh other considerations, the appeal to a moral right is frequently the best of all justifications for demanding that we change our ways. The civil rights movement and the women's rights movement, both of which justified their demands for legal reform by appealing to moral rights, have eliminated or at least reduced many of the grave injustices traditionally suffered by African-Americans and females in our society. Thus the assertion of new moral rights has had very real merit.

There is, however, reason to be skeptical of moral claims based on asserted moral rights. Not all such moral demands are justified, and some of those that are justified are not justified by the moral rights alleged. The demands of Serbs and Croats for territory in what was Bosnia are not justified at all, not even by the alleged right of a people to self-determination. Again what justifies the moral demand for laws prohibiting cruelty to animals is not the recently alleged animal right not to be tortured but simply the fact that the inhumane treatment of animals causes them unnecessary suffering.

In any event, asserting a moral right is only the first step in a complete justification for demanding any change in personal conduct or social institutions. One most go further and seek the moral reasons that ground this alleged right. Only if one can identify such reasons and finds them sufficient to justify asserting the claimed right can one be confident that the moral demand has really been justified. I hazard no guess whether this has been true for most of the moral claims recently based on new alleged moral rights. Still, the moral improvements genuinely justified by this sort of moral reasoning have a value that seems to me to outweigh any incidental harms that may have resulted from unsound attempts to justify moral claims on the basis of alleged rights.

Egalitarian Justice

However important rights may be in moral reasoning, they are not the only morally relevant considerations. If I refuse to give any of my income to charity, I have failed to fulfill one of my moral obligations, even though no charitable organization or needy individual has a right to some portion of my wealth. And on some occasions it would be immoral not to sacrifice some important self-interest for the sake of a friend, even though this would be a supererogatory action: an act over and beyond the call of duty. In order to explain the limited role that rights play in morality, some moral philosophers maintain that the special and distinctive value of rights lies in their essential connection with justice. If so, an important merit of the recent proliferation of alleged moral rights has presumably been their contribution to egalitarian justice in our society.

This merit probably does not accompany all rights. Some of the recently asserted moral rights do not seem to involve egalitarian justice in any way. The moral right to die may well be genuine, but what is at stake here is a merciful release from a life that has become intolerable for the patient not any social inequality or denial of rights enjoyed by one's oppressors. Still, the fact that so many of the recently asserted moral rights have challenged social or political inequality testifies to how important the proliferation of asserted moral rights has been to the advancement of egalitarian justice both in our country and, taking human rights into consideration, in the world.

The way the assertion of new moral rights has advanced the cause of justice is best illustrated by the civil rights movement. For instance, the right to nonsegregated public education was advocated on the ground that segregated schools are inherently unequal. Although the integration of public schools did not move forward with all deliberate speed and has been only partially accomplished at great cost, it has gone some way toward equalizing the educational opportunity of African-American and white children in the United States. And the right to interracial marriage has enabled mixed-race couples to exercise the same constitutional right to marry and raise a family that had been enjoyed only by same-race couples. At the same time, this right has reduced the racial purity of families that has sustained racial prejudice and perpetuated the oppression of whites over African-Americans for so long.

The civil rights movement has inspired a number of other movements—the women's rights movement, the patient's rights movement, the animal rights movement, and even the environmental rights movement. Although all of these have been beneficial on the whole, I believe that they are less analogous to the civil rights movement than many imagine.

Sexism is in some, but not all, ways similar to racism. Just as the oppression of African-Americans by whites has been defended by our prejudices concerning the nature and proper roles of African-Americans, so the subordination of women has seemed justified because of our stereotypes concerning the nature and proper roles of females. Women, like African-Americans, have traditionally suffered injustice and been denied an equal status in our society. Hence, the new women's rights have advanced the cause of egalitarian justice. Nevertheless, the analogy goes only so far. Whereas a color-blind society may be a moral ideal, it would be morally perverse to set up the ideal of a sex-blind society. Sexual differences are morally relevant in ways that racial differences are not. For example, the fact that only females can become pregnant and deliver a child explains why the abortion decision belongs to the mother rather than the biological father of the unborn child.

Just as the term "sexism" was introduced into our language by analogy with "racism," so the term "speciesism" was coined to suggest a similar oppression by human beings—who arbitrarily consider themselves to be members of the highest species, over the nonhuman animals—whom they assign to biologically lower species. Accordingly, the animal rights movement sometimes proclaimed animal liberation as its goal, presumably on the model of the liberation of African-Americans, who had been first enslaved and later oppressed. For example, Peter Singer's paper entitled "All Animals are Equal" begins as follows: "In recent years a number of oppressed groups have campaigned vigorously for equality. The classic instance is the Black Liberation movement, which demands an end to the prejudice and discrimination that has made blacks second-class citizens."[1] But the analogy he suggests in this passage does not hold.

The central demands of the civil rights movement were that African-Americans should enjoy the same civil rights enjoyed by white citizens and that the law ought to protect the fundamental moral rights of African-Americans, just as it does the moral rights of white persons. Nonhuman animals are neither citizens nor persons, and because they lack moral agency, I believe that they are incapable of possessing either legal or moral rights. In the end, even Singer does not defend the rights of animals. The equality for which he argues is the equal consideration of interests, not the equal respect for moral rights. But to speak of interests is to admit that what has made our treatment of nonhuman animals morally wrong, when it has been wrong, is the harms we have imposed upon them not any violation of their rights. And to admit this is in turn to concede that what is really at stake here is not egalitarian justice but unnecessary and unjustified cruelty—or so I believe. Therefore, I believe that the recent proliferation of alleged moral rights has gone too far.

A Balance Sheet

Many of the claimed moral rights do not exist. There cannot be any animal rights because nonhuman animals are not moral agents, and only moral agents could possibly possess a moral right. In spite of the *International Covenant on Economic, Social and Cultural Rights*, there is no universal human right to "the highest attainable standard of physical and mental health." If there were such a claim-right, it would impose a moral obligation upon every society to ensure that every one of its members enjoys this high level of medical care. But many societies lack the medical resources to make this possible, and there can be no moral obligation to do the impossible. Therefore, although the *International Covenant* may well define a valid moral ideal, it cannot describe a real moral right.

Whether I am correct depends upon the adequacy of the restrictive theory of moral rights that I have explained and defended in *Real Rights*. Of course, other moral philosophers have argued for much broader and less restrictive theories, according to which many more of the recently alleged moral rights are genuine. How should one decide which of these theories to accept? One criterion is whether the theory draws distinctions in a way that enables us both to understand more clearly the different kinds of moral judgments we make and to identify the moral reasons that count for or against each of these. Another consideration is how well each theory captures the practical importance that moral rights have in our lives. What difference does it make whether some alleged right really exists? And which theory of rights best explains the special value of moral rights?

Even if I am correct in believing that the recent proliferation of alleged moral rights has gone too far, this does not imply that its defects outweigh its merits. It has made us aware of many previously unrecognized moral wrongs; it has often, if not always, provided a rational basis for moral improvements in our society; and it has advanced the cause of egalitarian justice in our society and throughout the world. On balance, I believe that this strand in the proliferation of rights has been and continues to be beneficial.

Political Discourse

A third strand in the recent proliferation of rights has been the proliferation of the language of rights in political discourse. Increasingly, political issues have been debated in terms of rights rather than in terms of what would promote the public welfare or preserve civic virtue. This is probably both because the language of natural rights and of our fundamental constitutional rights has a long and venerable use in our society and because of the political impact of the more recent civil rights movement. Hence, the language of rights is a powerful instrument to use in promoting one's political goals, whatever these may be.

It is in political discourse that the first two strands of the proliferation of rights are intertwined, for moral reformers often demand the introduction of some new legal right as necessary to secure some previously unrecognized, or at least unprotected, moral right. Thus those who campaigned for an Equal Rights Amendment to the United States Constitution argued that this was necessary to enable women to enjoy their moral rights to equal pay for equal work, equal employment opportunity, and equal representation in state and federal legislatures. And the heated public debates over physician-assisted suicide, both in the courts and in the media, typically hinge upon whether a patient really does have any fundamental moral right to die and, if so, whether this entails any right to assistance from her physician.

Criticisms

Many social and political philosophers argue that the recent proliferation of the language of rights has been harmful because it has devalued that currency in public debate. Just as inflation gradually reduces the real value of one's savings because one can now purchase fewer goods and services with the same amount of money, so the rights inflation in political discourse has devalued any and every public appeal to rights.

Asserting the existence of unreal moral rights often leads to a skepticism concerning moral rights. For example, the assertion of a fundamental moral right to holidays with pay in the *Universal Declaration of Human Rights* suggested to some moral philosophers that none of the social and economic rights declared by the United Nations are real; and this assertion has caused others to wonder whether there really are any human rights at all. The fact both that some environmentalists can seriously assert that trees and ecosystems have moral rights and that their assertions are taken seriously by other moral philosophers seems to many a reductio ad absurdum of the very idea of moral rights.

Again, demanding legal protection for less important moral rights, even if they are real, often diverts public attention and social resources away from securing much more valuable rights. Although African-Americans may well have a moral right not to be segregated in our public schools, the new legal right to nonsegregated public education has diverted large amounts of public funding into bussing—thus making funds unavailable for the improvement of classroom education—and has stimulated white flight from urban cores—thus increasing the residential segregation that in turn increases the racial segregation in neighborhood schools. In retrospect, many believe that it would have been better not to insist on the legal protection of the moral right to nonsegregated public education. Instead we should have directed our political discourse toward the moral right both to residential nonsegregation and to a quality of education for African-Americans equal to that provided for white Americans. Accordingly, many argue that it would be better to resist the proliferation of the language of rights in political discourse and to reserve the appeal to moral rights for a few social issues, when this is necessary to win the most vital public debates.

To my mind, this line of criticism is only partially convincing. I would advocate a moderate skepticism regarding the moral rights asserted in political discourse. Because there is no effective and nonprejudicial way to prevent any public speaker from asserting any right that springs to her mind, what is needed is not an attempt to reduce the number or variety of asserted moral rights but an effort to greatly increase discussion within political discourse. This discussion would help us distinguish between genuine and illusory rights. Skepticism about alleged moral rights should not lead citizens to deny every, or even any, asserted moral right out of hand; but it should stimulate participants in public debate both to ask for the grounds of any asserted right and to look for any moral considerations that might show that the alleged right is not genuine.

Similarly, I would not omit consideration of less important moral rights in political discourse, much less try to exclude the mention of them. What is necessary is some realistic assessment of whether any moral right genuinely needs legal protection and, if so, whether this could be accomplished without diverting scarce public resources away from more urgent public projects. In short, it is not rights inflation per se that is objectionable but the failure to distinguish between real and illusory moral rights, on the one hand, and between those real moral rights that can be advantageously protected by the government and those where political action is unnecessary or would be ineffective, on the other.

A second criticism of the proliferation of the language of rights in political discourse is also expressed in an economic metaphor. Gresham's law is that bad money drives good money out of circulation. For example, if a government attempts to balance its budget by printing money, then prudent individuals will tend to spend their dollar bills before inflation reduces their real value and will tend to hoard silver dollars so that they can, if necessary, sell them for the value of the precious metal they contain. In a similar manner, the excessive appeal to moral rights, which are often bad or at least poor reasons for some political demand, has driven better reasons for moral reform out of political discourse.

Political controversy over laws guaranteeing maternity leave to female employees certainly should not be limited to debating the alleged moral right to maternity leave. Equally crucial reasons for such legislation exist: for example, the contributions to business enterprises females could make after returning from a maternity leave; the value of preventing post-delivery medical complications by avoiding the mother's premature return to work; the need of newborn children for care by their mothers; and the social problems resulting from the poverty of families in which only the mother is employed. Although questions remain about each of these reasons and about whether together they are sufficient to justify a law guaranteeing maternity leave to female workers, many political philosophers argue that we should debate the issue in these terms, as well as in the language of rights.

I agree that there has been and continues to be a harmful preoccupation with rights in political discourse. Alleged moral rights should be discounted when their existence is dubious, and genuine moral rights should be given less weight when they are relatively unimportant. The most serious danger is that the strident voices of those demanding protection for moral rights may drown out the voices of those pointing to other relevant considerations. What is needed is a richer vocabulary of political discourse in which the language of rights plays a more limited, although still important, part in public debate.

A third, and probably the most serious, criticism of the proliferation of the language of rights in political discourse is that it invites dogmatism and inhibits any rational dialogue between those who disagree on social or legal issues. This is exceedingly harmful because it intensifies social conflict and prevents any reasonable solution to the most serious problems confronting one's society.

An unfortunate example of this defect is the appeal to animal rights. A number of the most radical members of the Straight Edge youth group in Utah have resorted to violence in the name of animal rights. They have fire-bombed a McDonalds restaurant, a Tandy leather and crafts supply store, and a mink feed cooperative. In the United Kingdom, public debate concerning experimentation on animals has become so violent that in a few instances animal rights advocates have even attached bombs to the vehicles of those who use animals in their medical research.

Why does the appeal to alleged moral rights inhibit dialogue and tend to exclude reasonable political debate? (1) Moral rights are typically thought to be the strongest of moral claims, and our fundamental moral rights are often assumed to be absolute. If rights are so strong that they override every other consideration, then it must be immoral to accept any compromise on any issue involving rights, because that would violate someone's right. (2) Each right is identified by a label, for example "the right to life" or "the right to liberty." Because we all know what the words "life" or "liberty" mean, we frequently assume that we know the content of any asserted right. Hence, the terms in which crucial moral and political issues are framed are set in advance, before critical reflection even begins. (3) Rights, especially fundamental moral rights, are often taken to be self-evident. Therefore, there seems to be no need to give any reasons to justify one's assertion that every human being has a moral right to life or that the pregnant woman has a moral right to bodily integrity or to privacy. Those few who attempt to present reasons for the rights they assert are not taken seriously in political debate because there is nothing even approaching a consensus on the kinds of moral reasons, if any, that ground rights. (4) Most pernicious is the way asserting a moral right discredits one's opponent. For example, many believe that anyone who favors abortion obviously fails to respect the moral right to life of the unborn child. One need not reason with such persons; one ought to condemn them and resist their efforts to further their immoral cause.

Potential Benefits

I must admit that the language of moral rights does tend to damage political discourse in these ways. Yet it ought not to do so because an alleged moral right really exists only if there are moral reasons sufficient to justify its assertion. Therefore, the appeal to rights ought to be an invitation to reason with one another. Why does it so often not function in this manner? Moral philosophers have advanced no convincing theory of the grounds of moral rights. Most political speakers and writers are partisans striving to advance some cause they believe important; they are not persons engaged in an impartial search for the moral truth. And the public is an uncritical audience for political discourse; typically either it is prejudiced for or against the proclaimed viewpoint or so uninterested in the debate as to be entirely unmotivated to question even the most dogmatic assertions. The solution, if there is one, is not to abandon the language of rights in political discourse but to use it with more restraint and to question its use more often. Whether this is possible depends upon the efficacy of moral and political education. I would be very happy, and somewhat surprised, if this little book were to make some small contribution to this education.

If the proliferation of the language of rights in political discourse really is defective in the ways that I and others maintain, why has it occurred? The assertion of moral rights is rhetorically effective. Rhetoric is speech or writing that is impressive or persuasive, and in politics the name of the game is persuasion. Hence, the vocabulary of rights is the language of choice for political disputes and is used to achieve one's goals in a democracy. This language strengthens the will of one's political allies, persuades the undecided, and puts one's adversary on the defensive. Whatever theoretical defects the language of rights may have, the purpose of politics is practical, and political discourse should be evaluated in terms of its practical consequences.

Is the rhetorical effectiveness of the language of rights a merit or defect in political discourse? It is beneficial in the right hands or mouths because it enables moral reformers to write or speak so as to change the laws and institutions of their societies in ways that reduce the violation, and enhance the enjoyment, of genuine moral rights. At the same time, it is harmful in the wrong hands because it can be used to resist urgently needed reform both by appealing to our traditional moral prejudices and by disguising foolish or selfish projects as morally justified causes. Unfortunately, the rhetorical effectiveness of the language of rights tends to discourage any attempt to distinguish between right and wrong, for it is only when one remains unpersuaded that one seriously questions or challenges what is asserted. It is not merely that the dogmatic assertion of an alleged moral right can deceive the public; it can disguise false causes from oneself and thereby mislead even the most conscientious leaders.

Moreover, the very power of the language of rights is often counterproductive, for it tempts one's opponents to fight fire with fire and provokes the assertion of one or more conflicting rights. Therefore, it typically engenders confrontation rather than cooperation, power struggle rather than rational discussion to achieve mutually satisfactory solutions to social problems, and social fragmentation rather than social cohesion and goodwill among fellow citizens. In short, the rhetorical effectiveness of the language of rights is both a merit and a defect in political discourse. Whether on balance it will be beneficial or harmful depends primarily upon whether the public to whom it is addressed is politically engaged, informed, and critical.

The Bottom Line

The bottom line is, taken literally, the lowest line on a financial statement showing the net income or loss of an enterprise. What one wants now is an analogous summing up of the merits and defects of all three strands in the recent proliferation of rights in our society and around the world. Taking everything into consideration, has this proliferation been on balance beneficial or harmful?

I believe that the assertion of alleged moral rights has been too indiscriminate, that it has asserted as many unreal rights as genuine ones. But it has stimulated jurists and moral philosophers to develop new and more sophisticated theories of rights. This development, if it continues, may enable us to distinguish between those rights assertions that are solidly grounded on moral reasons and those that are unjustified. Although political discourse has been dominated by the language of rights to an excessive degree, it has also made the public more sensitive to important moral considerations—even when these could be formulated more accurately in other terms—and has led to many needed moral reforms. These reforms have frequently consisted in the introduction of new legal rights. Most of these, as I have argued in the first section of this chapter, have eliminated or at least reduced serious moral wrongs and increased social justice in our society and in other nations. Because this is what matters most to the lives of countless human beings, this reduction of wrongs and increase of justice should weigh the most heavily in our overall assessment. Therefore, although seriously defective in many ways, the proliferation of rights has done much more good than harm. We should be grateful that it has flourished in our time and, while remaining critical of its excesses, sustain it where it is most needed and best justified.

Notes

1. Singer, Peter, "All Animals Are Equal," in *Animal Rights and Human Obligations*, 2d ed., eds. Tom Regan and Peter Singer (Englewood Cliffs N.J.: Prentice Hall, 1989), p. 73

Suggestions for Further Reading

Feinberg, Joel. 1992. *Freedom and Fulfillment: Philosophical* Essays. Princeton: Princeton University Press. Feinberg explains the social importance of moral rights and defends them against several criticisms on pages 220–244.

Frey, R. G. 1983. *Rights, Killing, and Suffering: Moral Vegetarianism and Applied Ethics*. Oxford: Basil Blackwell. On pages 46–66 Frey argues that nothing is gained and much is lost by discussing moral issues in terms of rights.

Nelson, William. 1976. "On the Alleged Importance of Moral Rights." *Ratio* 18, pp. 145–155. Nelson maintains that because there are no moral courts, Feinberg's legalistic theory of the nature and value of moral rights is inappropriate.

Raz, Joseph. 1986. *The Morality of Freedom*. Oxford: Clarendon Press. Raz argues on pages 193–216 that any narrow morality based entirely on rights cannot explain either our intrinsic duties or what makes life worthwhile and, ultimately, rights important.

Silverstein, Helena. 1996. *Unleashing Rights: Law, Meaning, and the Animal Rights Movement*. Ann Arbor: University of Michigan Press. On pages 81–122 Silverstein gives a balanced appraisal of the benefits and drawbacks of the language of rights.

Singer, Peter. 1989. "All Animals Are Equal." In *Animal Rights and Human Obligations*, 2d ed. Englewood Cliffs N.J.: Prentice Hall. Singer argues for the equal consideration of interests, not the equal respect for rights.

Tribe, Laurence H. 1992. *Abortion: The Clash of Absolutes*. New York: W. W. Norton and Company. Tribe describes on pages 139–160 and 229–242 the political conflict between the pro-choice and pro-life factions after *Roe v. Wade* and the harm that the appeal to absolute rights does to political dialogue.

Wellman, Carl. 1985. *A Theory of Rights*. Totowa, N.J.: Rowman and Allanheld. This book discusses the values and alleged disvalues of rights on pages 186–220.

———. 1995. *Real Rights*. New York: Oxford University Press. On pages 105–177 I argue that only moral agents are possible right-holders.

Index